The Step-by-Step Guide to

200
Crochet
Stitches

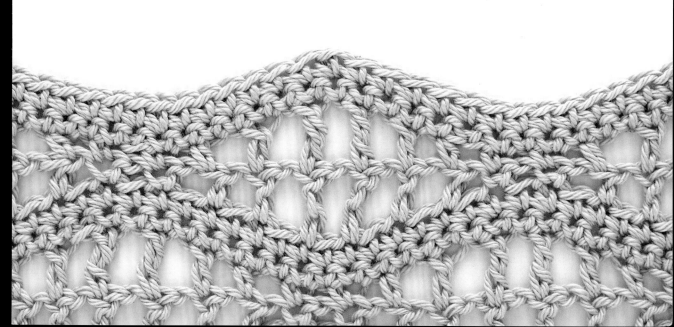

The Step-by-Step Guide to

200
Crochet
Stitches

Tracey Todhunter

Interweave®

A QUARTO BOOK

Copyright © 2019 Quarto Publishing plc

Interweave
An imprint of Penguin Random House LLC
penguinrandomhouse.com

Conceived, edited, and designed by
Quarto Publishing,
an imprint of The Quarto Group
The Old Brewery
6 Blundell Street
London N7 9BH
www.quartoknows.com

QUAR CRS2

ISBN 978-1-63250-657-3

Editor & designer: Michelle Pickering
Photographer: Phil Wilkins
Illustrator: Kuo Kang Chen
Technical editor: KJ Hay
Photoshop: Jackie Palmer
Editorial assistant: Cassie Lawrence
Art director: Jess Hibbert
Publisher: Samantha Warrington

Printed in China

3 5 7 9 10 8 6 4

Directory of Stitches   12

Basic Stitches

contents

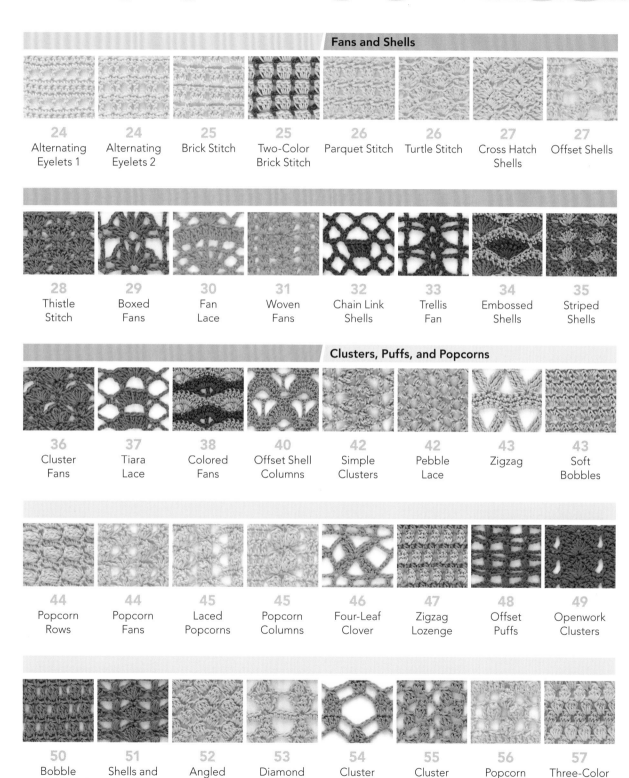

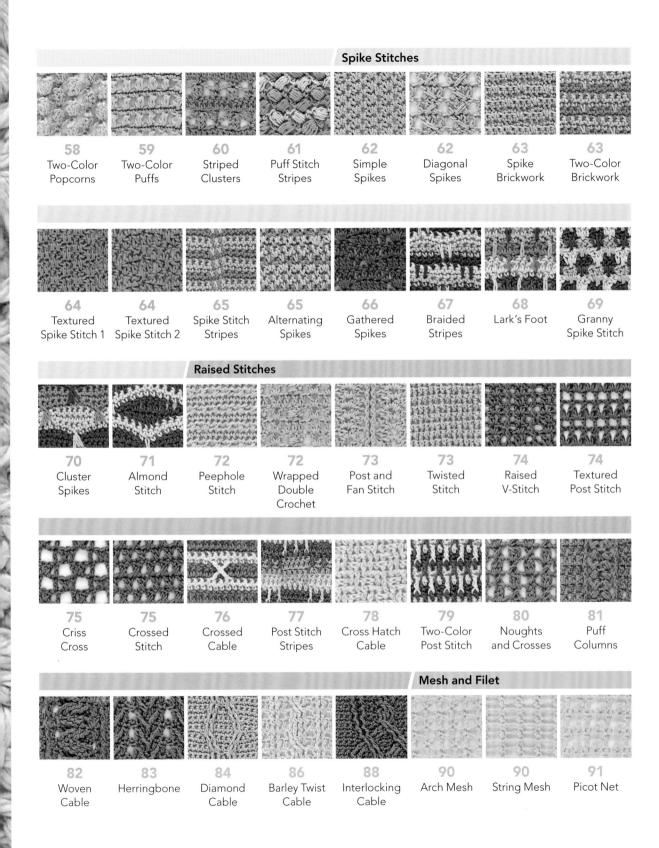

Spike Stitches

58	59	60	61	62	62	63	63
Two-Color Popcorns	Two-Color Puffs	Striped Clusters	Puff Stitch Stripes	Simple Spikes	Diagonal Spikes	Spike Brickwork	Two-Color Brickwork

64	64	65	65	66	67	68	69
Textured Spike Stitch 1	Textured Spike Stitch 2	Spike Stitch Stripes	Alternating Spikes	Gathered Spikes	Braided Stripes	Lark's Foot	Granny Spike Stitch

Raised Stitches

70	71	72	72	73	73	74	74
Cluster Spikes	Almond Stitch	Peephole Stitch	Wrapped Double Crochet	Post and Fan Stitch	Twisted Stitch	Raised V-Stitch	Textured Post Stitch

75	75	76	77	78	79	80	81
Criss Cross	Crossed Stitch	Crossed Cable	Post Stitch Stripes	Cross Hatch Cable	Two-Color Post Stitch	Noughts and Crosses	Puff Columns

Mesh and Filet

82	83	84	86	88	90	90	91
Woven Cable	Herringbone	Diamond Cable	Barley Twist Cable	Interlocking Cable	Arch Mesh	String Mesh	Picot Net

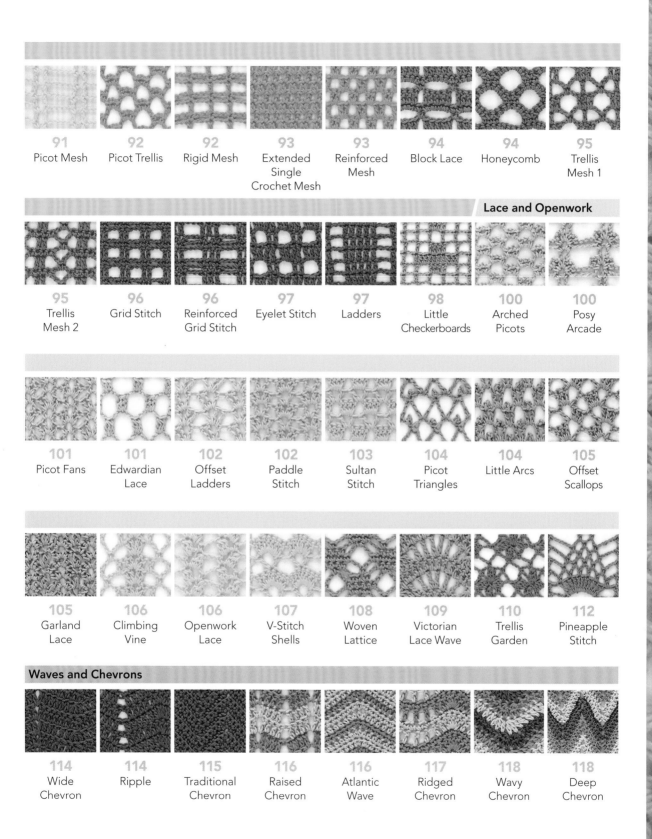

91 Picot Mesh

92 Picot Trellis

92 Rigid Mesh

93 Extended Single Crochet Mesh

93 Reinforced Mesh

94 Block Lace

94 Honeycomb

95 Trellis Mesh 1

Lace and Openwork

95 Trellis Mesh 2

96 Grid Stitch

96 Reinforced Grid Stitch

97 Eyelet Stitch

97 Ladders

98 Little Checkerboards

100 Arched Picots

100 Posy Arcade

101 Picot Fans

101 Edwardian Lace

102 Offset Ladders

102 Paddle Stitch

103 Sultan Stitch

104 Picot Triangles

104 Little Arcs

105 Offset Scallops

105 Garland Lace

106 Climbing Vine

106 Openwork Lace

107 V-Stitch Shells

108 Woven Lattice

109 Victorian Lace Wave

110 Trellis Garden

112 Pineapple Stitch

Waves and Chevrons

114 Wide Chevron

114 Ripple

115 Traditional Chevron

116 Raised Chevron

116 Atlantic Wave

117 Ridged Chevron

118 Wavy Chevron

118 Deep Chevron

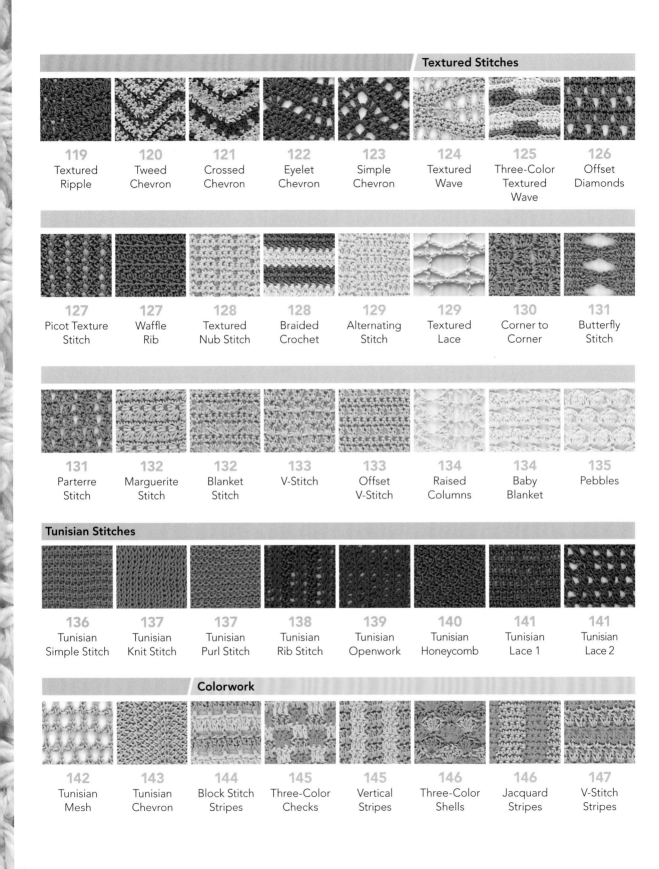

119 Textured Ripple

120 Tweed Chevron

121 Crossed Chevron

122 Eyelet Chevron

123 Simple Chevron

124 Textured Wave

125 Three-Color Textured Wave

126 Offset Diamonds

127 Picot Texture Stitch

127 Waffle Rib

128 Textured Nub Stitch

128 Braided Crochet

129 Alternating Stitch

129 Textured Lace

130 Corner to Corner

131 Butterfly Stitch

131 Parterre Stitch

132 Marguerite Stitch

132 Blanket Stitch

133 V-Stitch

133 Offset V-Stitch

134 Raised Columns

134 Baby Blanket

135 Pebbles

Tunisian Stitches

136 Tunisian Simple Stitch

137 Tunisian Knit Stitch

137 Tunisian Purl Stitch

138 Tunisian Rib Stitch

139 Tunisian Openwork

140 Tunisian Honeycomb

141 Tunisian Lace 1

141 Tunisian Lace 2

Colorwork

142 Tunisian Mesh

143 Tunisian Chevron

144 Block Stitch Stripes

145 Three-Color Checks

145 Vertical Stripes

146 Three-Color Shells

146 Jacquard Stripes

147 V-Stitch Stripes

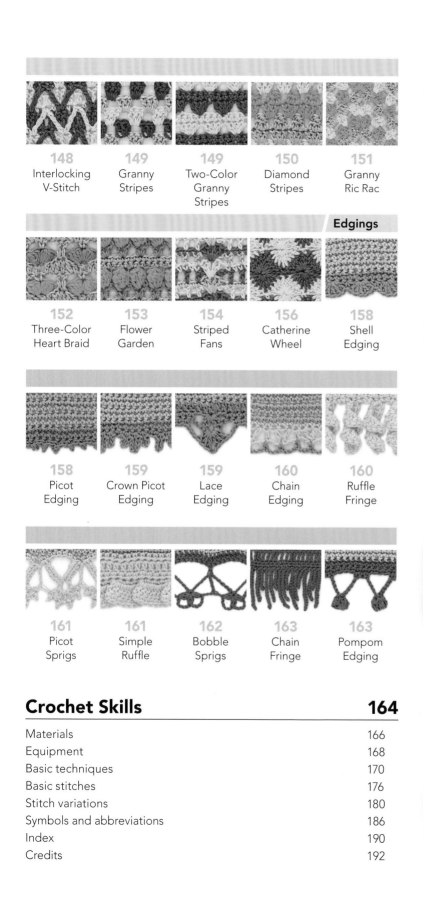

Crochet Skills 164

Foreword

I have always been fascinated by stitch dictionaries and the opportunities they offer to explore techniques and pattern. This book is a collection of some old favorites and some new ways to explore the creative possibilities crochet offers.

Each section of the stitch directory introduces a different technique: fine lace, chunky cables, and some deceptively simple colorwork. All you need is a hook and some yarn and you can dive in! Novice crocheters might like to start with the first section, which explores some creative ways to use the basic stitches, or you can dip into the book anywhere. Use the skills section at the back of the book if you need some help with basic techniques and crochet terminology.

Every stitch is accompanied by step-by-step photographs, charts, and swatches of the finished stitch. You will find suggestions on which stitches are best suited to particular yarns, plus advice on choosing hooks and project ideas you can make with your newly discovered stitches.

I hope that the 200 stitches in this book will inspire your own creativity and that you will enjoy trying something new. In choosing the stitches, I tested ideas on my friends and crochet pupils. As they worked through the swatches and techniques, they grew more confident and bolder in their choice of stitches; they discovered that by tackling each swatch one row at a time, they could master even the most "complicated" lace or cables.

I hope that you will use this book as an invitation to explore the creative opportunities crochet offers us and enjoy the simple pleasure of wrapping yarn over a hook to make something beautiful or practical for you and your friends.

Tracey Todhunter

About This Book

The main chapter of this book is the Directory of Stitches (pages 12–163), featuring step-by-step instructions for 200 crochet stitches ranging from shells, clusters, and spikes to mesh, lace, and Tunisian crochet. If you need to brush up any of your crochet skills at any point, at the back of the book you will find the Crochet Skills chapter (pages 164–189). There you will find information on crocheting basics, from choosing yarn and holding the hook to working basic stitches and stitch variations.

- **Step and row numbers:** For most of the stitches in this book, the step number is the same as the row number it describes. Where this is not the case, the row number appears in parentheses after the step number.
- **Special stitches:** Advanced or special stitches are explained with clear written instructions in the Special Stitch section at the end of each pattern when they are needed. These are also used to help make some patterns shorter or easier to follow and memorize.
- **Right and wrong side:** Where the first row of the stitch is worked from the right side, this is indicated at the start of the instructions and the first row of the chart begins on the right-hand side. The instructions also indicate when the first row is worked from the wrong side; these charts begin on the left-hand side.

Different colored yarns are allocated a letter.

Guidelines for the length of foundation chain required are listed. See page 171 for more on this.

Parentheses ( ) are used within the instructions for explanation or additional information. For example, "(RS)," "1dc in next dc (center of 5dc)," or "Ch1 (counts as 1dc)."

Reading the Patterns and Charts

The 200 crochet stitches that make up the stitch directory, with written instructions and charts, will help you master a wide range of crochet skills. Organized into 12 families of stitches and clearly numbered, you can dip in and out of the directory or work your way through a particular section to develop your skills in that area.

Stitches are divided into stitch families and clearly numbered.

Swatches shown at approximately actual size provide a great visual for how the finished stitch will look.

Symbol charts in the color of the swatch provide a visual map for working the stitch. Symbols indicate the different stitches and how they are placed in relation to each other. A full list of symbols can be found on pages 186–189. Charts show at least one full pattern repeat and represent the right side of the work. Right-side rows are numbered at the right and read from right to left. Wrong-side rows are numbered at the left and read from left to right.

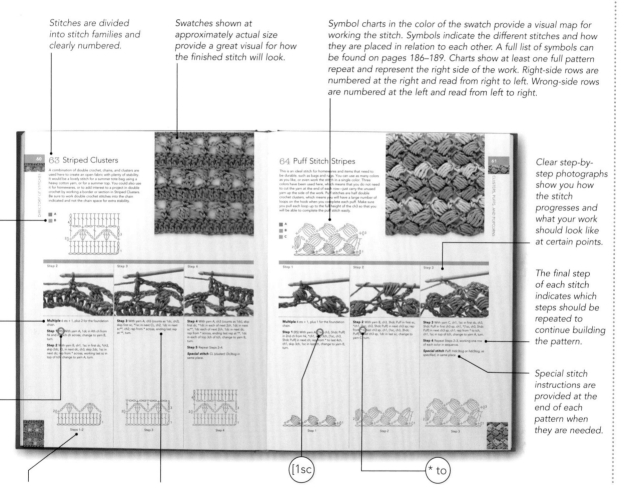

Clear step-by-step photographs show you how the stitch progresses and what your work should look like at certain points.

The final step of each stitch indicates which steps should be repeated to continue building the pattern.

Special stitch instructions are provided at the end of each pattern when they are needed.

The charts for some stitches are broken down to help you locate the specific part of the chart that relates to the instructions in that step or steps. Previous steps/rows are faintly shown so you can see how the chart and the stitch builds up.

Written step-by-step instructions guide you through the creation of the stitch. Make sure that you begin with the correct number of foundation chains and follow the instructions exactly. The terminology of crochet can be confusing at first. A full list of abbreviations is given on pages 186–189 at the back of the book.

[1sc]

Square brackets [ ] tell you to read the enclosed instructions as a group. For example, "skip [1sc, 1dc]" means that you should skip 1 single crochet and skip 1 double. Similarly, "[2dc in next dc, ch1] twice" indicates that you should work 2 doubles in the next double, chain 1, 2 doubles in the following double, chain 1.

* to)

*Asterisks * within the instructions indicate a point from which instructions are repeated. For example, "Rep from * across" means you should repeat the instructions after the * across the whole row to the end. Where instructions given after the * do not fit exactly or a different stitch is worked at the end of a row, the instruction will reflect this. For example, "*1sc in next sc**, 2dc in next sc; rep from * across, ending last rep at **, 1dc in last sc" means repeat the instructions after the * but end the last repeat at **, then work 1 double into the remaining single crochet.*

1 Directory of **stitches**

It's time to dive into the Directory of Stitches and the 200 crochet stitches that you'll find within. Learn how to build a sturdy and hard-wearing fabric from single crochet stitches, create a fun, multicolored pattern of spikes or chevrons, make a beautiful and delicate lace or mesh fabric, or embellish your pieces with clusters, popcorns, or cables. The directory is divided into 12 families of stitches to help you to easily find the perfect one to suit your project. Whether you dip in and out or work your way through a complete section to really master one technique, get ready to make some stunning crochet creations.

1 Slip Stitch Rib

Slip stitches can be tight to work, so it is best to use a hook that is larger than the one recommended on the ball band. Unlike taller stitches, there is no need to make a turning chain at the beginning of each row of slipped stitches. This stitch pattern tends to "lean" to one side, but can easily be straightened with blocking or when sewn to other squarer pieces.

2 Front Loop Slip Stitch

This stitch pattern produces a thin and stable fabric, and is often used for hats. There is no need to make a turning chain at the beginning of each row of slipped stitches.

Step 2

Step 3

Multiple Any number of sts.

Step 1 (RS) 1sc in 2nd ch from hk and in each ch across, turn.

Step 2 1sl st in each sc across, turn.

Step 3 Ch1, 1sc in each sl st across, turn.

Step 4 Repeat Steps 2–3.

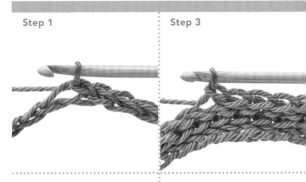

Step 1

Step 3

Multiple Any number of sts.

Step 1 (RS) 1sl st in first ch and in each ch across, turn.

Step 2 1FLsl st in each sl st across, turn.

Step 3 Repeat Step 2.

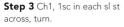

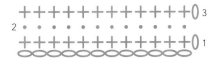

3 Back Loop Slip Stitch

This pattern closely resembles knitted fabric. It makes a strong and elastic rib suitable for cuffs, welts, and hat brims.

4 Purl Slip Stitch

Closely resembling knitted garter stitch, this stitch pattern has a defined texture and is ideal for sturdy projects such as edgings, bags, and homewares.

Step 2	Step 3

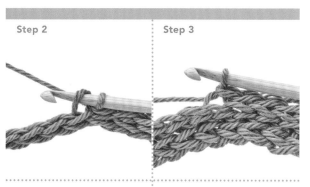

Step 2	Step 3

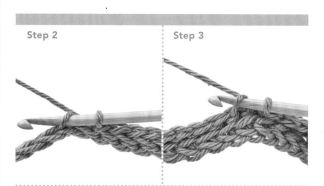

Multiple Any number of sts.

Step 1 (RS) 1sl st in first ch and in each ch across, turn.

Step 2 1BLsl st in each sl st across, turn.

Step 3 Repeat Step 2.

Multiple Any number of sts.

Step 1 (RS) 1sl st in first ch and in each ch across, turn.

Step 2 1BLsl st in each sl st across, turn.

Step 3 1FLsl st in each sl st across, turn.

Step 4 Repeat Steps 2–3.

5 Shallow Single Crochet

This pretty variation on traditional single crochet gives an effect similar to knitted stockinette stitch. It creates a slightly denser fabric that holds its shape well, and can be used for garments, homewares, and accessories.

6 Crossed Single Crochet

A simple stitch made using chains and single crochet, this pattern creates a fabric with a lovely texture and is best made using crisp cotton or smooth yarns.

Step 2	Step 3

insert hook here

Multiple Any number of sts.

Step 1 (RS) 1sc in 2nd ch from hk and in each ch across, turn.

Step 2 Ch1, 1Ssc in each sc across, turn.

Step 3 Repeat Step 2.

Special stitch *Ssc (shallow sc): Insert hk between the two vertical bars of stitch below and complete sc as usual.*

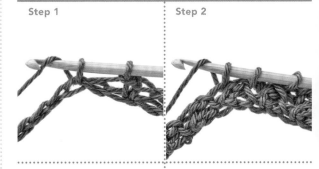

Step 1	Step 2

Multiple 2 sts, plus 1 for the foundation chain.

Step 1 (RS) 1sc in 3rd ch from hk, *ch1, skip 1ch, 1sc in next ch; rep from * across, turn.

Step 2 Ch2 (counts as 1sc, ch1), sc2tog over first and 2nd ch sp, *ch1, sc2tog over previous and next ch sp; rep from * to last sc, sc2tog over previous ch sp and tch sp, sc2tog over tch sp and first ch of tch, turn.

Step 3 Repeat Step 2.

7 Alternate Stitch

This pattern uses a combination of techniques and stitches to create beautiful texture and drape. Use smooth wool or cotton yarn to show off the texture. The stitch would be ideal for making a scarf.

8 Pin Tuck Ridges

The pleated effect of this stitch looks great for scarves and blankets. It is very effective if worked in combination with rows of single crochet.

Step 1

Step 2

Multiple An even number of sts, plus 1 for the foundation chain.

Step 1 (RS) Skip first 2ch, *sc2tog over next 2ch, ch1; rep from * to last ch, 1hdc in last ch, turn.

Step 2 Ch2 (counts as 1hdc), *BLsc2tog over next ch and sc2tog, ch1; rep from * to tch, 1hdc in top of tch, turn.

Step 3 Repeat Step 2.

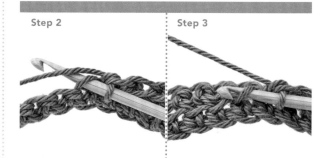

Step 2

Step 3

Multiple Any number of sts.

Step 1 (WS) 1sc in 2nd ch from hk and in each ch across, turn.

Step 2 Ch1, 1FLsc in each sc across, turn.

Step 3 Ch1, 1FLsc in each sc two rows below, turn.

Step 4 Ch1, 1sc in each sc of previous row, turn.

Step 5 Ch1, 1sc in each sc across, turn.

Step 6 Repeat Steps 2–5.

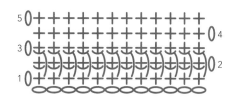

9 Rocking Stitch

Also known as Trinity Stitch, this simple pattern has a lovely texture and is ideal for blankets, scarves, and wraps. It is best to use a smooth yarn so that your hook can easily identify the chain spaces and stitches.

10 Middle Bar Half Double Crochet

You can crochet into the middle horizontal bar of any stitch taller than single crochet. This creates a clearly defined middle line and a horizontal pattern that looks like knitting. Also known as Camel Stitch, half double crochet is the most popular and best-known version.

Step 1

Step 2

Step 2

Step 3

Multiple An even number of sts.

Step 1 (RS) Sc2tog over 2nd and 3rd ch from hk, *ch1, sc3tog over previous ch and next 2ch; rep from * to last ch, ch1, sc2tog over previous ch and last ch, turn.

Step 2 Ch1, sc2tog over first sc2tog and ch sp, *ch1, sc3tog over [previous ch sp, next sc3tog, and next ch sp]; rep from * to last sc2tog, ch1, sc2tog over previous ch sp and last sc2tog, turn.

Step 3 Repeat Step 2.

Multiple Any number of sts.

Step 1 (RS) 1hdc in 3rd ch from hk and in each ch across, turn.

Step 2 Ch2 (counts as 1hdc), skip first hdc, 1hdc in middle bar of each hdc across, 1hdc in top of tch, turn.

Step 3 Ch2 (counts as 1hdc), skip first hdc, 1hdc in each hdc across, 1hdc in top of tch, turn.

Step 4 Repeat Steps 2–3.

Special stitch *1hdc in middle bar: Yo, insert hk in horizontal bar on the wrong side of the stitch (formed by yo of previous row), just below the top loops, and complete hdc as usual.*

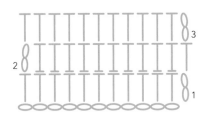

11 Wide Half Double Crochet

This is a simple variation of standard half double crochet, creating a lacy and open fabric with plenty of drape. It can be worked in textured or mohair yarn for scarves and wraps. It is best to use a hook one size larger for the foundation chain so that the stitches do not pucker.

12 Striped Wide Half Double Crochet

This version of Wide Half Double Crochet is worked in single-row stripes without cutting the yarn. Change to the new color on the last yarnover of the last stitch of the row. After the first three rows, the next color in the sequence will be waiting for you as you finish the row. Use this stitch for scarves, blankets, and projects where you will see both sides of the work.

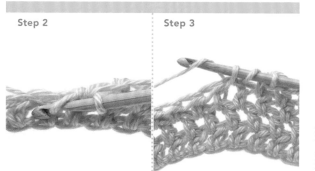

Step 2   Step 3

Multiple Any number of sts.

Step 1 (RS) 1hdc in 3rd ch from hk and in each ch across, turn.

Step 2 Ch2 (counts as 1hdc), 1hdc in each space between sts to last hdc, skip last hdc, 1hdc in top of tch, turn.

Step 3 Repeat Step 2.

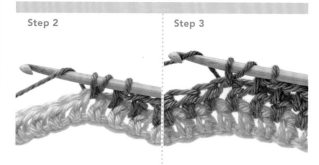

Step 2   Step 3

Multiple Any number of sts.

Step 1 (RS) With yarn A, 1hdc in 3rd ch from hk and in each ch across, change to yarn B, turn.

Step 2 With yarn B, ch2 (counts as 1hdc), 1hdc in each space between sts to last hdc, skip last hdc, 1hdc in top of tch, change to yarn C, turn.

Step 3 Repeat Step 2, working one row of each color in sequence.

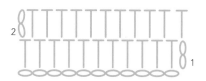

- A
- B
- C

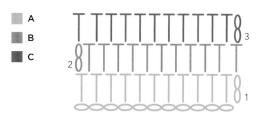

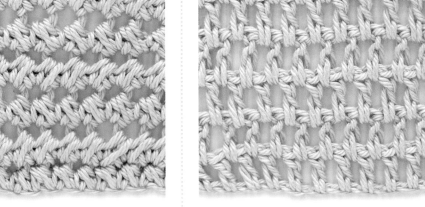

13 Crossed Half Double Crochet

This is a simple stitch with plenty of stability because of the crossed stitches. It is suitable for projects where you can see both the front and the back, such as blankets and scarves.

14 Wide Double Crochet

A simple variation of standard double crochet, this pattern creates a lacy and open fabric with plenty of drape. It is best to use a hook one size larger for the foundation chain so that the stitches do not pucker.

Step 1

Step 2

Step 2

Step 3

Multiple Any number of sts.

Step 1 (RS) Hdc2tog over 3rd and 4th ch from hk, *hdc2tog over previous ch and next ch; rep from * to last ch, 1hdc in last ch, turn.

Step 2 Ch2 (counts as 1hdc), hdc2tog over first hdc and hdc2tog, *hdc2tog over previous and next hdc2tog; rep from * to tch, 1hdc in top of tch, turn.

Step 3 Repeat Step 2.

Multiple Any number of sts.

Step 1 (RS) 1dc in 4th ch from hk and in each ch across, turn.

Step 2 Ch3 (counts as 1dc), 1dc each space between sts to last dc, skip last dc, 1dc in top of tch, turn.

Step 3 Repeat Step 2.

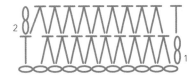

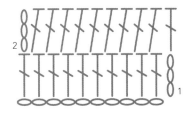

15 Griddle Stitch

This very effective combination of single and double crochet is easy to memorize, making it suitable for the novice crocheter. Use thick, chunky yarns for textured accessories and blankets.

16 Track Stitch

Combining rows of tall stitches with single crochet, this pattern creates an open fabric with lots of drape. It is most effective in natural fibers, such as linen and cotton, and can be used to make a very simple wrap or scarf. It would also work well for a lightweight summer beach cover-up.

Step 1

Step 2

Step 2

Step 3

Multiple An even number of sts.

Step 1 (RS) 1sc in 4th ch from hk, *1dc in next ch, 1sc in next ch; rep from * across, turn.

Step 2 Ch3 (counts as 1dc), skip first sc, *1sc in next dc, 1dc in next sc; rep from * across, 1sc in top of tch, turn.

Step 3 Repeat Step 2.

Multiple Any number of sts.

Step 1 (RS) 1sc in 3rd ch from hk and in each ch across, turn.

Step 2 Ch5 (counts as 1dtr), skip first sc, 1dtr in each sc across, 1dtr in top of tch, turn.

Step 3 Ch1 (counts as 1sc), skip first dtr, 1sc in each dtr across, 1sc in top of tch, turn.

Step 4 Ch1 (counts as 1sc), skip first sc, 1sc in each sc across, 1sc in tch, turn.

Step 5 Work as Step 4.

Step 6 Repeat Steps 2–5.

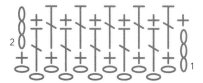

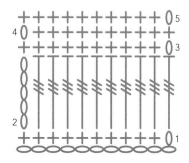

17 Double Crunch

This is another example where stitches of different heights are used together to give texture to the crochet fabric. It would be a good choice for garments. There is no need to make a turning chain on rows that begin with a slip stitch.

18 Tall Alternate Stitch

This combination of single crochet and extended single crochet creates texture and drape. It is a good choice for smooth yarns and has many uses. Try making a scarf in chunky wool or use it for a sweater. Extended stitches are made by working an extra yarnover, and the same technique can be used to make an extended version of any of the basic crochet stitches (see page 177).

Step 2

Step 3

Step 2

Step 4

Multiple An odd number of sts.

Step 1 (RS) 1dc in 4th ch from hk and in each ch across, turn.

Step 2 1sl st in first dc, *1dc in next dc, 1sl st in next dc; rep from * across, working last sl st in top of tch, turn.

Step 3 Ch3 (counts as 1dc), skip first sl st, 1dc in each st across, turn.

Step 4 Repeat Steps 2–3.

Multiple An odd number of sts, plus 1 for the foundation chain.

Step 1 (WS) 1sc in 2nd ch from hk and in each ch across, turn.

Step 2 Ch1, 1sc in first sc, *1exsc in next sc, 1sc in next sc; rep from * across, turn.

Step 3 Ch1, 1sc in each sc and exsc across, turn.

Step 4 Ch1, 1sc in each of first 2sc, *1exsc in next sc, 1sc in next sc; rep from * to last sc, 1sc in last sc, turn.

Step 5 Ch1, 1sc in each sc and exsc across, turn.

Step 6 Repeat Steps 2–5.

Special stitch *Exsc (extended sc): Insert hk in st, yo and pull a loop through, yo and pull through 1 loop on hk, yo and pull through both loops on hk.*

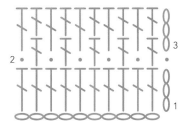

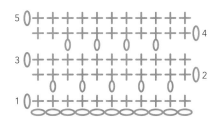

19 Staggered Double Crochet

An easy stitch combining double crochet and chain spaces, this pattern creates an open, textured fabric that has excellent drape, but also holds its shape well. It is suitable for homewares, garments, and accessories.

20 Easy Mock Bobbles

Give your crochet a subtle bobble effect without the effort by using this combination of tall stitches and double crochet. It is very easy to work, making it suitable for the novice crocheter. Use smooth yarns to accentuate the texture.

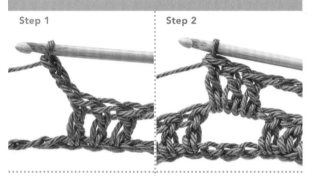

Step 1   **Step 2**

Multiple 6 sts + 2, plus 2 for the foundation chain.

Step 1 (RS) 1dc in 4th ch from hk, 1dc in each of next 2ch, *ch3, skip 3ch, 1dc in each of next 3ch; rep from * to last 4ch, ch3, skip 3ch, 1dc in last ch, turn.

Step 2 Ch3 (counts as 1dc), *3dc in next ch sp, ch3; rep from * to tch, 1dc in top of tch, turn.

Step 3 Repeat Step 2.

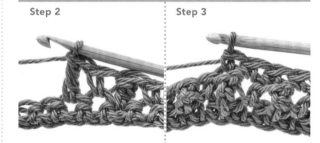

Step 2   **Step 3**

Multiple 2 sts + 1, plus 1 for the foundation chain.

Step 1 (RS) 1sc in 2nd ch from hk and in each ch across, turn.

Step 2 Ch1, 1sc in first sc, *1tr in next sc, 1sc in next sc; rep from * across, turn.

Step 3 Ch1, 1sc in each sc and tr across, turn.

Step 4 Ch1, 1sc in each sc across, turn.

Step 5 Work as Step 4.

Step 6 Repeat Steps 2–5.

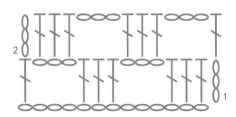

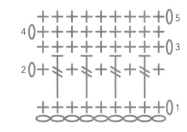

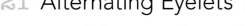

21 Alternating Eyelets 1

Alternating rows of different-height stitches are used to create this sturdy and attractive fabric. Shown here in a single color, you can also use your own choice of stripe sequence for bold accessories and blankets. Use a lightweight yarn and larger hook than usual for the yarn weight to crochet a wrap with excellent drape.

22 Alternating Eyelets 2

This version of Alternating Eyelets creates a very stable fabric. Use it for any project that requires a strong but lightweight fabric. You can use smooth or textured yarn for this stitch.

 Step 4

Step 5

Multiple 2 sts + 1, plus 1 for the foundation chain.

Step 1 (RS) 1sc in 2nd ch from hk and in each ch across, turn.

Step 2 Ch1, 1sc in each sc across, turn.

Step 3 Work as Step 2.

Step 4 Ch3 (counts as 1hdc, ch1), skip first 2sc, 1hdc in next sc, *ch1, skip 1sc, 1hdc in next sc; rep from * across, turn.

Step 5 Ch1, 1sc in first hdc, *1sc in next ch1 sp, 1sc in next hdc; rep from * to tch, 1sc in tch sp, 1sc in 2nd ch of tch, turn.

Step 6 Repeat Steps 2–5.

 Step 2

Step 3

Multiple 3 sts, plus 1 for the foundation chain.

Step 1 (RS) 1sc in 2nd ch from hk and in each ch across, turn.

Step 2 Ch4 (counts as 1dc, ch1), skip first 2sc, *1dc in each of next 2sc, ch1, skip 1sc; rep from * to last sc, 1dc in last sc, turn.

Step 3 Ch1, 1sc in first dc, *1sc in next ch1 sp, 1sc in each of next 2dc; rep from * to tch, 1sc in tch sp, 1sc in 3rd ch of tch, turn.

Step 4 Repeat Steps 2–3.

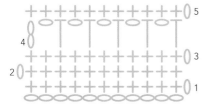

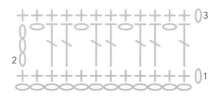

23 Brick Stitch

This is a good example of how simple stitches can be combined to create pleasing textures. Using a combination of single and double crochet, this pattern is ideal for garments and blankets because it holds its shape well. It is also easy to memorize.

24 Two-Color Brick Stitch

This is worked in the same way as Brick Stitch, but using two colors. The effect is very pleasing and would suit accessories and homewares. For added interest, try using a smooth yarn for the single crochet rows and textured yarn for the double crochet rows. You will need to cut the yarn at the end of each row, so it is helpful if you crochet over the yarn tails as you work.

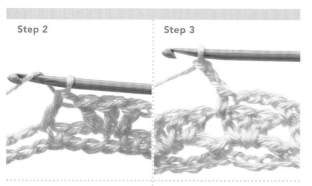

Step 2

Step 3

Multiple 4 sts + 1, plus 1 for the foundation chain.

Step 1 (WS) 1sc in 2nd ch from hk, *ch3, skip 3ch, 1sc in next ch; rep from * across, turn.

Step 2 Ch3 (counts as 1dc), 3dc in each ch3 sp across, 1dc in last sc, turn.

Step 3 Ch1, 1sc in first dc, ch3, skip 3dc, *1sc in space between previous and next dc, ch3, skip 3dc; rep from * to tch, 1sc in top of tch, turn.

Step 4 Repeat Steps 2–3.

Step 3

Step 4

Multiple 4 sts + 1, plus 1 for the foundation chain.

Step 1 (WS) With yarn A, 1sc in 2nd ch from hk, *ch3, skip 3ch, 1sc in next ch; rep from * across, change to yarn B, turn.

Step 2 With yarn B, ch3 (counts as 1dc), 3dc in each ch3 sp across, 1dc in last sc, change to yarn A, turn.

Step 3 With yarn A, ch1, 1sc in first dc, ch3, skip 3dc, *1sc in space between previous and next dc, ch3, skip 3dc; rep from * to tch, 1sc in top of tch, change to yarn B, turn.

Step 4 Repeat Steps 2–3.

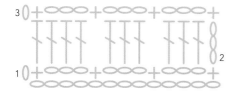

A
B

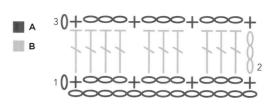

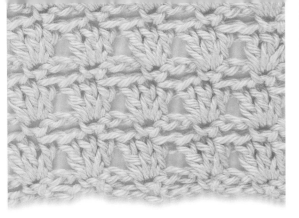

25 Parquet Stitch

This simple shell pattern looks striking in chunky yarns.
It is a very pretty stitch and is robust enough for homewares.
It also works for items that require a reversible fabric, such
as scarves.

26 Turtle Stitch

Working into the front and back loops produces a fabric with
good stability and drape. This pattern is easy to memorize,
making it ideal for a novice.

Step 2

Step 3

Step 2

Step 3

Multiple 3 sts + 1, plus 2 for
the foundation chain.

Step 1 (WS) 1sc in 6th ch
from hk, *ch2, skip 2ch, 1sc in
next ch; rep from * across,
turn.

Step 2 Ch3 (counts as 1dc),
1dc in first sc, *Shell in next sc;
rep from * to tch, skip 2ch, 2dc
in next ch, turn.

Step 3 Ch3 (counts as 1sc,
ch2), skip first 3dc, *1sc in
center dc of next Shell, ch2;
rep from * to tch, 1sc in top of
tch, turn.

Step 4 Repeat Steps 2–3.

Special stitch *Shell: 3dc in
same place.*

Multiple 6 sts + 4, plus 3 for
the foundation chain.

Step 1 (RS) 2dc in 4th ch from
hk, skip 2ch, *1sc in next ch,
skip 2ch, Shell in next ch, skip
2ch; rep from * to last ch, 1sc
in last ch, turn.

Step 2 Ch3 (counts as 1dc),
2FLdc in first sc, *1FLsc in
center dc of next Shell,
FL Shell in next sc; rep from *
to tch, 1sc in top of tch, turn.

Step 3 Ch3 (counts as 1dc),
2BLdc in first sc, *1BLsc in
center dc of next Shell,
BL Shell in next sc; rep from *
to tch, 1sc in top of tch, turn.

Step 4 Repeat Steps 2–3.

Special stitch *Shell: 5dc in
same place, working into front
loop (FL) or back loop (BL)
where specified.*

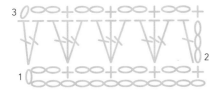

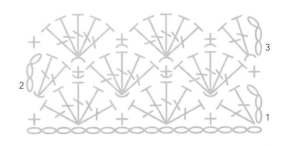

27 Cross Hatch Shells

28 Offset Shells

Cross Hatch Shells is very attractive and lends itself to several kinds of projects, including garments, blankets, and accessories. Choose a smooth yarn to show off the construction of the shell stitches.

This pretty stitch is suitable for many weights of yarn. Use lightweight wool or silk to make airy wraps and scarves, or use chunky yarn to make stylish blankets and throws. The shells are staggered on each row, making the pattern appear more complex than it is—with only one row to memorize, it is suitable for all skill levels.

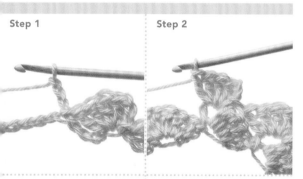

Step 1 — Step 2

Step 1 — Step 2

Multiple 6 sts + 1, plus 1 for the foundation chain.

Step 1 (RS) Shell in 4th ch from hk, skip 3ch, *[1sl st, ch3, Shell] in next ch, skip 3ch; rep from * to last ch, 1sl st in last ch, turn.

Step 2 Ch5, Shell in 4th ch from hk, *[1sl st, ch3, Shell] in space between last dc of next Shell and next ch3; rep from * to tch, 1sl st in top of tch, turn.

Step 3 Repeat Step 2.

Special stitch *Shell: 4dc in same place.*

Multiple 11 sts + 5, plus 2 for the foundation chain.

Step 1 (RS) 1dc in 4th ch from hk, 1dc in each of next 3ch, *skip 2ch, Shell in next ch, ch2, skip 3ch, 1dc in each of next 5ch; rep from * across, turn.

Step 2 Ch3 (counts as 1dc), skip first dc, 1dc in each of next 4dc, *Shell in first dc of next Shell, ch2, skip last 4dc of same Shell, 1dc in each of next 5dc; rep from * across, working last dc in top of tch, turn.

Step 3 Repeat Step 2.

Special stitch *Shell: 5dc in same place.*

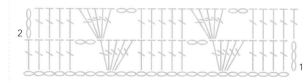

29 Thistle Stitch

The double crochet stitches between the shells give this stitch pattern plenty of stability, so it is ideal for a baby blanket or pillow cover. On Steps 2 and 3, double crochet stitches are worked in the spaces between stitches instead of into the top of the stitch.

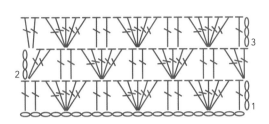

Step 1

Step 2

Step 3

Multiple 7 sts + 2, plus 2 for the foundation chain.

Step 1 (RS) 1dc in 4th ch from hk, *skip 2ch, Shell in next ch, skip 2ch, 1dc in each of next 2ch; rep from * across, turn.

Step 2 Ch3 (counts as 1dc), 2dc in first dc, skip 3dc, *1dc in space between 2nd and 3rd dc of next Shell, 1dc in space between 3rd and 4th dc of same Shell, skip 3dc**, Shell in space between last skipped dc and next dc, skip 3dc; rep from * across, ending last rep at **, 3dc in space between last dc and tch, turn.

Step 3 Ch3 (counts as 1dc), 1dc between first 2dc, *skip 3dc, Shell in space between last skipped dc and next dc, skip 3dc**, 1dc in space between 2nd and 3rd dc of next Shell, 1dc in space between 3rd and 4th dc of same Shell; rep from * across, ending last rep at **, 2dc in space between last dc and tch, turn.

Step 4 Repeat Steps 2–3.

Special stitch *Shell: 5dc in same place.*

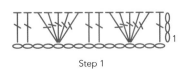

Step 1

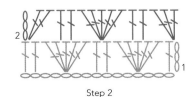

Step 2

Step 3

30 Boxed Fans

Rows of clusters alternate with chain spaces to create a stitch with plenty of drape. The columns of fans work well for items such as blankets and scarves. It is very effective when worked in a smooth yarn for the best stitch definition. You can also achieve a pleasing effect with a variegated yarn.

Step 2

Step 3

Step 4

Multiple 10 sts + 1, plus 1 for the foundation chain.

Step 1 (WS) 1sc in 2nd ch from hk, *ch3, skip 3ch, 1sc in next ch, ch3, skip 1ch, 1sc in next ch, ch3, skip 3ch, 1sc in next ch; rep from * across, turn.

Step 2 Ch1, 1sc in first sc, *ch1, skip next ch sp, Fan in next ch sp, ch1, skip next ch sp, 1sc in next sc; rep from * across, turn.

Step 3 Ch7 (counts as 1tr, ch3), *1sc in 2nd ch3 sp of next Fan, ch3, 1sc in next ch3 sp of same Fan, ch3, 1tr in next sc**, ch3; rep from * across, ending last rep at **, turn.

Step 4 Ch1, 1sc in first tr, *ch1, skip next ch sp, Fan in next ch sp, ch1, skip next ch sp, 1sc in next tr; rep from * across, working last sc in 4th ch of tch, turn.

Step 5 Repeat Steps 3–4.

Special stitch Fan: [(Dc2tog, ch3) 4 times, dc2tog] in same place.

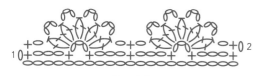

Steps 1–2

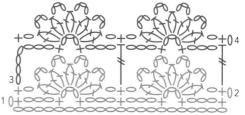

Steps 3–4

31 Fan Lace

This is a striking, large-scale pattern that works up quickly. Use soft cottons or yarns with plenty of drape to make a pretty wrap or casual accessory. This stitch could also be used to make a table runner or throw. Take care to work into the correct point of the turning chain to keep the edges straight and maintain the correct stitch count.

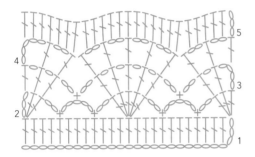

Step 2

Step 3

Step 5

Multiple 12 sts + 1, plus 2 for the foundation chain.

Step 1 (RS) 1dc in 4th ch from hk and in each ch across, turn.

Step 2 Ch3 (counts as 1dc), 2dc in first dc, ch2, skip 3dc, 1sc in next dc, ch5, skip 3dc, 1sc in next dc, ch2, skip 3dc, *5dc in next dc, ch2, skip 3dc, 1sc in next dc, ch5, skip 3dc, 1sc in next dc, ch2, skip 3dc; rep from * to tch, 3dc in top of tch, turn.

Step 3 Ch4 (counts as 1dc, ch1), skip first dc, 1dc in next dc, ch1, 1dc in next dc, ch2, 1sc in next ch5 sp, ch2, *[1dc in next dc, ch1] 4 times, 1dc in next dc, ch2, 1sc in next ch5 sp, ch2; rep from * to last 2dc, [1dc in next dc, ch1] twice, 1dc in top of tch, turn.

Step 4 Ch5 (counts as 1dc, ch2), skip first dc, 1dc in next dc, ch2, 1dc in next dc, *skip 1sc, [1dc in next dc, ch2] 4 times, 1dc in next dc; rep from * to last sc, skip last sc, [1dc in next dc, ch2] twice, 1dc in 3rd ch of tch, turn.

Step 5 Ch3 (counts as 1dc), skip first dc, 2dc in first ch2 sp, 1dc in next dc, 2dc in next ch2 sp, skip 1dc, 1dc in next dc, *[2dc in next ch2 sp, 1dc in next dc] 3 times, 2dc in next ch2 sp, skip 1dc, 1dc in next dc; rep from * to last ch2 sp, 2dc in last ch2 sp, 1dc in next dc, 2dc in tch sp, 1dc in 3rd ch of tch, turn.

Step 6 Repeat Steps 2–5.

Steps 1–2

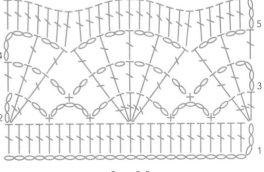

Steps 3–5

32 Woven Fans

This is a very decorative stitch, with the clusters forming vertical columns. This stitch would work in a variety of yarns and has excellent drape. The instructions may appear daunting, but the two-row repeat is quick to memorize.

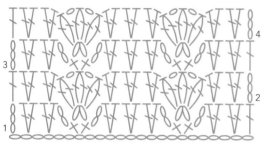

Step 1	Step 2	Step 3

Multiple 10 sts + 3, plus 3 for the foundation chain.

Step 1 (WS) 2dc in 5th ch from hk (2dc group made), skip 1ch, 2dc in next ch, *ch2, skip 2ch, [1sc, ch2, 1sc] in next ch, ch2, skip 2ch, 2dc in next ch**, [skip 1ch, 2dc in next ch] twice; rep from * across, ending last rep at **, skip 1ch, 2dc in next ch, 1dc in last ch, turn.

Step 2 Ch3 (counts as 1dc), skip first dc, [2dc in space between sts in center of next 2dc group] twice, *skip next ch sp, Fan in next ch sp, skip next ch sp**, [2dc in space between sts in center of next 2dc group] 3 times; rep from * across, ending last rep at **, [2dc in space between sts in center of next 2dc group] twice, 1dc in top of tch, turn.

Step 3 Ch3 (counts as 1dc), skip first dc, [2dc in space between sts in center of next 2dc group] twice, *ch2, [1sc, ch2, 1sc] in center dc2tog of next Fan, ch2**, [2dc in space between sts in center of next 2dc group] 3 times; rep from * across, ending last rep at **, [2dc in space between sts in center of next 2dc group] twice, 1dc in top of tch, turn.

Step 4 Repeat Steps 2–3.

Special stitch *Fan: [(Dc2tog, ch1) twice, dc2tog] in same place.*

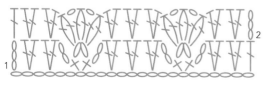

Steps 1–2

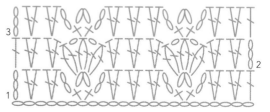

Step 3

33 Chain Link Shells

This light and airy stitch is ideal for summer garments and accessories. This is a stitch where you will need to pay attention to work into the correct chain at the end of each row in order to keep the edges of the work straight and give stability to the crochet fabric. It grows quickly and is a satisfying stitch for the novice crocheter to make.

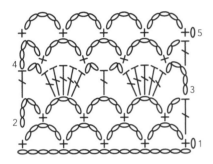

Step 2

Step 3

Step 4

Multiple 8 sts + 1, plus 1 for the foundation chain.

Step 1 (RS) 1sc in 2nd ch from hk, *ch5, skip 3ch, 1sc in next ch; rep from * across, turn.

Step 2 Ch5 (counts as 1dc, ch2), 1sc in first ch sp, *ch5, 1sc in next ch sp; rep from * to last sc, ch2, 1dc in last sc, turn.

Step 3 Ch5 (counts as 1dc, ch2), Shell in first ch5 sp, *ch2, 1dc in next ch5 sp, ch2, Shell in next ch5 sp; rep from * to tch sp, ch2, 1dc in 3rd ch of tch, turn.

Step 4 Ch5 (counts as 1dc, ch2), 1sc in first ch sp, *ch5, 1sc in next ch sp; rep from * across, working last sc in tch sp, ch2, 1dc in 3rd ch of tch, turn.

Step 5 Ch1, 1sc in first dc, *ch5, 1sc in next ch5 sp; rep from * across, working last sc in 3rd ch of tch, turn.

Step 6 Repeat Steps 2–5.

Special stitch *Shell: 5dc in same place.*

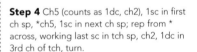

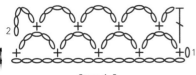

Steps 1–2

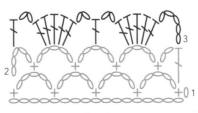

Step 3

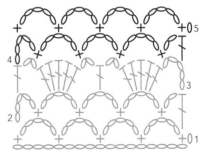

Steps 4–5

34 Trellis Fan

Trellis Fan is a traditional stitch, and is often made using a smooth, lightweight yarn. You can experiment with a heavier, textured yarn such as a DK-weight alpaca or mohair blend to make pretty accessories with good drape.

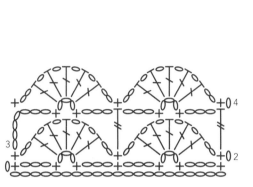

Step 2

Step 3

Step 4

Multiple 10 sts + 1, plus 1 for the foundation chain.

Step 1 (WS) 1sc in 2nd ch from hk, *ch3, skip 3ch, 1sc in next ch, ch3, skip 1ch, 1sc in next ch, ch3, skip 3ch, 1sc in next ch; rep from * across, turn.

Step 2 Ch1, 1sc in first sc, *ch2, skip next ch3 sp, Fan in next ch3 sp, ch2, skip next ch3 sp, 1sc in next sc; rep from * across, turn.

Step 3 Ch7 (counts as 1tr, ch3), *1sc in 2nd ch1 sp of next Fan, ch3, 1sc in next ch1 sp of same Fan, ch3, 1tr in next sc**, ch3; rep from * across, ending last rep at **, turn.

Step 4 Ch1, 1sc in first tr, *ch2, skip next ch3 sp, Fan in next ch3 sp**, ch2, skip next ch3 sp, 1sc in next tr; rep from * across, ending last rep at **, ch2, 1sc in 4th ch of tch, turn.

Step 5 Repeat Steps 3–4.

Special stitch Fan: [(1dc, ch1) 4 times, 1dc] in same place.

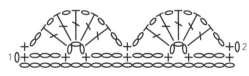

Steps 1–2

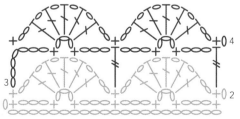

Steps 3–4

35 Embossed Shells

This is a bold stitch that works well in two or more colors. It works in all weights of yarn and is ideal for accessories and homewares. The yarn should be cut when changing colors and the ends woven in as you work across the row. For smooth color transitions, change to the new color on the last yarnover of the last stitch of the row.

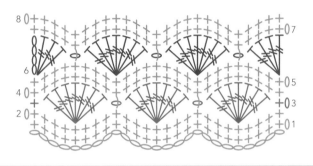

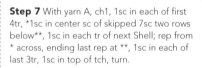

A
B
C

Step 3

Step 4

Step 7

Multiple 8 sts + 1, plus 1 for the foundation chain.

Step 1 (RS) With yarn A, 1sc in 2nd ch from hk and in each ch across, turn.

Step 2 With yarn A, ch1, 1sc in each sc across, change to yarn B, turn.

Step 3 With yarn B, ch1, 1sc in first sc, skip 3sc, *Shell in next sc, ch1, skip 7sc; rep from * to last 5sc, Shell in next sc, skip 3sc, 1sc in last sc, change to yarn A, turn.

Step 4 With yarn A, ch1, 1sc in first sc, *1sc in each tr of next Shell, 1sc in center sc of skipped 7sc two rows below; rep from * across, working last sc in last sc of previous row, turn.

Step 5 With yarn A, ch1, 1sc in each sc across, change to yarn C, turn.

Step 6 With yarn C, ch4 (counts as 1tr), 3tr in first sc, *ch1, skip 7sc, Shell in next sc; rep from * to last 8sc, ch1, skip 7sc, 4tr in last sc, change to yarn A, turn.

Step 7 With yarn A, ch1, 1sc in each of first 4tr, *1sc in center sc of skipped 7sc two rows below**, 1sc in each tr of next Shell; rep from * across, ending last rep at **, 1sc in each of last 3tr, 1sc in top of tch, turn.

Step 8 Work as Step 5.

Step 9 Repeat Steps 3–8.

Special stitch Shell: 7tr in same place.

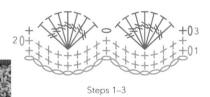

Steps 1–3

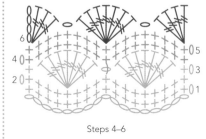

Steps 4–6

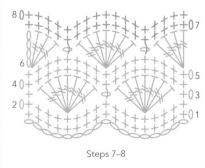

Steps 7–8

36 Striped Shells

This shell pattern uses two colors to create a bold fabric. Choose a smooth yarn that is not too bulky. The stitch can be used for homewares, garments, and accessories. You will need to cut the yarn at the end of each row, so weave in the yarn tails as you work the following row for a neater finish.

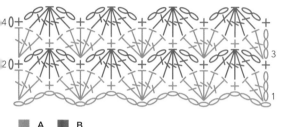

■ A   ■ B

Step 1

Multiple 6 sts + 1, plus 3 for the foundation chain.

Step 1 (RS) With yarn A, 2dc in 4th ch from hk, skip 2ch, 1sc in next ch, *skip 2ch, Shell in next ch, skip 2ch, 1sc in next ch; rep from * to last 3ch, skip 2ch, 3dc in last ch, change to yarn B, turn.

Step 2

Step 2 With yarn B, ch1, 1sc in first dc, *ch2, dc5tog over next [2dc, 1sc, 2dc], ch2, 1sc in next dc (center dc of Shell); rep from * across, working last sc in top of tch, change to yarn A, turn.

Step 3

Step 3 With yarn A, ch3 (counts as 1dc), 2dc in first sc, *1sc in next dc5tog**, Shell in next sc; rep from * across, ending last rep at **, 3dc in last sc, change to yarn B, turn.

Step 4 Repeat Steps 2–3.

Special stitch Shell: 5dc in same place.

Step 1

Step 2

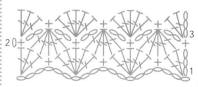

Step 3

37 Cluster Fans

An elegant textured fabric made using half double crochet clusters, this dense stitch is ideal for blankets. The clusters look most attractive in a smooth yarn, and also look very effective worked in a crisp, cotton yarn.

Step 2	Step 3	Step 5
 |  |

Multiple 8 sts + 1, plus 1 for the foundation chain.

Step 1 (RS) 1sc in 2nd ch from hk, *ch1, skip 3ch, Fan in next ch, ch1, skip 3ch, 1sc in next ch; rep from * across, turn.

Step 2 Ch3 (counts as 1dc), 1dc in first sc, *ch2, 1sc in center hdc3tog of next Fan, ch2**, 3dc in next sc; rep from * across, ending last rep at **, 2dc in last sc, turn.

Step 3 Ch2 (counts as 1hdc), [1hdc, ch2, hdc3tog] in first dc, *ch1, skip 1dc, 1sc in next sc, ch1, skip 1dc**, Fan in next dc; rep from * across, ending last rep at **, [hdc3tog, ch2, hdc2tog] in top of tch, turn.

Step 4 Ch1, 1sc in hdc2tog, *ch2, 3dc in next sc, ch2, 1sc in center hdc3tog of next Fan; rep from * across, working last sc in top of tch, turn.

Step 5 Ch1, 1sc in first sc, *ch1, skip 1dc, Fan in next dc, ch1, skip 1dc, 1sc in next sc; rep from * across, turn.

Step 6 Repeat Steps 2–5.

Special stitch Fan: [(Hdc3tog, ch2) twice, hdc3tog] in same place.

Steps 1–2

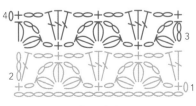

Steps 3–4

Step 5

38 Tiara Lace

This is a pretty stitch that works well in a variety of yarns. The interlocking chains make it stable enough for a wrap made in fine mohair. Try using a smooth cotton yarn first, and then experiment with different weights and textures. The two-row repeat is easy to memorize, making this an ideal stitch for a novice to try.

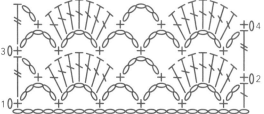

Step 1

Step 2

Step 3

Multiple 12 sts.

Step 1 (WS) 1sc in 2nd ch from hk, *ch5, skip 3ch, 1sc in next ch; rep from * to last 2ch, ch2, skip 1ch, 1dc in last ch, turn.

Step 2 Ch1, 1sc in first dc, *Shell in next ch5 sp, 1sc in next ch5 sp**, ch5, 1sc in next ch5 sp; rep from * across, ending last rep at **, ch2, 1tr in last sc, turn.

Step 3 Ch1, 1sc in first tr, *ch5, 1sc in 2nd dc of next Shell, ch5, 1sc in 6th dc of same Shell**, ch5, 1sc in next ch5 sp; rep from * across, ending last rep at **, ch2, 1tr in last sc, turn.

Step 4 Repeat Steps 2–3.

Special stitch *Shell: 7dc in same place.*

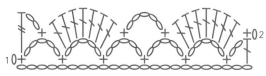

Steps 1–2

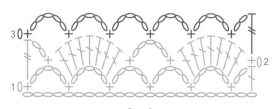

Step 3

39 Colored Fans

This striking and attractive stitch suits large-scale projects such as wraps. The stitch can be made in a single color, but using two or more colors shows off the fan pattern and adds visual interest. A smooth lightweight yarn is best for this stitch. Change color on the last yarnover of the last stitch of the row to ensure smooth color transitions. There is no need to cut the yarn; simply carry the unused yarn up the side of the work.

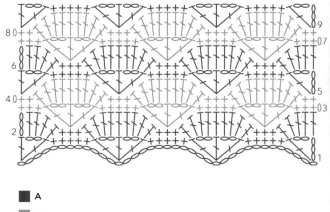

■ A
■ B

Step 1

Step 2

Step 3

Multiple 12 sts + 1, plus 5 for the foundation chain.

Step 1 (RS) With yarn A, 1dc in 6th ch from hk, skip 3ch, 1sc in each of next 5ch, skip 3ch, *Fan in next ch, skip 3ch, 1sc in each of next 5ch, skip 3ch; rep from * to last ch, [1dc, ch2, 1dc] in last ch, turn.

Step 2 With yarn A, ch3 (counts as 1dc), 3dc in first ch sp, 1dc in next dc, *skip 1sc, 1sc in each of next 3sc, skip 1sc**, 9dc Arch over next Fan; rep from * across, ending last rep at **, 1dc in last dc, 3dc in tch sp, 1dc in 3rd ch of tch, change to yarn B, turn.

Step 3 With yarn B, ch1, 1sc in each of first 3dc, *skip 2dc and 1sc, Fan in next sc, skip 1sc and 2dc**, 1sc in each of next 5dc (center 5dc of Arch); rep from * across, ending last rep at **, 1sc in each of last 2dc, 1dc in top of tch, turn.

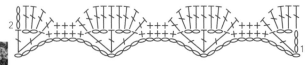

Steps 1–2

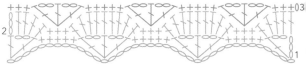

Step 3

Step 4 With yarn B, ch1, 1sc in each of first 2sc, *skip 1sc, 9dc Arch over next Fan, skip 1sc**, 1sc in each of next 3sc; rep from * across, ending last rep at **, 1sc in each of last 2sc, change to yarn A, turn.

Step 5 With yarn A, ch5 (counts as 1dc, ch2), 1dc in first sc, *skip 1sc and 2dc, 1sc in each of next 5dc (center 5dc of Arch), skip 2dc and 1sc**, Fan in next sc; rep from * across, ending last rep at **, [1dc, ch2, 1dc] in last sc, turn.

Step 6 Repeat Steps 2–5.

Special stitch *Fan: [(1dc, ch2) twice, 1dc] in same place.*

Special stitch *9dc Arch: 1dc in first dc of Fan, [3dc in next ch sp, 1dc in next dc] twice in same Fan.*

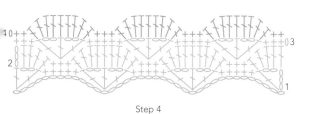

Step 4

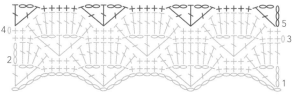

Step 5

40 Offset Shell Columns

This striking fabric is an excellent choice for smooth sport-weight yarns. It is made up of several different stitches, so be sure to read the pattern carefully before you begin. Novice crocheters may feel daunted by the length of the pattern, but if you follow each step in turn, you will soon become more confident.

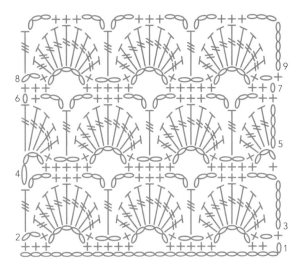

Step 2

Step 3

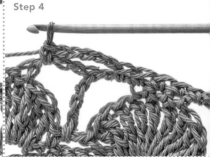

Step 4

Multiple 8 sts + 1, plus 1 for the foundation chain.

Step 1 (RS) 1sc in 3rd ch from hk, 1sc in next ch, *ch5, skip 3ch, 1sc in each of next 5ch; rep from * to last 6ch, ch5, skip 3ch, 1sc in each of last 3ch, turn.

Step 2 Ch2 (counts as 1sc, ch1), skip first 2sc, *1sc in next sc, Shell in next ch sp, 1sc in next sc**, ch2, skip 3sc; rep from * across, ending last rep at **, ch1, skip last sc, 1sc in top of tch, turn.

Step 3 Ch8 (counts as 1dtr, ch3), *1sc in each of center 3tr of next Shell, ch3**, 1dtr in next ch2 sp, ch3; rep from * across, ending last rep at **, 1dtr in first ch of tch, turn.

Step 4 Ch4 (counts as 1sc, ch3), skip first dtr, *1sc in next ch3 sp, 1sc in each of next 3sc**, 1sc in next ch3 sp, ch5; rep from * across, ending last rep at **, 1sc in tch sp, ch3, 1sc in 5th ch of tch, turn.

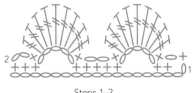

Steps 1–2

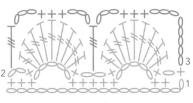

Step 3

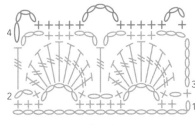

Step 4

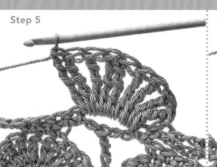

Step 5

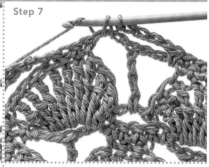

Step 6

Step 7

Step 5 Ch4 (counts as 1tr), skip first sc, 4tr in ch3 sp, *1sc in next sc, ch2, skip 3sc, 1sc in next sc**, Shell in next ch5 sp; rep from * across, ending last rep at **, 5tr in tch sp, turn.

Step 6 Ch1 (counts as 1sc), skip first tr, 1sc in next tr, *ch3, 1dtr in next ch2 sp, ch3**, 1sc in each of center 3tr of next Shell; rep from * across, ending last rep at **, 1sc in last tr, 1sc in top of tch, turn.

Step 7 Ch1 (counts as 1sc), skip first sc, 1sc in next sc, *1sc in next ch sp, ch5, 1sc in next ch sp**, 1sc in each of next 3sc; rep from * across, ending last rep at **, 1sc in last sc, 1sc in tch, turn.

Step 8 Repeat Steps 2–7.

Special stitch Shell: 9tr in same place.

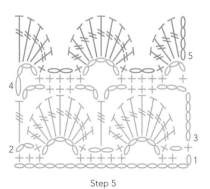

Step 5

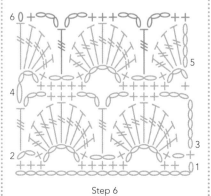

Step 6

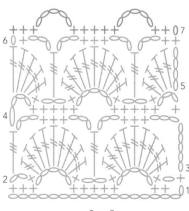

Step 7

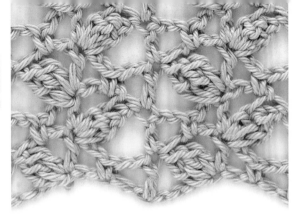

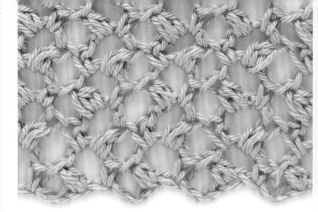

41 Simple Clusters

Made up of columns of clusters set at alternating angles, this versatile and striking stitch suits a crisp, smooth yarn. There is only one row to memorize, so it is simpler than it first appears and is suitable for beginners.

42 Pebble Lace

This is a simple but effective way to create a textured fabric. You can use it for scarves and wraps, which will drape well and show off the attractive pattern.

Step 1   Step 2

Step 2   Step 3

Multiple 8 sts + 1, plus 6 for the foundation chain.

Step 1 (RS) CL in 7th ch from hk, skip 3ch, 1dc in next ch, *ch2, skip 1ch, 1sc in next ch, ch2, skip 1ch**, [1dc, ch3, CL] in next ch, skip 3ch, 1dc in next ch; rep from * across, ending last rep at **, 1dc in last ch, turn.

Step 2 Ch6 (counts as 1dc, ch3), CL in first dc, *1dc in next dc, ch2, 1sc in next ch3 sp, ch2, [1dc, ch3, CL] in next dc; rep from * to last dc, 1dc in last dc, ch2, 1sc in tch sp, ch2, 1dc in 3rd ch of tch, turn.

Step 3 Repeat Step 2.

Special stitch CL (cluster): Dc3tog in same place.

Multiple 4 sts + 1, plus 1 for the foundation chain.

Step 1 (RS) 1sc in 2nd ch from hk, *ch3, Puff in next ch, ch1, skip 2ch, 1sc in next ch; rep from * across, turn.

Step 2 Ch4, hdc2tog over first and 2nd ch just worked, ch1, *[1sc, ch3, Puff] in next ch3 sp, ch1; rep from * to last ch3 sp, 1sc in last ch3 sp, ch2, hdc3tog working 2hdc in last ch3 sp and 1hdc in last sc, turn.

Step 3 Ch1, 1sc in hdc3tog, ch3, Puff in next ch2 sp, ch1, *[1sc, ch3, Puff] in next ch3 sp, ch1; rep from * to tch, 1sc in top of tch, turn.

Step 4 Repeat Steps 2–3.

Special stitch Puff: Hdc2tog in same place.

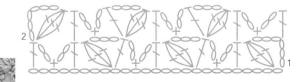

43 Zigzag

An easy way to add visual interest to plain projects, you can use this stitch pattern on blankets, scarves, and wraps, where it looks very effective between rows of plain stitches. You can also experiment with working the cluster groups in contrasting colors.

44 Soft Bobbles

This beautiful textured stitch is ideal for large-scale projects such as baby blankets. It is important to read the pattern carefully before you start, so that you know where to place the hook for each stitch. Note that the turning chain does not count as a stitch.

Step 3	Step 4

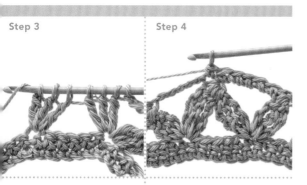

Step 2	Step 3

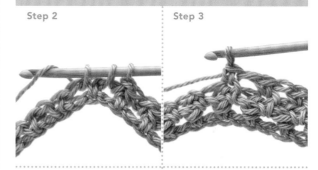

Multiple 6 sts + 1, plus 1 for the foundation chain.

Step 1 (RS) 1sc in 2nd ch from hk and in each ch across, turn.

Step 2 Ch1, 1sc in each sc across, turn.

Step 3 Ch5 (counts as 1dtr), skip first 3sc, dtr3tog in next sc, ch5, *CL pair, ch5; rep from * to last 3sc, dtr3tog in same sc as last dtr3tog, skip 2sc, 1dtr in last sc, turn.

Step 4 Ch1, 1sc in first dtr, 5sc in next ch sp, *1sc in next CL pair, 5sc in next ch sp; rep from * to tch, 1sc in top of tch, turn.

Step 5 Work as Step 2.

Step 6 Repeat Steps 2–5.

Special stitch CL (cluster) pair: Starting in same sc as last dtr3tog, work dtr3tog to last yo, skip 5sc, dtr3tog in next sc, pulling final yo through all loops on hk.

Multiple 2 sts + 1, plus 1 for the foundation chain.

Step 1 (WS) 1sc in 2nd ch from hk, *ch1, skip 1ch, 1sc in next ch; rep from * across, turn.

Step 2 Ch1, 1sc in first sc, ch1, sc2tog over next two ch sps, ch1, *sc2tog over previous and next ch sp, ch1; rep from * to last sc, 1sc in last sc, turn.

Step 3 Ch1, 1sc in first sc, *ch1, 1sc in next sc2tog; rep from * to last sc, ch1, 1sc in last sc, turn.

Step 4 Repeat Steps 2–3.

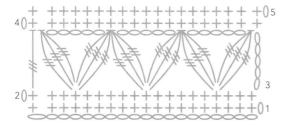

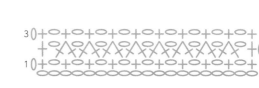

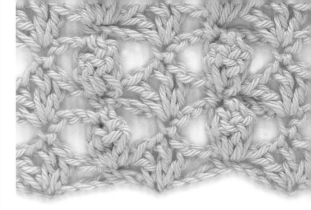

45 Popcorn Rows

This is a stitch with plenty of texture and visual interest. It is stable enough for blankets and accessories where one side of the project is visible. Use a smooth yarn to show off the three-dimensional texture for the best effect.

46 Popcorn Fans

Popcorns can be made in different sizes by varying the number of stitches used to create the popcorn. In this case four double crochet stitches are made and then a chain stitch is worked to secure the popcorn.

Step 1

Step 3

Step 2

Step 3

Multiple 4 sts + 1, plus 1 for the foundation chain.

Step 1 (RS) [1sc, ch3, PC] in 2nd ch from hk, *skip 3ch, [1sc, ch3, PC] in next ch; rep from * to last 4ch, skip 3ch, 1sc in last ch, turn.

Step 2 Ch3 (counts as 1dc), *[2sc, 1hdc] in next ch sp, 1dc in next sc; rep from * across, turn.

Step 3 Ch1, [1sc, ch3, PC] in first dc, *skip 1hdc and 2sc**, [1sc, ch3, PC] in next dc; rep from * across, ending last rep at **, 1sc in top of tch, turn.

Step 4 Repeat Steps 2–3.

Special stitch PC (popcorn): 5dc in same place, withdraw hk from loop, insert hk in top of first of these 5dc, catch empty loop and pull it through dc.

Multiple 8 sts + 1, plus 1 for the foundation chain.

Step 1 (RS) 1sc in 2nd ch from hk, *ch1, skip 3ch, Fan in next ch, ch1, skip 3ch, 1sc in next ch; rep from * across, turn.

Step 2 Ch6 (counts as 1dc, ch3), *1sc in center dc of next Fan, ch3**, PC in next sc, ch3; rep from * across, ending last rep at **, 1dc in last sc, turn.

Step 3 Ch1, 1sc in first dc, *ch1, Fan in next sc, ch1, 1sc in next PC; rep from * across, working last sc in 3rd ch of tch, turn.

Step 4 Repeat Steps 2–3.

Special stitch Fan: [1dc, ch1, 1dc, ch1, 1dc] in same place.

Special stitch PC (popcorn): 4dc in same place, withdraw hk from loop, insert hk in top of first of these 4dc, catch empty loop and pull it through dc, ch1.

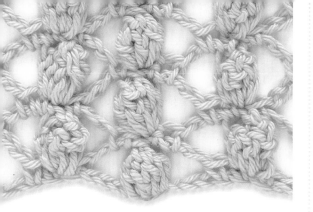

47 Laced Popcorns

The beautiful open texture of this pattern produces a fabric with plenty of drape, making it ideal for summer garments. Use a smooth lightweight yarn to show off the texture. The popcorns are made on both right-side and wrong-side rows, so as you complete each popcorn, be sure to push it through to the right side of the fabric.

48 Popcorn Columns

This highly textured stitch creates a fabric with excellent drape that is ideal for blankets and throws.

Step 2	Step 3

Step 2	Step 3

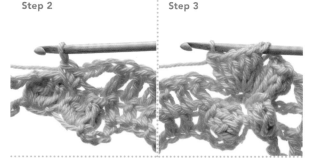

Multiple 10 sts + 1, plus 5 for the foundation chain.

Step 1 (RS) 1sc in 10th ch from hk, 1sc in each of next 2ch, *ch3, skip 3ch, PC in next ch, ch3, skip 3ch, 1sc in each of next 3ch; rep from * to last 4ch, ch3, skip 3ch, 1dc in last ch, turn.

Step 2 Ch1, 1sc in first dc, *1sc in next ch sp, ch3, skip 1sc, PC in next sc, ch3, skip 1sc**, 1sc in next ch sp, 1sc in next PC; rep from * across, ending last rep at **, skip 2ch, 1sc in each of next 2ch, turn.

Step 3 Ch6, (counts as 1dc, ch3), *1sc in next ch sp, 1sc in next PC, 1sc in next ch sp, ch3**, skip 1sc, PC in next sc, ch3, skip 1sc; rep from * across, ending last rep at **, 1dc in last sc, turn.

Step 4 Repeat Steps 2–3.

Special stitch PC (popcorn): 5dc in same place, withdraw hk from loop, insert hk in top of first of these 5dc, catch empty loop and pull it through dc, ch1.

Multiple 11 sts + 3, plus 2 for the foundation chain.

Step 1 (RS) 1dc in 4th ch from hk, 1dc in next ch, *ch2, skip 3ch, PC in next ch, ch1, PC in next ch, ch1, skip 3ch, 1dc in each of next 3ch; rep from * across, turn.

Step 2 Ch3 (counts as 1dc), skip first dc, 1dc in each of next 2dc, *ch3, 2sc in ch1 sp between next 2PC, ch3, 1dc in each of next 3dc; rep from * across, working last dc in top of tch, turn.

Step 3 Ch3 (counts as 1dc), skip first dc, 1dc in each of next 2dc, *ch2, PC in next sc, ch1, PC in next sc, ch1, 1dc in each of next 3dc; rep from * across, working last dc in top of tch, turn.

Step 4 Repeat Steps 2–3.

Special stitch PC (popcorn): 5dc in same place, withdraw hk from loop, insert hk in top of first of these 5dc, catch empty loop and pull it through dc.

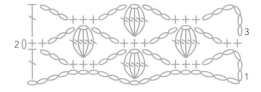

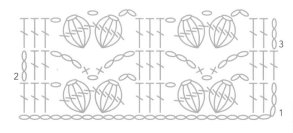

49 Four-Leaf Clover

Use this pretty stitch as a border or between rows of plain stitches to add visual interest. You can also use it for lightweight summer garments or as a border along the hem of baby sweaters and cardigans. It is a great pattern for making a mesh shopping bag, too.

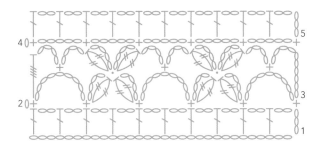

Step 2

Step 3

Step 5

Multiple 12 sts + 7, plus 4 for the foundation chain.

Step 1 (RS) 1dc into 8th ch from hk, *ch2, skip 2ch, 1dc in next ch; rep from * across, turn.

Step 2 Ch1, 1sc in first dc, *ch9, skip 1dc, [1sc, ch4, CL] in next dc, skip 1dc, [CL, ch4, 1sc] in next dc; rep from * to last dc, ch9, skip last dc, skip 2ch of tch, 1sc in next ch, turn.

Step 3 Ch10 (counts as 1trtr, ch4), 1sc in first ch9 sp, *ch4, [CL, ch4, 1sl st, ch4, CL] in next CL, skip next CL, ch4, 1sc in next ch9 sp; rep from * to last sc, ch4, 1trtr in last sc, turn.

Step 4 Ch1, 1sc in first trtr, *ch5, 1sc in next CL; rep from * across, ch5, 1sc in 6th ch of tch, turn.

Step 5 Ch5 (counts as 1dc, ch2), *1dc in next ch sp, ch2, 1dc in next sc**, ch2; rep from * across, ending last rep at **, turn.

Step 6 Repeat Steps 2–5.

Special stitch CL (cluster): Tr2tog in same place.

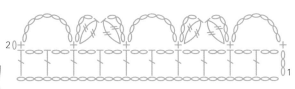

Steps 1–2

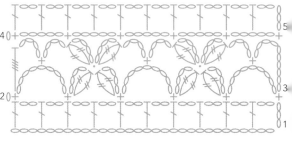

Steps 3–5

50 Zigzag Lozenge

This pretty stitch lends itself to a variety of projects. You can use it with a chunky yarn to make blankets, or use a lightweight yarn for sweaters and cardigans. This pattern features two colors. Cut the yarn each time you change color and weave in the ends as you go.

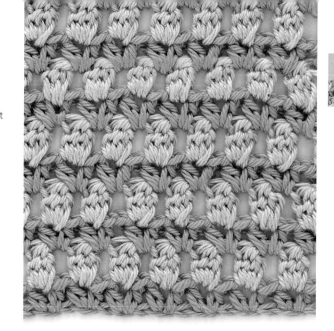

■ A
■ B

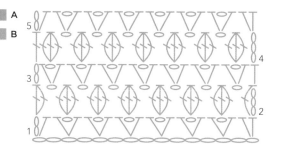

Step 2

Step 3

Step 5

Multiple 2 sts + 1, plus 2 for the foundation chain.

Step 1 (WS) With yarn A, 1hdc in 3rd ch from hk, *skip 1ch, [1hdc, ch1, 1hdc] in next ch; rep from * to last 2ch, skip 1ch, 2hdc in last ch, change to yarn B, turn.

Step 2 With yarn B, ch3 (counts as 1dc), 1dc in first hdc, *ch1, 3dc CL in next ch sp; rep from * to tch, ch1, 2dc CL in top of tch, change to yarn A, turn.

Step 3 With yarn A, ch2 (counts as 1hdc), [1hdc, ch1, 1hdc] in each ch1 sp across, 1hdc in top of tch, change to yarn B, turn.

Step 4 With yarn B, ch3 (counts as 1dc), 3dc CL in first ch1 sp, *ch1, 3dc CL in next ch1 sp; rep from * to tch, 1dc in top of tch, change to yarn A, turn.

Step 5 With yarn A, ch2 (counts as 1hdc), 1hdc in first dc, [1hdc, ch1, 1hdc] in each ch1 sp across, 2hdc in top of tch, change to yarn B, turn.

Step 6 Repeat Steps 2–5.

Special stitch 2dc or 3dc CL (cluster): Dc2tog or dc3tog in same place.

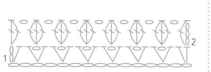

Steps 1–2

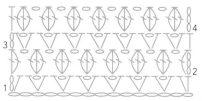

Steps 3–4

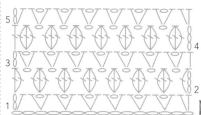

Step 5

51 Offset Puffs

This stitch has plenty of visual appeal and always looks attractive. Use a smooth, lightweight yarn for shawls and wraps, or a thick, chunky, or textured yarn to really make the puff stitches stand out.

Step 2

Step 3

Step 5

Multiple 6 sts + 1, plus 1 for the foundation chain.

Step 1 (RS) 1sc in 2nd ch from hk, *ch3, skip 2ch, Puff in next ch, ch4, skip 2ch, 1sc in next ch; rep from * across, turn.

Step 2 Ch1, 1sc in first sc, *ch3, 1sc in next Puff, ch3, 1sc in next sc; rep from * across, turn.

Step 3 Ch6 (counts as 1dc, ch3), skip first sc, 1sc in next sc, *ch3, Puff in next sc, ch4, 1sc in next sc; rep from * to last sc, ch3, 1dc in last sc, turn.

Step 4 Ch1, 1sc in first dc, *ch3, 1sc in next sc, ch3, 1sc in next Puff; rep from * across, working last sc in 3rd ch of tch, turn.

Step 5 Ch1, 1sc in first sc, *ch3, Puff in next sc, ch4, 1sc in next sc; rep from * across, turn.

Step 6 Repeat Steps 2–5.

Special stitch Puff: Hdc3tog in same place.

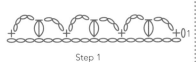

Step 1

Steps 2–3

Steps 4–5

52 Openwork Clusters

This simple but effective stitch has excellent stability. The position of the double crochet clusters creates the impression of a much taller stitch. The resulting fabric can be used to make scarves, blankets, and garments. Be sure to make the required number of chains between each cluster or your work will pucker.

Step 1 | **Step 2** | **Step 3**

Multiple 8 sts + 1, plus 1 for the foundation chain.

Step 1 (RS) 1sc in 2nd ch from hk, *skip 3ch, Shell in next ch, skip 3ch, 1sc in next ch; rep from * across, turn.

Step 2 Ch5 (counts as 1tr, ch1), *CL group over next Shell, ch1; rep from * to last sc, 1tr in last sc, turn.

Step 3 Ch1, 1sc in first tr, *Shell in center sc of next CL group, 1sc in next ch1 sp; rep from * across, working last sc in 4th ch of tch, turn.

Step 4 Repeat Steps 2–3.

Special stitch Shell: 9dc in same place.

Special stitch CL (cluster) group: Skip first dc of Shell, dc3tog over next 3dc, ch3, 1sc in next dc, ch3, dc3tog over next 3dc, skip last dc of Shell.

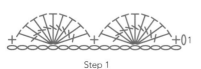
Step 1

Step 2

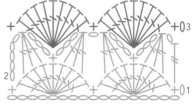
Step 3

53 Bobble Texture Stitch

Very simple to work, this stitch creates a bold, highly textured fabric that will suit a variety of projects. Experiment with different weights of yarn. You can make simple but attractive accessories such as cowls and scarves using this stitch, or use a chunky yarn to make a blanket.

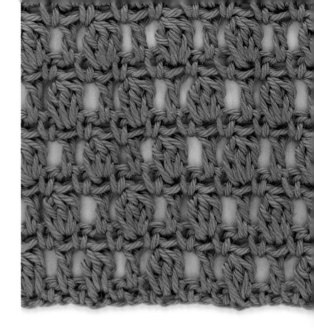

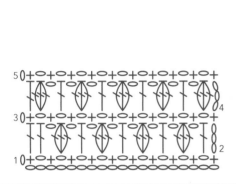

Step 2

Step 4

Step 5

Multiple 4 sts + 3, plus 1 for the foundation chain.

Step 1 (WS) 1sc in 2nd ch from hk, *ch1, skip 1ch, 1sc in next ch; rep from * across, turn.

Step 2 Ch3 (counts as 1dc), 1dc in first ch sp, *ch1, CL in next ch sp, ch1, 1dc in next ch sp; rep from * to last sc, 1dc in last sc, turn.

Step 3 Ch1, 1sc in first dc, *ch1, 1sc in next ch sp; rep from * to tch, ch1, 1sc in top of tch, turn.

Step 4 Ch3 (counts as 1dc), *CL in next ch sp, ch1, 1dc in next ch sp, ch1; rep from * to last ch sp, CL in last ch sp, 1dc in last sc, turn.

Step 5 Work as Step 3.

Step 6 Repeat Steps 2–5.

Special stitch CL (cluster): Dc3tog in same place.

Steps 1–2

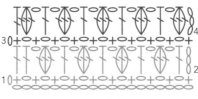

Steps 3–4

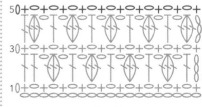

Step 5

54 Shells and Puffs

This pattern combines two techniques to create a delicate yet stable crochet fabric. You can use it for a variety of projects, such as scarves and blankets.

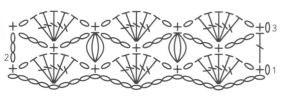

Step 1

Step 2

Step 3

Multiple 8 sts + 1, plus 1 for the foundation chain.

Step 1 (RS) 1sc in 2nd ch from hk, *ch1, skip 3ch, Shell in next ch, ch1, skip 3ch, 1sc in next ch; rep from * across, turn.

Step 2 Ch6 (counts as 1dc, ch3), 1sc in center dc of first Shell, *ch3, Puff in next sc, ch3, 1sc in center dc of next Shell; rep from * to last sc, ch3, 1dc in last sc, turn.

Step 3 Ch1, 1sc in first dc, *ch1, Shell in next sc, ch1**, 1sc in next Puff; rep from * across, ending last rep at **, 1sc in 3rd ch of tch, turn.

Step 4 Repeat Steps 2–3.

Special stitch *Shell: 5dc in same place.*

Special stitch *Puff: Hdc4tog in same place.*

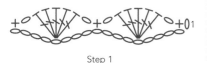

Step 1

Step 2

Step 3

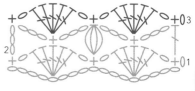

55 Angled Clusters

Rows of stitches angled in opposite directions create a pretty, textured fabric that is well-suited to accessories such as scarves. It is also suitable for homewares that need to be durable and retain their shape.

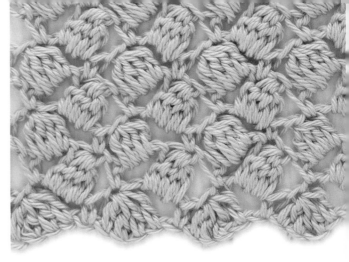

Step 1

Step 2

Step 3

Multiple 5 sts + 1, plus 3 for the foundation chain.

Step 1 (RS) 1sc in 4th ch from hk, *ch3, CL over next 4ch, ch1, 1sc in next ch; rep from * across, turn.

Step 2 Ch5, *1sc in next CL, ch3, CL in next ch3 sp, ch1; rep from * to last sc, 1dc in last sc, turn.

Step 3 Ch1, *1sc in next CL, ch3, CL in next ch3 sp, ch1; rep from * to tch sp, 1sc in tch sp, turn.

Step 4 Repeat Steps 2–3.

Special stitch CL (cluster): Dc4tog in place indicated.

Step 1

Step 2

Step 3

56 Diamond Braid

This open stitch is best suited to accessories or as a decorative feature between rows of single crochet. It will hold its shape well and can be worked in all weights and textures of yarn to achieve different effects.

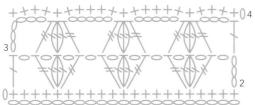

Step 2	Step 3	Step 4

Multiple 6 sts + 3, plus 1 for the foundation chain.

Step 1 (WS) 1sc in 2nd ch from hk and in each ch across, turn.

Step 2 Ch4 (counts as 1dc, ch1), skip first 4sc, *CL Fan in next sc, ch1, skip 5sc; rep from * to last 5sc, CL Fan in next sc, ch1, skip 3sc, 1dc in last sc, turn.

Step 3 Ch6 (counts as 1dc, ch3), skip first dc and ch sp, *CL Dec over next CL Fan**, ch5; rep from * across, ending last rep at **, ch3, 1dc in 3rd ch of tch, turn.

Step 4 Ch1, 1sc in first dc, 3sc in ch3 sp, *1sc in next CL Dec**, 5sc in next ch5 sp; rep from * across, ending last rep at **, 3sc in tch sp, 1sc in 3rd ch of tch, turn.

Step 5 Repeat Steps 2–4.

Special stitch CL (cluster): Dc3tog in same place.

Special stitch CL Fan (cluster fan): [1tr, ch1, CL, ch1, 1tr] in same place.

Special stitch CL Dec (cluster decrease): Working over sts of CL Fan, 1tr in first tr up to last yo (2 loops on hk), dc3tog in CL up to last yo (5 loops on hk), 1tr in 2nd tr up to last yo (6 loops on hk), yo and pull through all loops on hk.

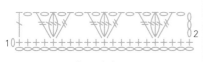

Steps 1–2

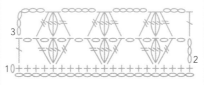

Step 3

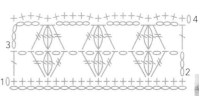

Step 4

57 Cluster Rings

This is a stitch where blocking your work really makes a difference—you only see the pattern of rings once you block it. You can use this stitch for accessories, such as scarves and wraps. Like many open or lacy stitches, you may find it helpful to refer to the chart alongside the written pattern to visualize what the fabric will look like, and to help you place stitches correctly in the first pattern repeat.

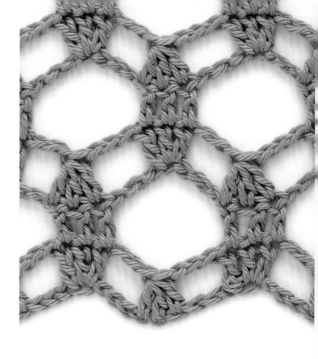

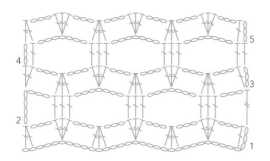

Step 2

Step 3

Step 5

Multiple 10 sts + 1, plus 2 for the foundation chain.

Step 1 (RS) 1dc in 4th ch from hk, *ch3, skip 3ch, 3dc in next ch, ch3, skip 3ch**, dc3tog over next 3ch; rep from * across, ending last rep at **, dc2tog over last 2ch, turn.

Step 2 Ch7 (counts as 1tr, ch3), skip dc2tog, *1dc in each of next 3dc**, ch7, skip dc3tog; rep from * across, ending last rep at **, ch3, skip last dc, 1tr in top of tch, turn.

Step 3 Ch3 (counts as 1dc), 1dc in first tr, *ch3, dc3tog over next 3dc, ch3**, 3dc in center ch of next ch7; rep from * across, ending last rep at **, 2dc in 4th ch of tch, turn.

Step 4 Ch3 (counts as 1dc), skip first dc, 1dc in next dc, *ch7, skip dc3tog**, 1dc in each of next 3dc; rep from * across, ending last rep at **, 1dc in last dc, 1dc in top of tch, turn.

Step 5 Ch3 (counts as 1dc), skip first dc, 1dc in next dc, *ch3, 3dc in center ch of next ch7, ch3**, dc3tog over next 3dc; rep from * across, ending last rep at **, dc2tog over last dc and top of tch, turn.

Step 6 Repeat Steps 2–5.

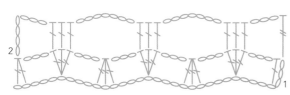

Steps 1–2

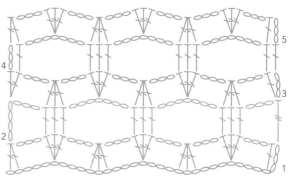

Steps 3–5

58 Cluster Mesh

Simple and easy to memorize, this stitch is suitable for less experienced crocheters. It has plenty of stability, making it suitable for many kinds of projects. Be sure to work the yarnovers on each cluster stitch quite loosely so that you can pass them over the hook to complete the stitch. This is an effective stitch to use with metallic yarns to create striking accessories such as scarves.

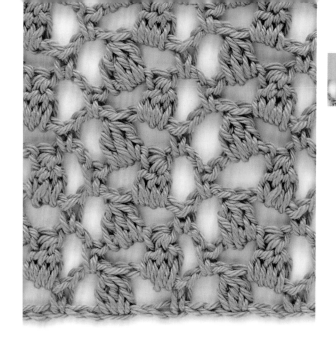

Step 1

Step 2

Step 3

Multiple 6 sts + 1, plus 1 for the foundation chain

Step 1 (RS) 1sc in 2nd ch from hk, *ch3, skip 2ch, CL in next ch, ch3, skip 2ch, 1sc in next ch; rep from * across, turn.

Step 2 Ch5 (counts as 1dc, ch2), *1sc in next ch sp, ch3, CL in next ch sp; rep from * to last sc, 1dc in last sc, turn.

Step 3 Ch1, 1sc in first dc, *ch3, CL in next ch sp, ch3, 1sc in next ch sp; rep from * across, working last sc in 3rd ch of tch, turn.

Step 4 Repeat Steps 2–3.

Special stitch CL (cluster): Dc3tog in same place.

Step 1

Step 2

Step 3

59 Popcorn Mesh

This is a very open stitch that lends itself to large-scale projects. The popcorns are set within a structure of double crochet mesh, so the fabric is more stable than you would expect. Popcorns are made on both right-side and wrong-side rows, so be sure to push all the popcorns through to the right side as you make them.

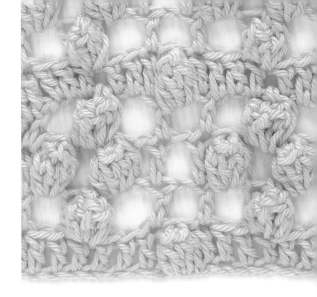

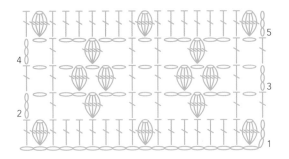

Step 2

Step 3

Step 5

Multiple 8 sts + 3, plus 2 for the foundation chain.

Step 1 (RS) PC in 4th ch from hk, *1dc in each of next 7ch, PC in next ch; rep from * to last ch, 1dc in last ch, turn.

Step 2 Ch4 (counts as 1dc, ch1), skip first dc and PC, 1dc in next dc, *ch2, skip 2dc, PC in next dc, ch2, skip 2dc, 1dc in next dc, ch1, skip PC, 1dc in next dc; rep from * across, working last dc in top of tch, turn.

Step 3 Ch4 (counts as 1dc, ch1), skip first dc, 1dc in next dc, *[ch1, PC in next ch2 sp] twice, [ch1, 1dc in next dc] twice; rep from * across, working last dc in 3rd ch of tch, turn.

Step 4 Ch4 (counts as 1dc, ch1), skip first dc, 1dc in next dc, *ch2, PC in ch1 sp between next 2PC, ch2, 1dc in next dc, ch1, 1dc in next dc; rep from * across, working last dc in 3rd ch of tch, turn.

Step 5 Ch3 (counts as 1dc), skip first dc, *PC in next ch1 sp, 1dc in next dc, 1dc in each of next 2ch, 1dc in next PC, 1dc in each of next 2ch, 1dc in next dc; rep from * to tch sp, PC in tch sp, 1dc in 3rd ch of tch, turn.

Step 6 Repeat Steps 2–5.

Special stitch PC (popcorn): 5dc in same place, withdraw hk from loop, insert hk in top of first of these 5dc, catch empty loop and pull it through dc, ch1.

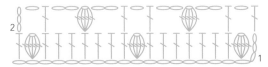

Steps 1–2

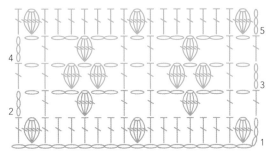

Steps 3–5

60 Three-Color Bobbles

Choose any number or combination of colors, or even a single color, to make this pattern. If you dislike weaving in ends, choosing three colors is a good option because there is no need to cut the yarn when you change color. After the first three rows, the correct color in the sequence will be waiting for you at the end of the row, and you can carry the unused yarn up the side of the work.

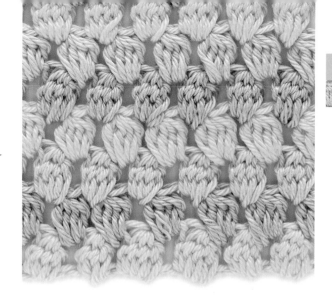

 A
 B
C

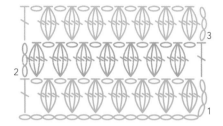

Step 1

Step 2

Step 3

Multiple An even number of sts, plus 2 for the foundation chain.

Step 1 (RS) With yarn A, CL in 4th ch from hk, *ch1, skip 1ch, CL in next ch; rep from * to last 2ch, ch1, skip 1ch, 1dc in last ch, change to yarn B, turn.

Step 2 With yarn B, ch3 (counts as 1dc), *CL in next ch1 sp, ch1; rep from * to tch, 1dc in top of tch, change to yarn C, turn.

Step 3 Repeat Step 2, working one row of each color in sequence.

Special stitch *CL (cluster): Dc4tog in same place.*

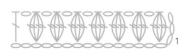

Step 1

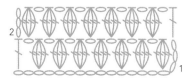

Step 2

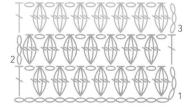

Step 3

61 Two-Color Popcorns

This pattern is unusual because it is worked with the right side always facing. At the end of each row, instead of turning, you fasten off your work and join the new color of yarn to the first stitch of the previous row. It is an ideal stitch for blankets and homewares because the bulky texture makes a warm and hard-wearing fabric. The sample shown is made in two colors, but you can use any combination of colors you like. There will be lots of ends to weave in, so you might prefer to weave them in after every few rows rather than waiting until the project is completed.

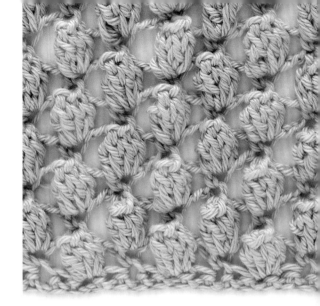

A
B

Step 2

Step 3

Step 4

Multiple 4 sts + 5, plus 1 for the foundation chain.

Step 1 (WS) With yarn A, 1sc in 2nd ch from hk and in each ch across, turn.

Step 2 (RS) With yarn A, ch1, 1sc in each of first 2sc, *ch2, skip 1sc, PC in next sc, ch2, skip 1sc, 1sc in next sc; rep from * to last 3sc, ch2, skip 1sc, PC in next sc, 1dc in last sc, do not turn. Fasten off yarn A.

Step 3 With RS facing, join yarn B with sl st to first sc, ch1, 1sc in first sc, *ch2, PC in next sc, ch2, 1sc in next PC; rep from * to last dc, 1dc in last dc, do not turn. Fasten off yarn B.

Step 4 With RS facing, join yarn A with sl st to first sc, ch1, 1sc in each of first [sc, ch sp, PC], *ch2, PC in next sc, ch2, 1sc in next PC; rep from * to last sc, ch2, PC in last sc, 1dc in last dc, do not turn. Fasten off yarn A.

Step 5 Repeat Steps 3–4.

Special stitch PC (popcorn): 5dc in same place, withdraw hk from loop, insert hk in top of first of these 5dc, catch empty loop and pull it through dc, ch1.

Steps 1–2

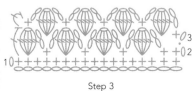

Step 3

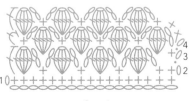

Step 4

62 Two-Color Puffs

The soft texture of this stitch pattern is ideal for scarves and cowls, and can be worked in a single color if you prefer. Your puff stitches will be easier to work if you pull the loops up a little longer than when working a standard half double crochet stitch. This pattern works in many different yarns. An interesting effect can be achieved by using a mohair yarn for the puff stitch rows, and a smooth yarn for the single crochet rows.

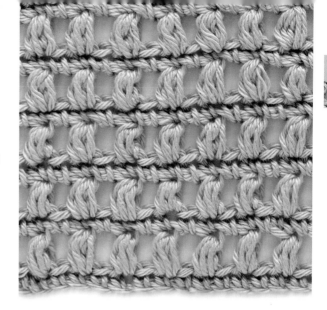

A
B

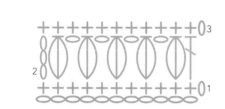

CLUSTERS, PUFFS, AND POPCORNS

Step 1

Step 2

Step 3

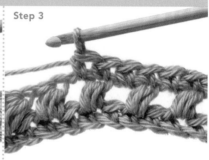

Multiple 2 sts + 1, plus 1 for the foundation chain.

Step 1 (RS) With yarn A, 1sc in 2nd ch from hk and in each ch across, change to yarn B, turn.

Step 2 With yarn B, ch3 (counts as 1dc), skip first sc, Puff in next sc, *ch1, skip 1sc, Puff in next sc; rep from * to last sc, 1dc in last sc, change to yarn A, turn.

Step 3 With yarn A, ch1, 1sc in first dc, 1sc in each Puff and ch sp across, 1sc in top of tch, change to yarn B, turn.

Step 4 Repeat Steps 2–3.

Special stitch *Puff:* Hdc3tog in same place.

Step 1

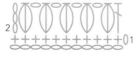

Step 2

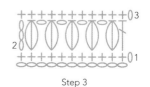

Step 3

63 Striped Clusters

A combination of double crochet, chains, and clusters are used here to create an open fabric with plenty of stability. It would be a lovely stitch for a summer tote bag using a heavy cotton yarn, or for a summer top. You could also use it for homewares, or to add interest to a project in double crochet by working a border or section in Striped Clusters. Be sure to work double crochet stitches into the chain indicated and not the chain space for extra stability.

■ A
■ B

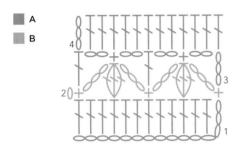

Step 2

Step 3

Step 4

Multiple 6 sts + 1, plus 2 for the foundation chain.

Step 1 (RS) With yarn A, 1dc in 4th ch from hk and in each ch across, change to yarn B, turn.

Step 2 With yarn B, ch1, 1sc in first dc, *ch3, skip 2dc, CL in next dc, ch3, skip 2dc, 1sc in next dc; rep from * across, working last sc in top of tch, change to yarn A, turn.

Step 3 With yarn A, ch5 (counts as 1dc, ch2), skip first sc, *1sc in next CL, ch2, 1dc in next sc**, ch2; rep from * across, ending last rep at **, turn.

Step 4 With yarn A, ch3 (counts as 1dc), skip first dc, *1dc in each of next 2ch, 1dc in next sc**, 1dc each of next 2ch, 1dc in next dc; rep from * across, ending last rep at **, 1dc in each of top 3ch of tch, change to yarn B, turn.

Step 5 Repeat Steps 2–4.

Special stitch *CL (cluster): Dc3tog in same place.*

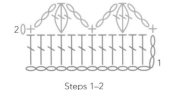

Steps 1–2

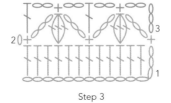

Step 3

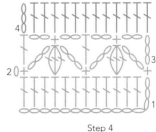

Step 4

64 Puff Stitch Stripes

This is an ideal stitch for homewares and items that need to be durable, such as bags and rugs. You can use as many colors as you like, or even work the stitch in a single color. Three colors have been used here, which means that you do not need to cut the yarn at the end of each row—just carry the unused yarn up the side of the work. Puff stitches are half double crochet clusters, which means you will have a large number of loops on the hook when you complete each puff. Make sure you pull each loop up to the full height of the ch3 so that you will be able to complete the puff stitch easily.

Step 1

Multiple 4 sts + 1, plus 1 for the foundation chain.

Step 1 (RS) With yarn A, [1sc, ch3, 5hdc Puff] in 2nd ch from hk, *ch1, skip 3ch, [1sc, ch3, 5hdc Puff] in next ch; rep from * to last 4ch, ch1, skip 3ch, 1sc in last ch, change to yarn B, turn.

Step 2

Step 2 With yarn B, ch3, 3hdc Puff in first sc, *ch1, [1sc, ch3, 5hdc Puff] in next ch3 sp; rep from * to last ch3 sp, ch1, [1sc, ch3, 3hdc Puff] in last ch3 sp, 1dc in last sc, change to yarn C, turn.

Step 3

Step 3 With yarn C, ch1, 1sc in first dc, ch3, 5hdc Puff in first ch3 sp, ch1, *[1sc, ch3, 5hdc Puff] in next ch3 sp, ch1; rep from * to tch, ch1, 1sc in top of tch, change to yarn A, turn.

Step 4 Repeat Steps 2–3, working one row of each color in sequence.

Special stitch Puff: Hdc3tog or hdc5tog, as specified, in same place.

Step 1

Step 2

Step 3

65 Simple Spikes

This stitch makes a dense and firm fabric that is suited to homewares and garments that need to hold their shape well.

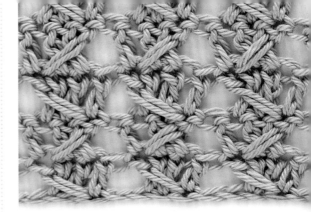

66 Diagonal Spikes

A simple variation of plain double crochet, this spike stitch pattern is created by working into a previous stitch on the same row instead of a previous row. When you work each spike stitch, be sure to draw the yarn up to the full height of the double crochet, so that your stitches are not squashed.

Step 2

Step 4

Multiple 2 sts + 1, plus 1 for the foundation chain.

Step 1 (RS) 1sc in 2nd ch from hk and in each ch across, turn.

Step 2 Ch1, 1sc in first sc, *1Spike sc in next st two rows below, 1sc in next sc; rep from * across, turn.

Step 3 Ch1, 1sc in each of first 2sc, *1Spike sc in next sc two rows below, 1sc in next sc; rep from * to last sc, 1sc in last sc, turn.

Step 4 Repeat Steps 2–3.

Special stitch *Spike sc: Work sc in specified st two rows below (on row 2 work into foundation ch).*

Step 1

Step 2

Multiple 4 sts + 2, plus 2 for the foundation chain.

Step 1 (RS) 1dc in 4th ch from hk, 1dc in each of next 2ch, *1Diagonal Spike dc in same ch as first of 3dc just made, skip 1ch, 1dc in each of next 3ch; rep from * to last 2ch, skip 1ch, 1dc in last ch, turn.

Step 2 Ch3 (counts as 1dc), skip first dc, *1dc in each of next 3dc, 1Diagonal Spike dc in same st as first of 3dc just made, skip 1dc; rep from * to tch, 1dc in top of tch, turn.

Step 3 Repeat Step 2.

Special stitch *Diagonal Spike dc: Work dc in specified st earlier in same row (on row 1 work into foundation ch).*

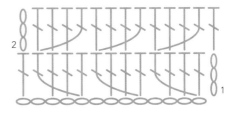

67 Spike Brickwork

Use this pattern as a simple way to add texture to your crochet projects. The spike stitches are worked into stitches two rows below the row you are currently working; you can use the chart to help you visualize where to put your hook. It helps if you do not pull the spike stitches too tight.

68 Two-Color Brickwork

This pattern uses two colors to add texture and visual interest. You will be changing colors every two rows, so there is no need to cut the yarn; simply carry the unused yarn up the side of the work. Change color on the last yarnover of the last stitch of the row to ensure neat and tidy color changes.

Step 3

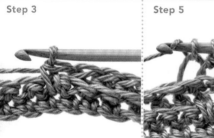

Step 5

Step 3

Step 5

Multiple 4 sts + 3, plus 1 for the foundation chain.

Step 1 (RS) 1sc in 2nd ch from hk and in each ch across, turn.

Step 2 Ch1, 1BLsc in each sc across, turn.

Step 3 Ch1, *1BLsc in each of next 3sc, 1Spike sc in next sc two rows below; rep from * to last 3sc, 1BLsc in each of last 3sc, turn.

Step 4 Work as Step 2.

Step 5 Ch1, 1BLsc in first sc, *1Spike sc in next sc two rows below**, 1BLsc in each of next 3sc; rep from * across, ending last rep at **, 1BLsc in last sc, turn.

Step 6 Repeat Steps 2–5.

Special stitch Spike sc: Work sc in specified st two rows below.

Multiple 4 sts + 3, plus 1 for the foundation chain.

Step 1 (RS) With yarn A, 1sc in 2nd ch from hk and in each ch across, turn.

Step 2 With yarn A, ch1, 1sc in each sc across, change to yarn B, turn.

Step 3 With yarn B, ch1, *1sc in each of next 3sc, 1Spike sc in next sc two rows below; rep from * to last 3sc, 1sc in each of last 3sc, turn.

Step 4 With yarn B, ch1, 1sc in each sc across, change to yarn A, turn.

Step 5 With yarn A, ch1, 1sc in first sc, *1Spike sc in next sc two rows below**, 1sc in each of next 3sc; rep from * across, ending last rep at **, 1sc in last sc, turn.

Step 6 Repeat Steps 2–5.

Special stitch Spike sc: Work sc in specified st two rows below.

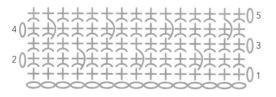

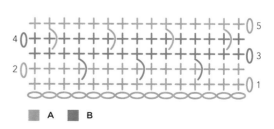

69 Textured Spike Stitch 1

This is an attractive way to use spike stitches. The elongated double crochet stitches create a fabric with excellent drape and textural interest. The chain spaces help you to locate the correct placement of the hook, and the simple repeat means this is an excellent stitch for the novice crocheter. You can use most yarn weights and experiment with different textures for accessories and blankets.

70 Textured Spike Stitch 2

The attractive texture of this spike stitch works best in a medium-weight yarn. It would be ideal for masculine accessories, such as scarves and cowls. You can achieve interesting effects using a variegated yarn for this stitch. To ensure your work does not pucker, be sure to pull the loops up loosely as you work each spike stitch.

Step 2

Step 4

Step 2

Step 3

Multiple 4 sts, plus 2 for the foundation chain.

Step 1 (RS) 1dc in 4th ch from hk, 1dc in next ch, *ch2, skip 2ch, 1dc in each of next 2ch; rep from * to last ch, 1dc in last ch, turn.

Step 2 Ch5 (counts as 1dc, ch2), skip first 3dc, *1Spike dc in each of skipped 2 sts two rows below, ch2, skip 2dc; rep from * to tch, 1dc in top of tch, turn.

Step 3 Ch3 (counts as 1dc), skip first dc, *1Spike dc in each of skipped 2dc two rows below**, ch2, skip 2dc; rep from * across, ending last rep at **, 1dc in 3rd ch of tch, turn.

Step 4 Repeat Steps 2–3.

Special stitch *Spike dc: Work dc in skipped st two rows below (on row 2 work into foundation ch).*

Multiple 6 sts + 5, plus 2 for the foundation chain.

Step 1 (RS) 1dc in 4th ch from hk, *ch1, skip 1ch, 1dc in each of next 5ch; rep from * to last 3ch, skip 1ch, 1dc in each of last 2ch, turn.

Step 2 Ch3 (counts as 1dc), skip first dc, 1dc in next dc, *1Spike dc in skipped st two rows below**, 1dc in each of next 2dc, ch1, skip 1dc, 1dc in each of next 2dc; rep from * across, ending last rep at **, 1dc in last dc, 1dc in top of tch, turn.

Step 3 Ch3 (counts as 1dc), skip first dc, 1dc in next dc, *ch1, skip 1dc, 1dc in each of next 2dc, 1Spike dc in skipped dc two rows below, 1dc in each of next 2dc; rep from * to last 2dc, ch1, skip 1dc, 1dc in last dc, 1dc in top of tch, turn.

Step 4 Repeat Steps 2–3.

Special stitch *Spike dc: Work dc in skipped st two rows below (on row 2 work into foundation ch).*

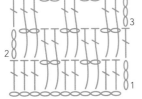

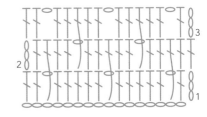

71 Spike Stitch Stripes

Spike stitches create visually interesting stripe patterns. Use toning colors for subtle stripes or contrasting colors for a busier surface texture. There is no need to cut the yarn when you change colors; simply carry the unused yarn up the side of the work. For smooth color transitions, change color on the last turnover of the last stitch of the row.

72 Alternating Spikes

The use of three colors—one stronger color plus two subtly toning colors—gives this simple stitch visual interest and texture. When changing colors, there is no need to cut the yarn; after the first three rows, the correct color will be waiting for you at the end of each row. Just carry the unused yarn up the side of the work.

Step 3	Step 5

Multiple 8 sts, plus 1 for the foundation chain.

Step 1 (RS) With yarn A, 1sc in 2nd ch from hk and in each ch across, turn.

Step 2 With yarn A, ch1, 1sc in each sc across, change to yarn B, turn.

Step 3 With yarn B, ch1, 1sc in each of first 3sc, *1Spike sc in each of next 2sc two rows below**, 1sc in each of next 6sc; rep from * across, ending last rep at **, 1sc in each of last 3sc, turn.

Step 4 With yarn B, ch1, 1sc in each sc across, change to yarn A, turn.

Step 5 Repeat Steps 3–4, working two rows of each color in sequence.

Special stitch Spike sc: *Work sc in specified st two rows below.*

Step 3 (row 3)	Step 3 (row 4)

Multiple An even number of sts, plus 1 for the foundation chain.

Step 1 (RS) With yarn A, 1sc in 3rd ch from hk and in each ch across, turn.

Step 2 With yarn A, ch1 (counts as 1sc), skip first sc, *1sc in next sc, 1Spike sc in next st two rows below; rep from * to tch, 1sc in top of tch, change to yarn B, turn.

Step 3 Repeat Step 2, working one row of each color in sequence.

Special stitch Spike sc: *Work sc in specified st two rows below (on row 2 work into foundation ch).*

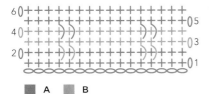

A   B

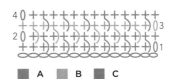

A   B   C

73 Gathered Spikes

This attractive stitch combines double crochet spikes and chain spaces to create beautiful drape and interesting texture. It works best in a smooth, medium-weight yarn and would be a good choice for a summer garment. The pattern is quite subtle, so it is best to use a single color rather than a variegated yarn for this stitch.

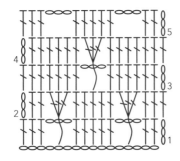

Step 2

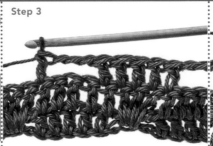

Step 3

Step 6

Multiple 8 sts + 1, plus 2 for the foundation chain.

Step 1 (RS) 1dc in 4th ch from hk, 1dc in next ch, *ch3, skip 3ch, 1dc in each of next 5ch; rep from * to last 6ch, ch3, skip 3ch, 1dc in each of last 3ch, turn.

Step 2 Ch3 (counts as 1dc), skip first dc, 1dc in each of next 2dc, *3dc Spike in center st of skipped 3 sts two rows below**, 1dc in each of next 5dc; rep from * across, ending last rep at **, 1dc in each of last 2dc, 1dc in top of tch, turn.

Step 3 Ch3 (counts as 1dc), skip first dc, 1dc in each of next 6dc, *ch3, skip 3dc, 1dc in each of next 5dc; rep from * to last dc, 1dc in last dc, 1dc in top of tch, turn.

Step 4 Ch3 (counts as 1dc), skip first dc, 1dc in each of next 6dc, *3dc Spike in center dc of skipped 3dc two rows below, 1dc in each of next 5dc; rep from * to last dc, 1dc in last dc, 1dc in top of tch, turn.

Step 5 Ch3 (counts as 1dc), skip first dc, 1dc in each of next 2dc, *ch3, skip 3dc, 1dc in each of next 5dc; rep from * to last 5dc, ch3, skip 3dc, 1dc in each of last 2dc, 1dc in top of tch, turn.

Step 6 Repeat Steps 2–5.

Special stitch 3dc Spike: Work 3dc in center st of skipped 3 sts two rows below (on row 2 work into foundation ch).

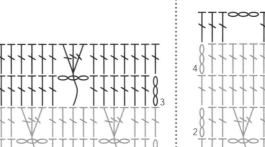

Steps 1–2

Steps 3–4

Step 5

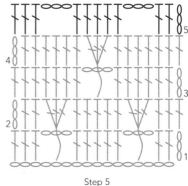

74 Braided Stripes

This pattern shows how easy it can be to create a fabric with plenty of visual interest using simple stitches. Although it is worked in three colors, you do not need to cut the yarn and so there are few ends to weave in. The pattern does not create a reversible fabric, but you can still use it for projects where the back will be seen, such as scarves and blankets. Always change yarn color on the last yarnover of the last stitch of the row for smooth color transitions.

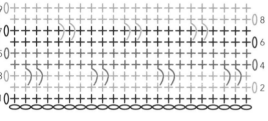

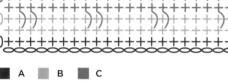

A **B** **C**

Step 3

Step 4

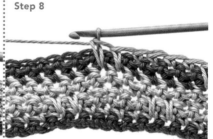
Step 8

Multiple 6 sts + 4, plus 1 for the foundation chain.

Step 1 (WS) With yarn A, 1sc in 2nd ch from hk and in each ch across, change to yarn B, turn.

Step 2 With yarn B, ch1, 1sc in each sc across, turn.

Step 3 With yarn B, 1sc in each sc across, change to yarn C, turn.

Step 4 With yarn C, ch1, 1sc in first sc, *1Spike sc in each of next 2sc two rows below**, 1sc in each of next 4sc; rep from * across, ending last rep at **, 1sc in last sc, turn.

Step 5 With yarn C, 1sc in each sc across, change to yarn A, turn.

Step 6 With yarn A, 1sc in each sc across, turn.

Step 7 With yarn A, 1sc in each sc across, change to yarn B, turn.

Step 8 With yarn B, ch1, 1sc in each of first 4sc, *1Spike sc in each of next 2sc two rows below, 1sc in each of next 4sc; rep from * across, turn.

Step 9 With yarn B, 1sc in each sc across, change to yarn A, turn.

Step 10 Repeat Steps 2–9, working two rows of each color in sequence.

Special stitch *Spike sc: Work sc in specified st two rows below.*

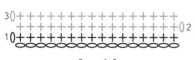
Steps 1–3

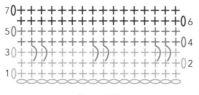
Steps 4–7

Steps 8–9

75 Lark's Foot

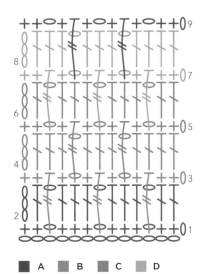

■ A ■ B ■ C ■ D

This striking interlocking stitch looks most effective in several colors. Instead of a traditional spike stitch, the pattern calls for an extra-tall stitch to be worked into a previous row. You can either cut the yarn each time you change color, and weave in the ends as you work the next row, or carry the unused yarn up the side of the work. For smooth color transitions, change color on the last yarnover of the last stitch of the row.

Step 3

Step 5

Step 6 (row 7)

Multiple 4 sts + 1, plus 1 for the foundation chain.

Step 1 (RS) With yarn A, 1sc in 2nd ch from hk, 1sc in next ch, *ch1, skip 1ch, 1sc in each of next 3ch; rep from * to last 3ch, ch1, skip 1ch, 1sc in each of last 2ch.

Step 2 With yarn A, ch3 (counts as 1dc), skip first sc, 1dc in next sc, *ch1, skip 1ch**, 1dc in each of next 3 sts; rep from * across, ending last rep at **, 1dc in each of last 2sc, change to yarn B, turn.

Step 3 With yarn B, ch1, 1sc in each of first 2dc, *1Spike tr in skipped st three rows below**, 1sc in next dc, ch1, skip 1dc, 1sc in next dc; rep from * across, ending last rep at **, 1sc in top of tch, turn.

Step 4 With yarn B, ch3 (counts as 1dc), skip first sc, 1dc in each of next 3 sts, *ch1, skip 1ch, 1dc in each of next 3 sts; rep from * to last sc, 1dc in last sc, change to yarn C, turn.

Step 5 With yarn C, ch1, 1sc in each of first 2dc, *ch1, skip 1dc, 1sc in next dc, 1Spike tr in skipped dc three rows below, 1sc in next dc; rep from * to last 2dc, ch1, skip 1dc, 1sc in last dc, 1sc in top of tch, turn.

Step 6 Repeat Steps 2–5, working next row in yarn C and then working two rows of each color in sequence.

Special stitch Spike tr: Work tr in skipped st three rows below (on row 3 work into foundation ch).

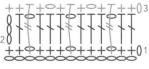

Steps 1–3

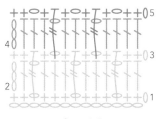

Steps 4–5

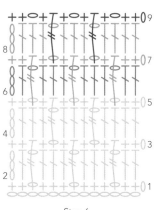

Step 6

76 Granny Spike Stitch

Use this simple stitch to add color and texture to your crochet projects. You will be changing color at the end of each row, but you do not need to cut the yarn. After the first three rows, the correct color in the sequence will be waiting for you. For neat and tidy color changes, change color on the last yarnover of the last stitch of the row.

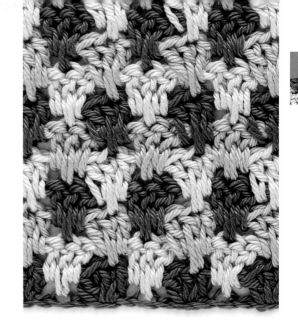

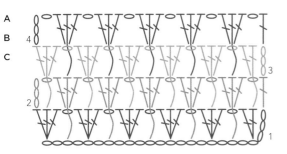

A
B
C

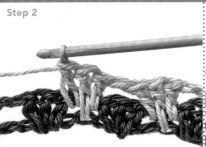

Step 2

Step 3

Step 4 (row 5)

Multiple 4 sts + 3, plus 1 for the foundation chain.

Step 1 (RS) With yarn A, 2dc in 4th ch from hk, *ch1, skip 3ch, 3dc in next ch; rep from * across, change to yarn B, turn.

Step 2 With yarn B, ch4 (counts as 1dc, ch1), skip first 3dc, *1dc in next ch1 sp, 1Spike dc in center st of skipped 3 sts two rows below, 1dc in same ch1 sp, ch1**, skip 3dc; rep from * across, ending last rep at **, skip 2dc, 1dc in top of tch, change to yarn C, turn.

Step 3 With yarn C, ch3 (counts as 1dc), skip first dc, 1Spike dc in first skipped dc two rows below, 1dc in first ch1 sp, *ch1, skip 3dc, 1dc in next ch1 sp, 1Spike dc in center st of skipped 3dc two rows below, 1dc in same ch1 sp; rep from * across, working 1dc on each side of last Spike dc into tch sp, change to yarn A, turn.

Step 4 Repeat Steps 2–3, working one row of each color in sequence.

Special stitch Spike dc: Work dc in specified skipped st two rows below (on row 2 work into foundation ch).

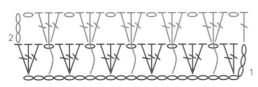

Steps 1–2

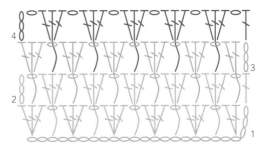

Steps 3–4

77 Cluster Spikes

This bold pattern does require some concentration to make sure the spike stitches are placed correctly. After the first repeat, their position will become clearer. The pattern is worked over a color sequence of four rows in each color. You can either cut the yarn each time you change color and weave in the ends as you go, or carry the unused yarn up the side of the work.

■ A
■ B
■ C

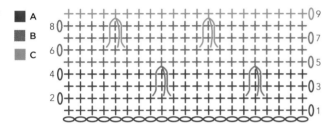

Step 2

Step 5

Step 9

Multiple 8 sts + 5, plus 1 for the foundation chain.

Step 1 (RS) With yarn A, 1sc in 2nd ch from hk and in each ch across, turn.

Step 2 With yarn A, ch1, 1sc in each sc across, turn.

Step 3 With yarn A, ch1, 1sc in each sc across, turn.

Step 4 With yarn A, ch1, 1sc in each sc across, change to yarn B, turn.

Step 5 With yarn B, ch1, 1sc in each of first 4sc, *Spike CL, 1sc in each of next 7sc; rep from * to last sc, 1sc in last sc, turn.

Step 6 With yarn B, ch1, 1sc in each sc across, turn.

Step 7 With yarn B, ch1, 1sc in each sc across, turn.

Step 8 With yarn B, ch1, 1sc in each sc across, change to yarn C, turn.

Step 9 With yarn C, ch1, 1sc in each of first 8sc, *Spike CL, 1sc in each of next 7sc; rep from * to last 5sc, Spike CL, 1sc in each of last 4sc, turn.

Step 10 Repeat Steps 2–9, working four rows of each color in sequence.

Special stitch Spike CL (spike cluster): Insert hk in sc three rows directly below sc just made, yo and pull a loop through (2 loops on hk), [insert hk in next sc three rows below, yo and pull a loop through] twice (4 loops on hk), insert hk in next unworked sc on current row, yo and pull a loop through (5 loops on hk), yo and pull through all 5 loops on hk to complete cluster.

Steps 1–4

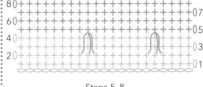

Steps 5–8

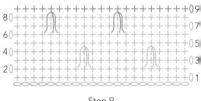

Step 9

78 Almond Stitch

This striking pattern can be used for many projects. Varying the height of the stitches creates an embossed effect that would add visual interest to homewares and accessories. Change color on the last turnover of the last stitch of the row. You can either carry the unused yarn up the side of the work, or cut the yarn and weave in the end as you work the next row so that you have fewer ends to weave in when you complete your project.

Step 2

Step 4

Step 8

Multiple 10 sts + 1, plus 1 for the foundation chain.

Step 1 (RS) With yarn A, 1sc in 2nd ch from hk and in each ch across, change to yarn B, turn.

Step 2 With yarn B, ch1, 1sc in first sc, *1sc in next sc, 1hdc in next sc, 1dc in each of next 5sc, 1hdc in next sc, 1sc in next sc**, ch1, skip 1sc; rep from * across, ending last rep at **, 1sc in last sc, turn.

Step 3 With yarn B, ch1, 1sc in first sc, *1sc in next sc, 1hdc in next hdc, 1dc in each of next 5dc, 1hdc in next hdc, 1sc in next sc**, ch1, skip 1ch; rep from * across, ending last rep at **, 1sc in last sc, turn.

Step 4 With yarn A, ch1, 1sc in first sc, *1sc in each of next 9 sts, 1Spike sc in skipped sc three rows below; rep from * to last 10 sts, 1sc in each of last 10 sts, turn.

Step 5 With yarn A, ch1, 1sc in each sc across, change to yarn B, turn.

Step 6 With yarn B, ch3 (counts as 1dc), skip first sc, *1dc in each of next 2sc, 1hdc in next sc, 1sc in next sc, ch1, skip 1sc, 1sc in next sc, 1hdc in next sc, 1dc in each of next 3sc; rep from * across, turn.

Step 7 With yarn B, ch3 (counts as 1dc), skip first dc, *1dc in each of next 2dc, 1hdc in next hdc, 1sc in next sc, ch1, skip 1ch, 1sc in next sc, 1hdc in next hdc, 1dc in each of next 3dc; rep from * across, working last dc in top of tch, change to yarn A, turn.

Step 8 With yarn A, ch1, 1sc in each of first 5 sts, *1Spike sc in skipped sc three rows below**, 1sc in each of next 9 sts; rep from * across, ending last rep at **, 1sc in each of last 4 sts, 1sc in top of tch, turn.

Step 9 With yarn A, ch1, 1sc in each sc across, change to yarn B, turn.

Step 10 Repeat Steps 2–9.

Special stitch Spike sc: Work sc in skipped st three rows below.

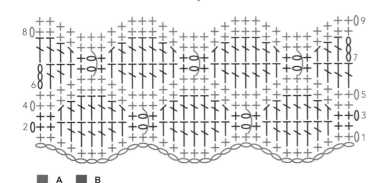

■ A ■ B

79 Peephole Stitch

This is a simple introduction to crossed stitches and creates a textured and versatile fabric. Use it for blankets, accessories, and homewares. Unlike traditional half double crochet, only one turning chain is worked, so be sure to draw the loop up to the full height of the stitch before beginning the row.

Step 1

Step 3

Multiple 2 sts, plus 1 for the foundation chain.

Step 1 (WS) 1hdc in 2nd ch from hk, *Crossed 2hdc over next 2ch; rep from * to last ch, 1hdc in last ch, turn.

Step 2 Ch1, 1FLsc in each hdc across, turn.

Step 3 Ch1, 1hdc in first sc, *Crossed 2hdc over next 2sc; rep from * to last sc, 1hdc in last sc, turn.

Step 4 Repeat Steps 2–3.

Special stitch Crossed 2hdc: Skip 1 st, 1hdc in next st, working in front of hdc just made, 1hdc in skipped st.

80 Wrapped Double Crochet

Changing the direction of your stitches is an easy way to add texture and visual interest to your crochet projects. The groups of V-stitches help to create a lacy, open fabric with excellent drape. Use smooth yarns to show off the stitches to their best. You can use this project for practical accessories, such as scarves and cowls, that require some stability.

Step 2

Step 3

Multiple 6 sts + 1, plus 2 for the foundation chain.

Step 1 (RS) 1dc in 4th ch from hk, *skip 1ch, V-st in next ch, skip 1ch**, 1dc in each of next 3ch; rep from * across, ending last rep at **, 1dc in each of last 2ch, turn.

Step 2 Ch3 (counts as 1dc), skip first dc, 1dc in next dc, V-st in next ch sp, *1dc in each of next 2dc between V-sts, wrapped CL around 2dc just worked, V-st in next ch sp; rep from * to last dc, 1 dc in last dc, 1dc in top of tch, turn.

Step 3 Ch3 (counts as 1dc), skip first dc, 1dc in next dc, V-st in next ch sp, *1dc in each of next 3dc between V-sts, V-st in next ch sp; rep from * to last dc, 1dc in last dc, 1dc in top of tch, turn.

Step 4 Repeat Steps 2–3.

Special stitch V-st (V-stitch): [1dc, ch1, 1dc] in same place.

Special stitch Wrapped CL (cluster): Inserting hk from front, work dc2tog around posts of specified sts.

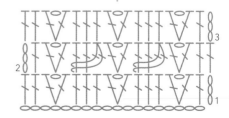

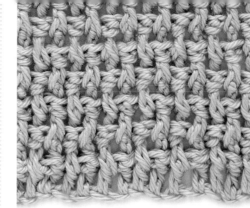

81 Post and Fan Stitch

This pretty stitch is an excellent introduction to post stitches, creating a fabric with enough stability for garments and accessories. Use a smooth yarn, so that the stitches can easily be located and to show off the stitch pattern.

82 Twisted Stitch

This stitch creates a beautiful texture, similar to woven fabric. The dense construction makes it ideal for hats, bags, and three-dimensional projects that need to hold their shape well.

Step 2	Step 3

Multiple 8 sts, plus 1 for the foundation chain.

Step 1 (RS) 2dc in 5th ch from hk, ch2, 2dc in next ch, skip 2ch, 1hdc in each of next 2ch, *skip 2ch, 2dc in next ch, ch2, 2dc in next ch, skip 2ch**, 2hdc in next ch; rep from * across, ending last rep at **, 1hdc in last ch, turn.

Step 2 Ch2 (counts as 1hdc), Fan in first ch sp, *skip 2dc, 1BPdc around each of next 2 sts, Fan in next ch sp; rep from * to tch, 1hdc in top of tch, turn.

Step 3 Ch2 (counts as 1hdc), Fan in first ch sp, *skip 2dc, 1FPdc around each of next 2 sts, Fan in next ch sp; rep from * to tch, 1hdc in top of tch, turn.

Step 4 Repeat Steps 2–3.

Special stitch Fan: [2dc, ch2, 2dc] in same place.

Special stitch FP or BPdc (front post or back post dc): Inserting hk from front or back as indicated, work dc around post of specified st.

Step 2	Step 3

Multiple An odd number of sts, plus 3 for the foundation chain.

Step 1 (RS) 1dc in 4th ch from hk and in each ch across, turn.

Step 2 Ch3 (counts as 1dc), skip first dc, *1FPdc around next dc, 1BPdc around next dc; rep from * to tch, 1dc in top of tch, turn.

Step 3 Ch3 (counts as 1dc), skip first dc, *1BPdc around next dc, 1FPdc around next dc; rep from * to tch, 1dc in top of tch, turn.

Step 4 Repeat Steps 2–3.

Special stitch FP or BPdc (front post or back post dc): Inserting hk from front or back as indicated, work dc around post of specified st.

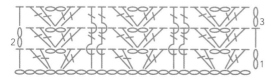

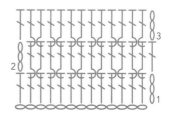

83 Raised V-Stitch

This pattern makes good use of post stitches to give stability to rows of V-stitch. You can use it for scarves and blankets, where the raised lines of post stitches look very attractive. The repeat is easy to memorize, as the post stitches are always made into the raised stitch of the row below. Use a lightweight yarn for a delicate, lacy fabric, or choose a chunky yarn for a scarf that will work up quickly.

84 Textured Post Stitch

This stitch creates a fabric with defined horizontal texture and good drape. You may find it easier to try this stitch in a smooth, medium-weight yarn before experimenting with different yarn weights and textures. You will need to pay attention for the first few rows to make sure you place the post stitches correctly.

Step 2

Step 4

Step 2

Step 3

Multiple 4 sts + 1, plus 1 for the foundation chain.

Step 1 (RS) 1sc in 2nd ch from hk and in each ch across, turn.

Step 2 Ch3 (counts as 1dc), skip first sc, *skip 1sc, V-st in next sc, skip 1sc, 1dc in next sc; rep from * across, turn.

Step 3 Ch3 (counts as 1dc), V-st in first ch sp, *1FPdc around next dc between V-sts, V-st in next ch sp; rep from * to tch, 1dc in top of tch, turn.

Step 4 Ch3 (counts as 1dc), V-st in first ch sp, *1BPdc around next dc between V-sts, V-st in next ch sp; rep from * to tch, 1dc in top of tch, turn.

Step 5 Repeat Steps 3–4.

***Special stitch** V-st (V-stitch): [1dc, ch1, 1dc] in same place.*

***Special stitch** FP or BPdc (front post or back post dc): Inserting hk from front or back as indicated, work dc around post of specified st.*

Multiple An odd number of sts, plus 4 for the foundation chain.

Step 1 (RS) 1dc in 5th ch from hk, *ch1, dc2tog working first leg of st in same ch as previous dc, then skip 1ch and work 2nd leg in next ch; rep from * across, turn.

Step 2 Ch4 (counts as 1dc, ch1), skip first dc2tog, *1FPdc around next dc2tog, ch1; rep from * to last dc, skip last dc, 1dc in top of tch, turn.

Step 3 Ch4 (counts as 1dc, ch1), dc2tog over first two ch sps, *ch1, dc2tog over previous and next ch sp; rep from * across, working last dc2tog over tch sp and 3rd ch of tch, turn.

Step 4 Repeat Steps 2–3.

***Special stitch** FPdc (front post dc): Inserting hk from front, work dc around post of specified st.*

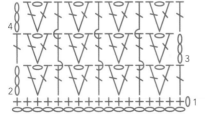

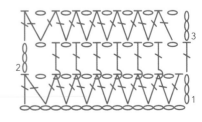

85 Criss Cross

his pattern creates a fabric with excellent drape. As there
only one row to memorize, it requires less concentration
an many crossed stitch patterns. You can use any weight of
arn—lightweight yarn will produce a lacy fabric with excellent
rape, while heavier yarn can be used for winter-weight
ccessories and blankets. The crossed stitches are worked into
e chains, not the chain spaces, so be sure to work the chains
osely so that you can insert the hook on the next row.

86 Crossed Stitch

This stitch makes an interesting fabric, with the stitches
appearing to move in different directions. The resulting fabric
is suited to many different weights and yarn textures. Use a
slightly larger hook than recommended for your yarn to ensure
the fabric has good drape.

Step 1	Step 3

Multiple 6 sts + 1, plus 2 for
the foundation chain.

Step 1 (RS) Crossed 2dc over
4th and 5th ch from hk, *1dc in
next ch, ch2, skip 2ch, 1dc in
next ch**, Crossed 2dc over
next 2ch; rep from * across,
ending last rep at **, turn.

Step 2 Ch3 (counts as 1dc),
skip first dc, *Crossed 2dc
over next 2ch, 1dc in next dc,
ch2, skip 2dc, 1dc in next dc;
rep from * across, working last
dc in top of tch, turn.

Step 3 Repeat Step 2.

Special stitch *Crossed 2dc:
Skip 1ch, 1dc in next ch,
working behind dc just made,
1dc in skipped ch.*

Multiple An even number of
sts, plus 2 for the foundation
chain.

Step 1 (RS) Crossed 2dc
over 4th and 5th ch from hk,
*Crossed 2dc over next 2ch;
rep from * to last ch, 1dc in
last ch, turn.

Step 2 Ch3 (counts as 1dc),
skip first dc, 1dc in next dc,
*Crossed 2dc over next 2dc;
rep from * to last dc, 1dc in
last dc, 1dc in top of tch, turn.

Step 3 Ch3 (counts as 1dc),
skip first dc, *Crossed 2dc
over next 2dc; rep from * to
tch, 1dc in top of tch, turn.

Step 4 Repeat Steps 2–3.

Special stitch *Crossed 2dc:
Skip 1 st, 1dc in next st,
working behind dc just made,
1dc in skipped st.*

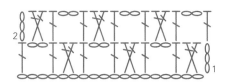 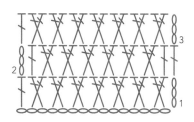

87 Crossed Cable

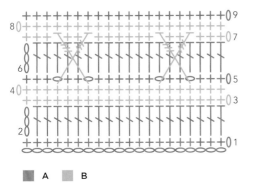

A ■   B ■

The raised crossed stitches in this pattern are crocheted in a contrasting color to make them really stand out. You can work this stitch in any smooth yarn, and it is particularly effective for homewares such as pillows and throws. Set against rows of single and double crochet, this stitch is much simpler than it might appear. For smooth color transitions, change color on the last yarnover of the last stitch of the row. You do not need to cut the yarn; simply carry the unused yarn up the side of the work.

Step 3

Multiple 10 sts, plus 1 for the foundation chain.

Step 1 (RS) With yarn A, 1sc in 2nd ch from hk and in each ch across, turn.

Step 2 With yarn A, ch3 (counts as 1dc), skip first sc, 1dc in each sc across, change to yarn B, turn.

Step 3 With yarn B, ch1, 1sc in each dc across, 1sc in top of tch, turn.

Step 4 With yarn B, ch1, 1sc in each sc across, change to yarn A, turn.

Step 5

Step 5 With yarn A, ch1, 1sc in each of first 3sc, *ch1, skip 1sc, 1sc in each of next 2sc, ch1, skip 1sc**, 1sc in each of next 6sc; rep from * across, ending last rep at **, 1sc in each of last 3sc, turn.

Step 6 With yarn A, ch3 (counts as 1dc), skip first sc, 1dc in each sc and ch (not ch sp) across, change to yarn B, turn.

Step 7 With yarn B, ch1, 1sc in each of first 3dc, *1dtr in 2nd skipped sc three rows below, skip 1dc (below dtr just made), 1sc in

Step 7

each of next 2dc, 1dtr in first skipped sc three rows below (forming crossed stitch), skip 1dc (below dtr just made)**, 1sc in each of next 6dc; rep from *across, ending last rep at **, 1sc in each of last 2dc, 1sc in top of tch, turn.

Step 8 With yarn B, ch1, 1sc in each sc and dtr across, change to yarn A, turn.

Step 9 With yarn A, ch1, 1sc in each sc across, turn.

Step 10 Repeat Steps 2–9.

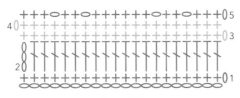

Steps 1–5

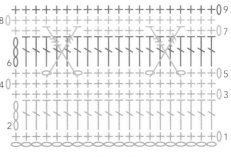

Steps 6–9

38 Post Stitch Stripes

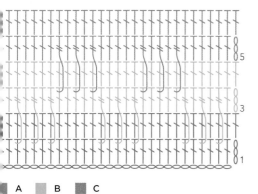

A ■ B ■ C

This stitch uses elongated post stitches to create an interesting stripe effect. It looks as though you are using two colors of yarn across each row, but in fact each row is worked in one color. The same color sequence is repeated throughout and you do not need to cut the yarn; simply carry the unused yarn up the side of the work until it is needed again. Change yarns in the usual way, on the last yarnover of the last stitch of the row.

Step 3

Step 5

Step 7

Multiple 10 sts + 9, plus 2 for the foundation chain.

Step 1 (RS) With yarn A, 1dc in 4th ch from hk and in each ch across, turn.

Step 2 With yarn A, ch3 (counts as 1dc), skip first dc, 1dc in each dc across, 1dc in top of tch, change to yarn B, turn.

Step 3 With yarn B, ch3 (counts as 1dc), skip first dc, 1dc in next dc, *[1FPtr around next dc two rows below, 1dc in next dc] 3 times**, 1dc in each of next 4dc; rep from * across, ending last rep at **, 1dc in top of tch, turn.

Step 4 With yarn B, ch3 (counts as 1dc), skip first dc, 1dc in each st across, 1dc in top of tch, change to yarn C, turn.

Step 5 With yarn C, ch3 (counts as 1dc), skip first dc, 1dc in each of next 6dc, *[1FPtr around next dc two rows below, 1dc in next dc] 3 times, 1dc in each of next 4dc; rep from * to last 2dc, 1dc in each of last 2dc, 1dc in top of tch, turn.

Step 6 With yarn C, ch3 (counts as 1dc), 1dc in each st across, 1dc in top of tch, change to yarn A, turn.

Step 7 Repeat Steps 3–6, working two rows of each color in sequence.

Special stitch FPtr (front post tr): Inserting hk from front, work tr around post of specified st.

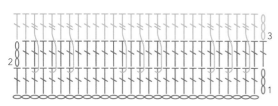

Steps 1–3

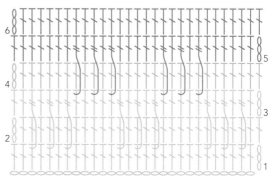

Steps 4–6

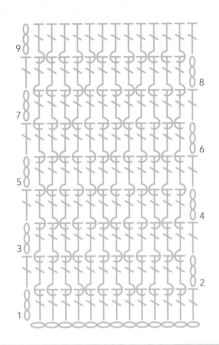

89 Cross Hatch Cable

The repeating post stitches used for this pattern are reminiscent of the ripples on water. Use a smooth, medium-weight yarn so you can really appreciate the texture of this stitch. It is best to use this stitch where only one side of the work will be visible, as it is not reversible.

Step 2

Step 4

Step 9

Multiple 4 sts + 2, plus 2 for the foundation chain.

Step 1 (WS) 1dc in 4th ch from hk and in each ch across, turn.

Step 2 Ch3 (counts as 1dc), skip first dc, *1FPdc around each of next 2dc, 1BPdc around each of next 2dc; rep from * to tch, 1dc in top of tch, turn.

Step 3 Ch3 (counts as 1dc), 1BPdc around next dc, *1FPdc around each of next 2dc**, 1BPdc around each of next 2dc; rep from * across, ending last rep at **, 1BPdc around last dc, 1dc in top of tch, turn.

Step 4 Ch3 (counts as 1dc), skip first dc, *1BPdc around each of next 2dc, 1FPdc around each of next 2dc; rep from * to tch, 1dc in top of tch, turn.

Step 5 Ch3 (counts as 1dc), skip first dc, 1FPdc around next dc, *1BPdc around each of next 2dc**, 1FPdc around each of next 2dc; rep from * across, ending last rep at **, 1FPdc around last dc, 1dc in top of tch, turn.

Steps 6–9 Work as Steps 4, 3, 2, and then 5.

Step 10 Repeat Steps 2–9.

Special stitch FP or BPdc (front post or back post dc): Inserting hk from front or back as specified, work dc around post of specified st.

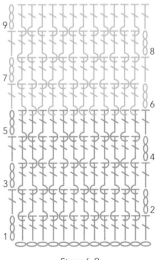

Steps 1–3

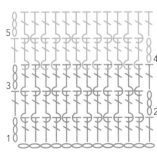

Steps 4–5

Steps 6–9

90 Two-Color Post Stitch

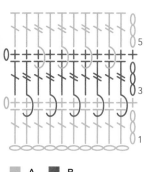

■ A   ■ B

This pattern uses taller post stitches to create a highly textured crochet fabric. You can work this stitch in a single color, or use two as shown here to add visual interest. This is an easy stitch to memorize and lends itself to homewares such as pillows. You might find the post stitches easier if you wrap the yarn over the hook more loosely than you usually would. As you will be changing color every two rows, there is no need to cut the yarn; simply carry the unused yarn up the side of the work. For smooth color transitions, change color on the last yarnover of the last stitch of the row.

Step 2

Step 3

Step 5

Multiple 2 sts + 1, plus 2 for the foundation chain.

Step 1 (RS) With yarn A, 1dc in 4th ch from hk and in each ch across, turn.

Step 2 With yarn A, ch1, 1sc in each dc across, 1sc in top of tch, change to yarn B, turn.

Step 3 With yarn B, ch3 (counts as 1dc), skip first sc, *1FPtr around next dc two rows below, 1dc in next sc; rep from * across, turn.

Step 4 With yarn B, ch1, 1sc in each dc and tr across, 1sc in top of tch, change to yarn A, turn.

Step 5 With yarn A, ch3 (counts as 1dc), skip first sc, *1dc in next sc, 1FPtr around next dc two rows below; rep from * to last 2sc, 1dc in each of last 2sc, change to yarn B, turn.

Step 6 Repeat Steps 2–5, working two rows of each color in sequence.

Special stitch FP or BPtr (front post or back post tr): Inserting hk from front or back as indicated, work tr around post of specified st.

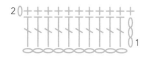

Steps 1–2

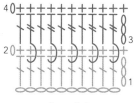

Steps 3–4

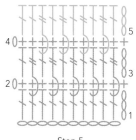

Step 5

91 Noughts and Crosses

The combination of crossed stitches and bobbles makes a very attractive textured fabric that is suitable for homewares and accessories. In this pattern, you will not be working directly into the top of stitches; instead, be sure to work the crossed stitches into the chain spaces, not into the chains. The bobble clusters are made into the space between the crossed stitches on the previous row. This stitch is good for projects where you see both sides of the fabric, such as scarves.

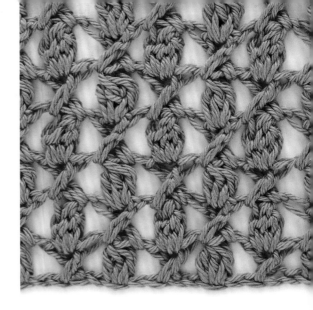

Step 1

Step 2

Step 4

Multiple 5 sts, plus 3 for the foundation chain.

Step 1 (RS) CL in 6th ch from hk, *ch1, skip 1ch, Crossed 2dc over next 2ch, ch1, skip 1ch, CL in next ch; rep from * to last 2ch, ch1, skip 1ch, 1dc in last ch, turn.

Step 2 Ch4 (counts as 1dc, ch1), *Crossed 2dc over next two ch1 sps, ch1, CL in space between sts in center of next Crossed 2dc, ch1; rep from * to last ch1 sp, Crossed 2dc over last ch1 sp and tch sp, ch1, skip 1ch of tch, 1dc in next ch, turn.

Step 3 Ch4 (counts as 1dc, ch1), *CL in space between sts in center of next Crossed 2dc, ch1**, Crossed 2dc over next two ch1 sps, ch1; rep from * across, ending last rep at **, ch1, 1dc in 3rd ch of tch, turn.

Step 4 Repeat Steps 2–3.

Special stitch *CL (cluster): Dc3tog in same place.*

Special stitch *Crossed 2dc: Skip ch1 sp, 1dc in next ch1 sp, working behind dc just made, 1dc in skipped ch1 sp (on row 1 work into foundation ch rather than ch sp).*

Step 1

Step 2

Step 3

92 Puff Columns

This is a stitch with lots of texture. By combining puff stitches with columns of double crochet, you will create a tactile fabric with a distinct vertical pattern. This lends itself to large-scale projects such as blankets and throws. The post stitches add stability and help to make the puff stitches "pop out" of the fabric. It is a very satisfying stitch to work.

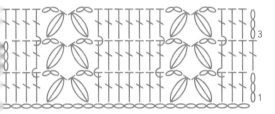

Step 1

Step 2

Step 3

Multiple 12 sts + 1, plus 2 for the foundation chain.

Step 1 (RS) 1dc in 4th ch from hk, 1dc in each of next 2ch, *ch2, Puff in next ch, skip 3ch, Puff in next ch, ch2**, 1dc in each of next 7ch; rep from * across, ending last rep at **, 1dc in each of last 4ch, turn.

Step 2 Ch3 (counts as 1dc), skip first dc, 1dc in each of next 2dc, *1BPdc around next dc, ch2, Puff in each of next two ch sps, ch2, 1BPdc around next dc**, 1dc in each of next 5dc; rep from * across, ending last rep at **, 1dc in each of last 2dc, 1dc in top of tch, turn.

Step 3 Ch3 (counts as 1dc), skip first dc, 1dc in each of next 2dc, *1FPdc around next dc, ch2, Puff in each of next two ch sps, ch2, 1FPdc around next dc**, 1dc in each of next 5dc; rep from * across, ending last rep at **, 1dc in each of last 2dc, 1dc in top of tch, turn.

Step 4 Repeat Steps 2–3.

Special stitch *Puff: Hdc3tog in same place.*

Special stitch *FP or BPdc (front post or back post dc): Inserting hk from front or back as indicated, work dc around post of specified st.*

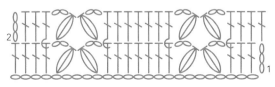

Steps 1–2

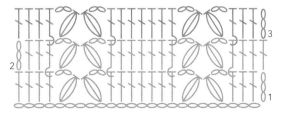

Step 3

93 Woven Cable

The twisted stitches in this cable panel create a highly textured vertical woven effect. Use a smooth, lightweight yarn to make wraps and accessories with excellent drape and structure, or crochet this stitch in a heavier yarn for a chunky scarf or homewares.

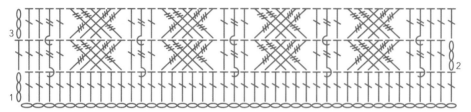

Step 2

Step 3

Step 3 (cont.)

Multiple 18 sts + 7, plus 2 for the foundation chain.

Step 1 (WS) 1dc in 4th ch from hk and in each ch across, turn.

Step 2 Ch3 (counts as 1dc), skip first dc, 1dc in each of next 2dc, 1FPtr around next st, 1dc in next dc, *C6B over next 6 sts, 1dc in next dc, 1FPtr around next st, 1dc in next dc, C6F over next 6 sts, 1dc in next dc, 1FPtr around next st, 1dc in next dc; rep from * to last dc, 1dc in last dc, 1dc in top of tch, turn.

Step 3 Ch3 (counts as 1dc), skip first dc, 1dc in each of next 2dc, 1BPtr around next tr, 1dc in next dc, *C6B over next 6 sts, 1dc in next dc, 1BPtr around next tr, 1dc in next dc, C6F over next 6 sts, 1dc in next dc, 1BPtr around next tr, 1dc in next dc; rep from * to last dc, 1dc in last dc, 1dc in top of tch, turn.

Step 4 Repeat Steps 2–3.

Special stitch FP or BPtr (front post or back post tr): Inserting hk from front or back as indicated, work tr around post of specified st.

Special stitch C6B (cross 6 back): Skip 3 sts, 1dtr in each of next 3 sts, working behind 3dtr just made, 1dtr in each of skipped 3 sts.

Special stitch C6F (cross 6 front): Skip 3 sts, 1dtr in each of next 3 sts, working in front of 3dtr just made, 1dtr in each of skipped 3 sts.

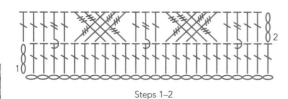

Steps 1–2

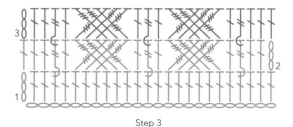

Step 3

94 Herringbone

This stitch creates a highly textured fabric that can be used for a variety of projects, including homewares and accessories. Making post stitches that lean to the left and the right creates a pattern of raised columns that look best in a smooth, medium-weight yarn.

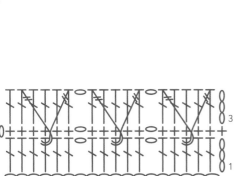

Step 2

Step 3

Step 3 (cont.)

Multiple 6 sts + 1, plus 2 for the foundation chain.

Step 1 (RS) 1dc in 4th ch from hk, 1dc in each of next 4ch, *ch1, skip 1ch, 1dc in each of next 5ch; rep from * to last ch, 1dc in last ch, turn.

Step 2 Ch1, 1sc in each of first 6 sts, *ch1, skip ch sp, 1sc in each of next 5 sts; rep from * to tch, 1sc in top of tch, turn.

Step 3 Ch3 (counts as 1dc), skip first sc, *1FPst Right in next sc, 1dc in each of next 3sc, 1FPst Left in next sc**, ch1; rep from * across, ending last rep at **, 1dc in last sc, turn.

Step 4 Repeat Steps 2–3.

Special stitch FPst Right (right-leaning front post st): Yo, insert hk in next sc on row below and pull a loop through, yo and pull through 2 loops on hk, yo twice, skip next sc, insert hk around post of next dc two rows below from front to back to front and pull a loop through, [yo and pull through 2 loops on hk] twice, yo and pull through all 3 loops on hk.

Special stitch FPst Left (left-leaning front post st): Yo twice, insert hk around post of same dc two rows below as previous FPst Right from front to back to front and pull a loop through, [yo and pull through 2 loops on hk] twice, yo, insert hk in next sc on row below and pull a loop through, yo and pull through 2 loops on hk, yo and pull through all 3 loops on hk.

Steps 1–2

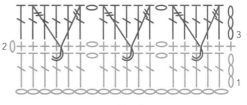

Step 3

95 Diamond Cable

Cable stitches often seem daunting because they look so complicated. However, by using basic stitches and inserting the hook to the left or the right, simple cable patterns can be formed that even a novice crocheter can master. It is essential to pay attention to the pattern because rows often combine different-height stitches. Cable stitches can be made in most weights of yarn, but use smooth yarns and paler colors to show the cables at their best. This cable panel can be worked on a background of single crochet (simply add an equal number of stitches to either side of the panel), or you can make a longer chain and repeat the panel for wider projects such as scarves and blankets.

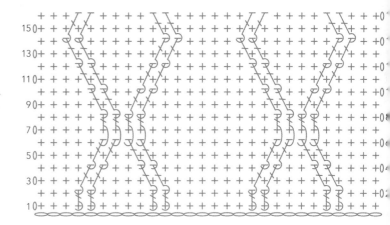

Step 2

Step 4

Step 8

Multiple 14 sts, plus 1 for the foundation chain.

Step 1 (WS) 1sc in 2nd ch from hk and in each ch across, turn.

Step 2 Ch1, *1sc in each of next 3sc, 1FPdc around each of next 2sc, 1sc in each of next 4sc, 1FPdc around each of next 2sc, 1sc in each of next 3sc; rep from * across, turn.

Step 3 Ch1, 1sc in each sc and dc across, turn.

Step 4 Ch1, *1sc in each of next 4sc, 1FPdc around each of first 2dc two rows below, skip 2sc, 1sc in each of next 2sc, 1FPdc around each of next 2dc two rows below, skip 2sc, 1sc in each of next 4sc; rep from * across, turn.

Step 5 Work as Step 3.

Step 6 Ch1, *1sc in each of next 5sc, 1FPdc around each of 4dc two rows below, skip 4sc, 1sc in each of next 5sc; rep from * across, turn.

Step 7 Work as Step 3.

Step 8 Ch1, *1sc in each of next 5sc, 1FPdc around each of 4dc two rows below, skip 4sc, 1sc in each of next 5sc; rep from * across, turn.

Step 9 Work as Step 3.

Step 10 Ch1, *1sc in each of next 4sc, 1FPdc around each of first 2dc two rows below, skip 2sc, 1sc in each of next 2sc, 1FPdc around each of next 2dc two rows below, skip 2sc, 1sc in each of next 4sc; rep from * across, turn.

Step 11 Work as Step 3.

Steps 1–3

Steps 4–7

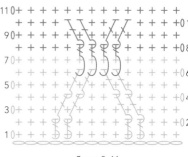

Steps 8–11

Step 12

Step 14

Step 16

Step 12 Ch1, *1sc in each of next 3sc, 1FPdc around each of first 2dc two rows below, skip 2sc, 1sc in each of next 4sc, 1FPdc around each of next 2dc two rows below, skip 2sc, 1sc in each of next 3sc; rep from * across, turn.

Step 13 Work as Step 3.

Step 14 Ch1, *1sc in each of next 2sc, 1FPdc around each of first 2dc two rows below, skip 2sc, 1sc in each of next 6sc, 1FPdc around each of next 2dc two rows below, skip 2sc, 1sc in each of next 2sc; rep from * across, turn.

Step 15 Work as Step 3.

Step 16 Ch1, *1sc in each of next 3sc, 1FPdc around each of first 2dc two rows below, skip 2sc, 1sc in each of next 4sc, 1FPdc around each of next 2dc two rows below, skip 2sc, 1sc in each of next 3sc; rep from * across, turn.

Step 17 Repeat Steps 3–16.

Special stitch *FPdc (front post dc): Inserting hk from front, work dc around post of specified st.*

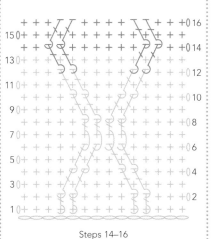

Steps 12–13

Steps 14–16

96 Barley Twist Cable

This is a classic cable pattern that adds plenty of texture and visual interest. Use a smooth, medium-weight yarn and a size larger hook than usual to make the cables easier. Set within columns of raised double crochet, this stitch is ideal for home accessories such as pillows, and can also be used for blankets and throws.

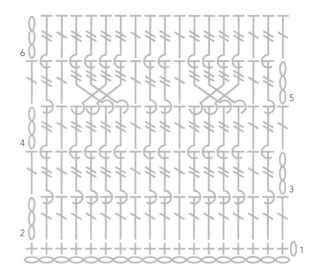

Step 2

Step 3

Step 4

Multiple 8 sts + 2, plus 1 for the foundation chain.

Step 1 (RS) 1sc in 2nd ch from hk and in each ch across, turn.

Step 2 Ch3 (counts as 1dc), skip first sc, 1dc in each sc across, turn.

Step 3 Ch3 (counts as 1dc), skip first dc, *1FPtr around next dc, 1dc in next dc, 1FPtr around each of next 4dc, 1dc in next dc, 1FPtr around next dc; rep from * to tch, 1dc in top of tch, turn.

Step 4 Ch3 (counts as 1dc), skip first dc, *1BPtr around next tr, 1dc in next dc, 1BPtr around each of next 4tr, 1dc in next dc, 1BPtr around next tr; rep from * to tch, 1dc in top of tch, turn.

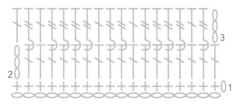

Steps 1–3

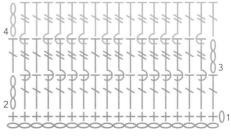

Step 4

Step 5

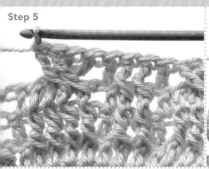

Step 6

Step 7

Step 5 Ch3 (counts as dc), skip first dc, *1FPtr around next tr, 1dc in next dc, skip 2tr, 1FPtr around each of next 2tr, 1FPtr around each of 2tr just skipped, 1dc in next dc, 1FPtr around next tr; rep from * to tch, 1dc in top of tch, turn.

Step 6 Ch3 (counts as 1dc), skip first dc, *1BPtr around next tr, 1dc in next dc, 1BPtr around each of next 4tr, 1dc in next dc, 1BPtr around next tr; rep from * to tch, 1dc in top of tch, turn.

Step 7 Repeat Steps 3–6.

Special stitch FP or BPtr (front post or back post tr): Inserting hk from front or back as indicated, work tr around post of specified st.

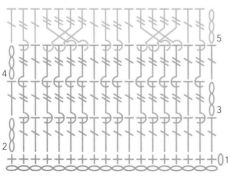

Step 5

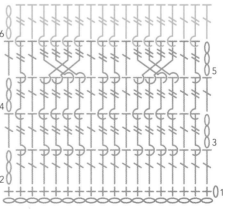

Step 6

97 Interlocking Cable

This attractive cable stitch can either be used as a panel on a background of single crochet, or repeated for large-scale projects such as sweaters and homewares. When working cables, using smooth yarns in pale colors and a size larger hook than usual for the yarn weight can help to make working the cables easier.

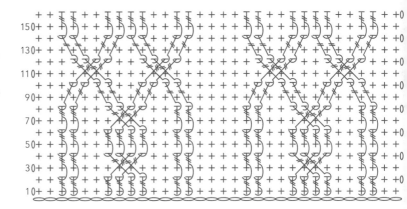

Step 2

Step 4

Step 6

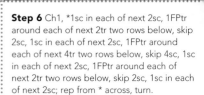

Multiple 16 sts, plus 1 for the foundation chain.

Step 1 (WS) 1sc in 2nd ch from hk and in each ch across, turn.

Step 2 Ch1, *1sc in each of next 2sc, 1FPtr around each of next 2sc, 1sc in each of next 2sc, 1FPtr around each of next 4sc, 1sc in each of next 2sc, 1FPtr around each of next 2sc, 1sc in each of next 2sc; rep from * across, turn.

Step 3 Ch1, 1sc in each sc and tr across, turn.

Step 4 Ch1, *1sc in each of next 2sc, 1FPtr around each of next 2tr two rows below, skip 2sc, 1sc in each of next 2sc, skip 2tr two rows below, 1FPtr around each of next 2tr two rows below, 1FPtr around each of skipped 2tr two rows below, skip 4sc, 1sc in each of next 2sc, 1FPtr around each of next 2tr two rows below, skip 2sc, 1sc in each of next 2sc; rep from * across, turn.

Step 5 Work as Step 3.

Step 6 Ch1, *1sc in each of next 2sc, 1FPtr around each of next 2tr two rows below, skip 2sc, 1sc in each of next 2sc, 1FPtr around each of next 4tr two rows below, skip 4sc, 1sc in each of next 2sc, 1FPtr around each of next 2tr two rows below, skip 2sc, 1sc in each of next 2sc; rep from * across, turn.

Step 7 Work as Step 3.

Steps 1–3

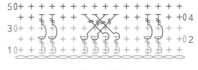
Steps 4–5

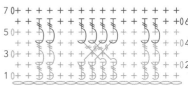
Steps 6–7

Step 8

Step 10

Step 12

Step 8 Work as Step 4.

Step 9 Work as Step 3.

Step 10 Ch1, *1sc in each of next 3sc,
[1FPtr around each of next 4tr two rows
below, skip 4sc, 1sc in each of next 2sc] twice,
1sc in next sc; rep from * across, turn.

Step 11 Work as Step 3.

Step 12 Ch1, *1sc in each of next 3sc, [skip
2tr two rows below, 1FPtr around each of
next 2tr two rows below, 1FPtr around each
of skipped 2tr two rows below, skip 4sc, 1sc
in each of next 2sc] twice, 1sc in next sc; rep
from * across, turn.

Step 13 Work as Step 3.

Step 14 Work as Step 6.

Step 15 Work as Step 3.

Step 16 Work as Step 6.

Step 17 Repeat Steps 3–16.

Special stitch *FPdtr (front post dtr):
Inserting hk from front, work dtr around post
of specified st.*

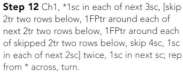

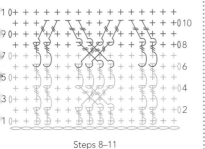

Steps 8–11

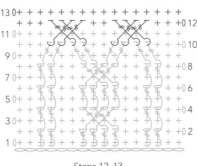

Steps 12–13

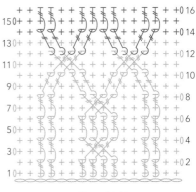

Steps 14–16

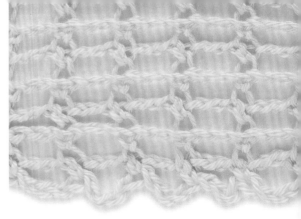

98 Arch Mesh

Combinations of chains and basic crochet stitches can be used to create lightweight fabrics with plenty of drape. This stitch works best in a smooth, lightweight yarn and is an excellent choice for shawls and wraps. Mesh and net patterns are also a great choice for making reusable shopping bags, beach cover-ups, and light breezy curtains.

99 String Mesh

This stitch is ideal for long, straight accessories such as scarves and wraps where both sides of the fabric will be visible. The single crochet stitches create a framework for the chain stitches and the overall effect is very pleasing. Use a lightweight or medium-weight yarn with a smooth texture to show the stitch off to its best.

Step 1

Step 2

Step 1

Step 2

Multiple 4 sts + 3, plus 1 for the foundation chain.

Step 1 (RS) 1sc in 2nd ch from hk, ch2, skip 1ch, 1dc in next ch, *ch2, skip 1ch, 1sc in next ch, ch2, skip 1ch, 1dc in next ch; rep from * across, turn.

Step 2 Ch1, 1sc in first dc, ch2, 1dc in next sc, *ch2, 1sc in next dc, ch2, 1dc in next sc; rep from * across, turn.

Step 3 Repeat Step 2.

Multiple 4 sts + 1, plus 1 for the foundation chain.

Step 1 (RS) 1sc in 2nd ch from hk, *ch3, skip 3ch, 1sc in next ch; rep from * across, turn.

Step 2 Ch1, 1BLsc in first sc, *ch3, 1BLsc in next sc; rep from * across, turn.

Step 3 Repeat Step 2.

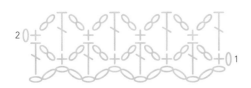

100 Picot Net

his is a very feminine stitch that looks best in a smooth yarn. e small picot stitches within a framework of chains and taller tches give the fabric plenty of stability.

101 Picot Mesh

Although it appears to be made almost entirely of chains, this stitch creates a beautiful lightweight fabric that can be used for several different projects. Use a medium-weight yarn in soft cotton to make a lightweight summer top, for example, or choose a lightweight silk or wool to make a light-as-air wrap.

Step 2

Step 3

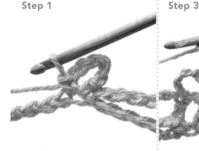

Step 1

Step 3

Multiple 3 sts + 1, plus 1 for the foundation chain.

Step 1 (RS) 1sc in 2nd ch from hk, 1sc in next ch, *Picot, 1sc in each of next 3ch; rep from * to last 2ch, Picot, 1sc in each of last 2ch, turn.

Step 2 Ch5 (counts as 1dc, ch2), skip first 3sc and Picot, 1dc in next sc, *ch2, skip next 2sc and Picot, 1dc in next sc; rep from *across, turn.

Step 3 Ch1, 1sc in first dc, *[1sc, Picot, 1sc] in next ch2 sp, 1sc in next dc; rep from * to tch, [1sc, Picot, 1sc] in tch sp, 1sc in 3rd ch of tch, turn.

Step 4 Repeat Steps 2–3.

Special stitch Picot: Ch4, 1sl st in 4th ch from hk.

Multiple 6 sts + 1, plus 3 for the foundation chain.

Step 1 (RS) 1dc in 4th ch from hk, *ch5, skip 5ch, Picot in next ch; rep from * to last 6ch, ch5, skip 5ch, 1dc in last ch, turn.

Step 2 Ch3 (counts as 1dc), 1dc in first dc, *ch5, Picot in ch sp of next Picot; rep from * to tch, ch5, 1dc in top of tch, turn.

Step 3 Repeat Step 2.

Special stitch Picot: [1sc, ch5, 1sc] in same place.

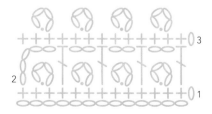

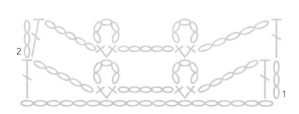

102 Picot Trellis

The small picot stitches set within arches of chains create a very pretty stitch that is suitable for summer accessories. Like all mesh and filet stitches, Picot Trellis needs to be firmly blocked to reveal the full effect of the pattern.

103 Rigid Mesh

This is an excellent stitch for accessories such as scarves. Working single crochet and double crochet on alternate rows gives the stitch stability and visual interest. Use a smooth, cotton yarn for this stitch and experiment with different yarn weights to achieve interesting textures.

Step 2

Step 3

Step 2

Step 3

Multiple 5 sts + 1, plus 1 for the foundation chain.

Step 1 (RS) 1sc in 2nd ch from hk, *ch5, skip 4ch, 1sc in next ch; rep from * across, turn.

Step 2 Ch6 (counts as 1tr, ch2), Picot in first ch5 sp, *ch5, Picot in next ch5 sp; rep from * to last sc, ch2, 1tr in last sc, turn.

Step 3 Ch1, 1sc in first tr, *ch5, Picot in next ch5 sp; rep from * to tch, ch5, 1sc in 4th ch of tch, turn.

Step 4 Repeat Steps 2–3.

Special stitch *Picot: [1sc, ch3, 1sc] in same place.*

Multiple Multiple 4 sts + 1, plus 1 for the foundation chain.

Step 1 (RS) 1dc in 10th ch from hk, *ch3, skip 3ch, 1dc in next ch; rep from * across, turn.

Step 2 Ch1, 1sc in first dc, *ch3, 1sc in next dc; rep from * to tch, ch3, skip 3ch of tch, 1sc in next ch, turn.

Step 3 Ch6 (counts as 1dc, ch3), skip first sc, 1dc in next sc, *ch3, 1dc in next sc; rep from * across, turn.

Step 4 Repeat Steps 2–3.

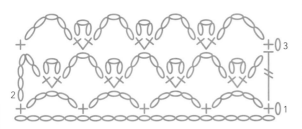

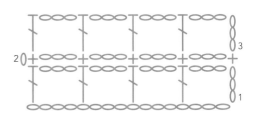

104 Extended Single Crochet Mesh

xtended single crochet is used to make a taller stitch with
ood stability that can be used for a variety of projects
cluding garments. The one-row repeat is suitable for
ocheters of all skill levels.

105 Reinforced Mesh

This stitch creates a fabric with a checkerboard effect that
is strong enough to use for accessories. After the first row,
stitches are made into the chain spaces, not into the double
crochet stitches, which gives the fabric stability and prevents
it from distorting.

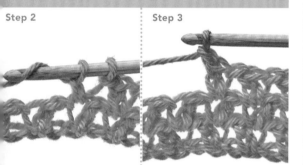

Step 2

Step 3

Step 2

Step 3

Multiple An even number
of sts + 1.

Step 1 (RS) 1exsc in 5th ch
from hk, *ch1, skip 1ch, 1exsc
in next ch; rep from * across,
turn.

Step 2 Ch3 (counts as 1exsc,
ch1), skip first exsc, *1exsc in
next exsc, ch1; rep from * to
tch, skip 1ch of tch, 1exsc in
next ch, turn.

Step 3 Repeat Step 2.

Special stitch *Exsc
(extended sc): Insert hk in
specified ch or st, yo and
pull a loop through, yo and
pull through 1 loop on hk,
yo and pull through both
loops on hk.*

Multiple 3 sts + 2, plus 2 for
the foundation chain.

Step 1 (RS) 1dc in 4th ch from
hk, *ch1, skip 1ch, 1dc in each
of next 2ch; rep from * across,
turn.

Step 2 Ch4 (counts as 1dc,
ch1), *2dc in next ch sp, ch1;
rep from * to tch, 1dc in top of
tch, turn.

Step 3 Ch3 (counts as 1dc),
1dc in first ch sp, *ch1, 2dc
in next ch sp; rep from * to
tch sp, ch1, 1dc in tch sp,
1dc in 3rd ch of tch, turn.

Step 4 Repeat Steps 2–3.

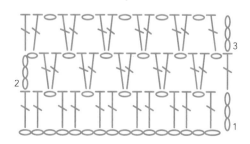

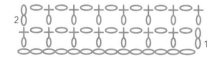

106 Block Lace

This is a very firm mesh pattern with a grid of chain spaces anchored between rows of single and double crochet. Use a smooth, crisp cotton for this stitch and block it well so that the chain spaces are clearly defined.

107 Honeycomb

This is a very stable stitch because the chain spaces are supported by single crochet arches, creating a very open and stable fabric that suits a variety of projects.

Step 2	Step 3

Step 3	Step 4

Multiple 6 sts + 1, plus 1 for the foundation chain.

Step 1 (RS) 1sc in 2nd ch from hk, *ch5, skip 5ch, 1sc in next ch; rep from * across, turn.

Step 2 Ch1, 1sc in first sc, *5sc in next ch sp, 1sc in next sc; rep from *across, turn.

Step 3 Ch3 (counts as 1dc), skip first sc, 1dc in each of next 5sc, *ch1, skip 1sc, 1dc in each of next 5sc; rep from * to last sc, 1dc in last sc, turn.

Step 4 Ch1, 1sc in first dc, *ch5, 1sc in next ch1 sp; rep from * across, working last sc in top of tch, turn.

Step 5 Repeat Steps 2–4.

Multiple 6 sts + 1, plus 1 for the foundation chain.

Step 1 (RS) 1sc in 2nd ch from hk, *ch6, skip 5ch, 1sc in next ch; rep from * across, turn.

Step 2 Ch1, 1sc in first sc, *7sc in next ch sp, 1sc in next sc; rep from * across, turn.

Step 3 Ch7 (counts as 1tr, ch3), skip first 3sc, 1sc in each of next 3sc, *ch6, skip 5sc, 1sc in each of next 3sc; rep from * to last 3sc, ch3, skip 2sc, 1tr in last sc, turn.

Step 4 Ch1, 1sc in first tr, 3sc in ch3 sp, *skip 1sc, 1sc in next sc, skip 1sc**, 7sc in ch6 sp; rep from * across, ending last rep at **, 3sc in tch sp, 1sc in 4th ch of tch, turn.

Step 5 Ch1, 1sc in each of first 2sc, *ch6, skip 5sc**, 1sc in each of next 3sc; rep from * across, ending last rep at **, 1sc in each of last 2sc, turn.

Step 6 Ch1, 1sc in first sc, *skip 1sc, 7sc in ch sp, skip 1sc, 1sc in next sc; rep from * across, turn.

Step 7 Repeat Steps 3–6.

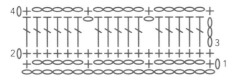

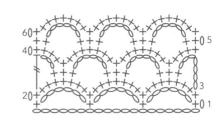

08 Trellis Mesh 1

is mesh pattern is made up of rows where the chains
erlock with each other, held in place by a series of single and
uble crochet stitches. The resulting fabric has a pleasing
xture that reveals itself when the crochet is blocked. This
tch lends itself to lightweight projects made in smooth
tural fibers such as cotton and bamboo.

109 Trellis Mesh 2

This is another example of a mesh stitch where the pattern
is built up over rows of interlinking chain stitches. It creates
a very pretty fabric with excellent drape and texture. This
pattern is suitable for garments and accessories as it holds
its shape well.

Step 2	Step 3

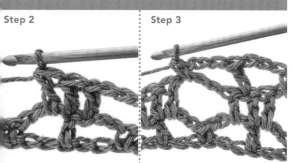

Step 2	Step 3

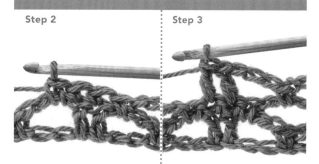

Multiple 6 sts + 1, plus 5 for
the foundation chain.

Step 1 (RS) 1sc in 9th ch from
hk, ch3, skip 2ch, 1dc in next
ch, *ch3, skip 2ch, 1sc in next
ch, ch3, skip 2ch, 1dc in next
ch; rep from * across, turn.

Step 2 Ch3 (counts as 1dc),
skip first dc, *1dc in next ch
sp, ch3**, 1dc in next ch sp,
1dc in next dc; rep from *
across, ending last rep at **,
1dc in tch sp, skip 3ch of tch,
1dc in next ch, turn.

Step 3 Ch6, (counts as 1dc,
ch3), skip first 2dc, *1sc in next
ch sp, ch3, skip 1dc, 1dc in
next dc**, ch3, skip 1dc; rep
from * across, ending last rep
at ** and working last dc in
top of tch, turn.

Step 4 Repeat Steps 2–3.

Multiple 7 sts, plus 5 for the
foundation chain.

Step 1 (RS) 1sc in 9th ch from
hk, ch3, skip 2ch, *1dc in each
of next 2ch, ch3, skip 2ch, 1sc
in next ch, ch3, skip 2ch; rep
from * to last ch, 1dc in last ch,
turn.

Step 2 Ch1, 1sc in first dc,
*1sc in next ch sp, ch3**, 1sc
in next ch sp, 1sc in each of
next 2dc; rep from * across,
ending last rep at **, 1sc in
tch sp, skip 3ch of tch, 1sc in
next ch, turn.

Step 3 Ch6 (counts as 1dc,
ch3), skip first 2sc, *1sc in next
ch sp, ch3, skip 1sc**, 1dc in
each of next 2sc, ch3, skip 1sc;
rep from * across, ending last
rep at **, 1dc in last sc, turn.

Step 4 Repeat Steps 2–3.

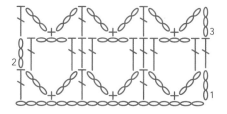

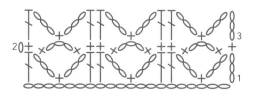

110 Grid Stitch

This stitch appears to form a series of square grids. By combining chains with single crochet and double crochet, a repeating pattern of squares appears. The pattern looks best in a smooth yarn, but you can experiment with different weights to make a light summer wrap or a chunky winter scarf.

Step 2	Step 3

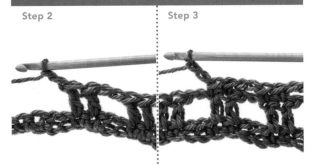

Multiple 4 sts + 2, plus 1 for the foundation chain.

Step 1 (RS) 1sc in 2nd ch from hk, 1sc in next ch, *ch2, skip 2ch, 1sc in each of next 2ch; rep from * across, turn.

Step 2 Ch3 (counts as 1dc), skip first sc, 1dc in next sc, *ch2, 1dc in each of next 2sc; rep from * across, turn.

Step 3 Ch1, 1sc in each of first 2dc, *ch2, 1sc in each of next 2dc; rep from * across, working last sc in top of tch, turn.

Step 4 Repeat Steps 2–3.

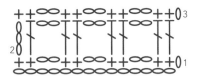

111 Reinforced Grid Stitch

This mesh stitch can be used with any weight of yarn. Use a very fine, lightweight yarn to make a simple wrap that will drape and lie over your shoulders, or use chunky yarns to make robust winter scarves. The simple repeat makes this a good stitch for all skill levels.

Step 2	Step 4

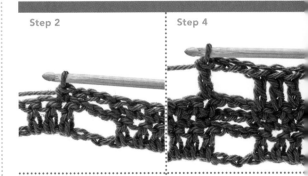

Multiple 6 sts + 3, plus 2 for the foundation chain.

Step 1 (RS) 1dc in 4th ch from hk, 1dc in next ch, *ch3, skip 3ch, 1dc in each of next 3ch; rep from * across, turn.

Step 2 Ch1, 1sc in each of first 3dc, *ch3, 1sc in each of next 3dc; rep from * across, working last sc in top of tch, turn.

Step 3 Ch1, 1sc in each of first 3sc, *ch3, 1sc in each of next 3sc; rep from * across, turn.

Step 4 Ch3 (counts as 1dc), skip first sc, 1dc in each of next 2sc, *ch3, 1dc in each of next 3sc; rep from * across, turn.

Step 5 Repeat Steps 2–4.

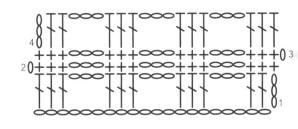

112 Eyelet Stitch

This stitch makes a regular pattern of horizontal eyelets. It can be used as a pattern in its own right for garments and accessories, or you can work a series of repeats within another project to make eyelet rows that can be threaded with cord or ribbon.

113 Ladders

This is a visually pleasing stitch that creates a vertical column of eyelets. It would suit many projects, including lightweight summer garments.

Step 2
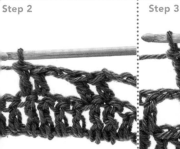

Step 3

Step 1

Step 3

Multiple 4 sts, plus 3 for the foundation chain.

Step 1 (RS) 1dc in 5th ch from hk, 1dc in next ch, *1tr in each of next 2ch, 1dc in each of next 2ch; rep from * to last ch, 1tr in last ch, turn.

Step 2 Ch5 (counts as 1dc, ch2), skip first 3 sts, *1dc in each of next 2tr, ch2, skip 2dc; rep from * to tch, 1dc in top of tch, turn.

Step 3 Ch4 (counts as 1tr), skip first dc, *2dc in next ch2 sp, 1tr in each of next 2dc; rep from * to tch, 2dc in tch sp, 1dc in 3rd ch of tch, turn.

Step 4 Repeat Steps 2–3.

Multiple 7 sts + 1, plus 2 for the foundation chain.

Step 1 (RS) 1dc in 4th ch from hk, 1dc in next ch, ch2, skip 2ch, *1dc in each of next 5ch, ch2, skip 2ch; rep from * to last 3ch, 1dc in each of last 3ch, turn.

Step 2 Ch3 (counts as 1dc), skip first dc, 1dc in each of next 2dc, ch2, *1dc in each of next 5dc, ch2; rep from * to last 2dc, 1dc in each of last 2dc, 1dc in top of tch, turn.

Step 3 Repeat Step 2.

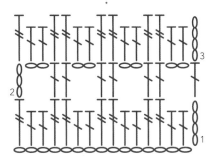

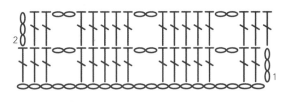

114 Little Checkerboards

Filet crochet is made from a regular series of alternating chains and double crochet stitches to form a design or repeating pattern. Designs and pictures of all kinds can be created using just a combination of double crochet and chain spaces. Patterns are usually followed from a special filet chart because the written pattern often has a large number of instructions and abbreviations. Filet charts are always followed from bottom to top, with odd-numbered rows worked right to left and even-numbered rows from left to right. This example for a simple checkerboard pattern includes written instructions and a filet chart to help you practice the basic filet techniques. The empty squares on the chart represent spaces and the solid ones represent blocks. A standard stitch chart is also provided so that you can see exactly how the blocks and spaces are worked. Traditionally, white or cream cotton yarn is used, but you can achieve interesting effects and stunning results using darker yarns.

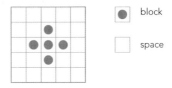

● block

☐ space

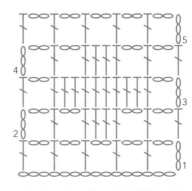

Filet chart

Standard chart

Step 1

Step 2

Step 3

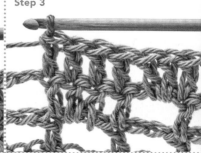

Multiple 3 sts + 1, plus 4 for the foundation chain.

Step 1 (RS) 1dc in 8th ch from hk, *ch2, skip 2ch, 1dc in next ch; rep from * across, turn.

Step 2 Ch5 (counts as 1dc, ch2), skip first dc, 1dc in next dc, *ch2, 1dc in next dc (space made), 2dc in next ch sp and 1dc in next dc (block made), ch2, 1dc in next dc**, [ch2, 1dc in next dc] twice; rep from * across, ending last rep at **, ch2, skip 2ch of tch, 1dc in next ch, turn.

Step 3 Ch5 (counts as 1dc, ch2), skip first dc, 1dc in next dc, *2dc in next ch sp, 1dc in each of next 4dc, 2dc in next ch sp, 1dc in next dc, ch2, 1dc in next dc**, ch2, 1dc in next dc; rep from * across, ending last rep at ** and working last dc in 3rd ch of tch, turn.

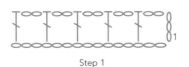

Step 1

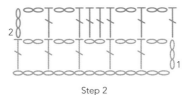

Step 2

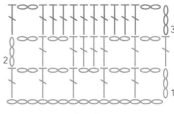

Step 3

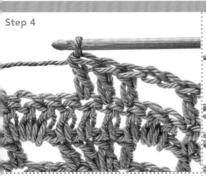

Step 4 Ch5 (counts as 1dc, ch2), skip first dc, 1dc in next dc, *ch2, skip 2dc, 1dc in each of next 4dc, ch2, skip 2dc, 1dc in next dc, ch2, 1dc in next dc**, ch2, 1dc in next dc; rep from * across, ending last rep at ** and working last dc in 3rd ch of tch, turn.

Step 5 Ch5 (counts as 1dc, ch2), skip first dc, 1dc in next dc, *ch2, 1dc in next dc, ch2, skip 2dc, 1dc in next dc, [ch2, 1dc in next dc] twice**, ch2, 1dc in next dc; rep from * across, ending last rep at ** and working last dc in 3rd ch of tch, turn.

Step 6 Repeat Steps 2–5.

Special technique To make a space: Ch2, skip 2ch or 2dc, 1dc in next ch or dc.

Special technique To make a block over the foundation chain or another block: 1dc in each of next 3ch or 3dc.

Special technique To make a block over a space, work either [2dc in next ch2 sp, 1dc in next dc] or [1dc in each of next 2ch, 1dc in next dc]. The first method is used in the sample shown.

Note When a block follows a space, it will look like 4dc because the first dc belongs to the adjacent space.

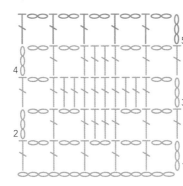

Step 4

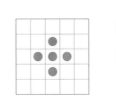

Step 5

block

space

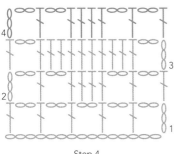

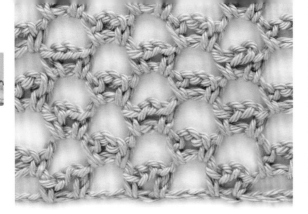

115 Arched Picots

This simple stitch is made by combining single crochet and chains. The one-row repeat is easy to memorize, and the resulting fabric is lacy and delicate. This pattern is ideal for cotton yarns and is suitable for making light and airy accessories with excellent drape.

116 Posy Arcade

In this stitch, groups of three picots are arranged to create a trefoil pattern that is reminiscent of tiny flowers. The stitch looks best in a crisp, cotton yarn, which helps to provide structure and show off the delicate pattern. Use smooth yarns in natural fibers to make lightweight shawls and wraps.

Step 1

Step 2

Step 2

Step 3

Multiple 4 sts.

Step 1 (RS) Picot over 4th and 5th ch from hk, *ch3, skip 2ch, Picot over next 2ch; rep from * to last 3ch, ch3, skip 2ch, 1sc in last ch, turn.

Step 2 Ch3, *Picot in next ch sp, ch3, skip next Picot; rep from * to tch, 1sc in top of tch, turn.

Step 3 Repeat Step 2.

Special stitch *Picot: In Step 1, work 1sc in next ch, ch3, 1sc in next ch. In Step 2, work [1sc, ch3, 1sc] in same ch sp.*

Multiple 7 sts + 2, plus 1 for the foundation chain.

Step 1 (RS) 1sc in 2nd ch from hk, ch2, skip 2ch, *1sc in next ch, ch3, skip 1ch, 1sc in next ch**, ch4, skip 4ch; rep from * across, ending last rep at **, ch2, skip 2ch, 1sc in last ch, turn.

Step 2 Ch1, 1sc in first sc, ch2, *Trefoil in next ch3 sp**, ch4; rep from * across, ending last rep at **, ch2, 1sc in last sc, turn.

Step 3 Ch6 (counts as 1tr, ch2), *[1sc, ch3, 1sc] in ch5 of next Trefoil**, ch4; rep from * across, ending last rep at **, ch2, 1tr in last sc, turn.

Step 4 Ch1, 1sc in first tr, ch2, *Trefoil in next ch3 sp**, ch4; rep from * across, ending last rep at **, ch2, 1sc in 4th ch of tch, turn.

Step 5 Repeat Steps 3–4.

Special stitch *Trefoil: [1sc, ch3, 1sc, ch5, 1sc, ch3, 1sc] in same place.*

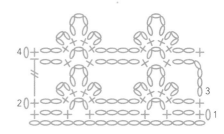

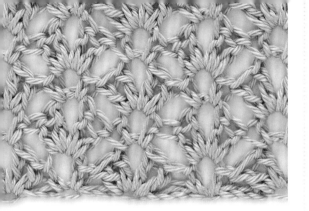

117 Picot Fans

This is a very pretty and versatile stitch. Use a thicker, chunky yarn to make a solid design, or use a lighter weight yarn to make a lacy fabric suitable for garments and accessories. The fan stitches are offset on each row, helping to give the crochet fabric stability. As you will be working into chain spaces, the fabric has excellent drape but holds its shape well.

118 Edwardian Lace

This stitch creates a very open fabric that holds its shape well because the clusters anchor themselves within the chain repeats. You can use this stitch with lightweight or heavier yarns and it is a good choice for lacy accessories. For extra stability, the clusters are worked into the chain stitch rather than into the chain space.

Step 2	Step 3
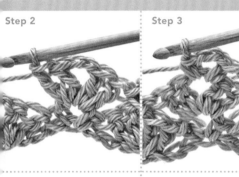	

Step 2	Step 3

Multiple 6 sts + 3, plus 1 for the foundation chain.

Step 1 (RS) 1sc in 4th ch from hk, *skip 2ch, Fan in next ch, skip 2ch**, Picot in next ch; rep from * across, ending last rep at **, [1sc, ch1, 1hdc] in last ch, turn.

Step 2 Ch3 (counts as 1dc), 2dc in first hdc, *Picot in ch2 sp of next Fan**, Fan in ch3 sp of next Picot; rep from * across, ending last rep at **, 3dc in top of tch, turn.

Step 3 Ch3 (counts as 1hdc, ch1), 1sc in first dc, *Fan in ch3 sp of next Picot**, Picot in ch2 sp of next Fan; rep from * across, ending last rep at **, [1sc, ch1, 1hdc] in top of tch, turn.

Step 4 Repeat Steps 2–3.

Special stitch Fan: [2dc, ch2, 2dc] in same place.

Special stitch Picot: [1sc, ch3, 1sc] in same place.

Multiple 5 sts + 1, plus 1 for the foundation chain.

Step 1 (RS) 1sc in 2nd ch from hk, *ch5, skip 4ch, 1sc in next ch; rep from * across, turn.

Step 2 Ch5 (counts as 1dc, ch2), *CL in 3rd ch of next ch5**, ch5; rep from * across, ending last rep at **, ch2, 1dc in last sc, turn.

Step 3 Ch1, 1sc in first dc, skip first 2ch, *ch5, CL in 3rd ch of next ch5; rep from * to tch, ch5, 1sc in 3rd ch of tch, turn.

Step 4 Repeat Steps 2–3.

Special stitch CL (cluster): Dc3tog in same place.

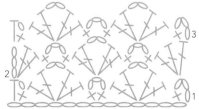

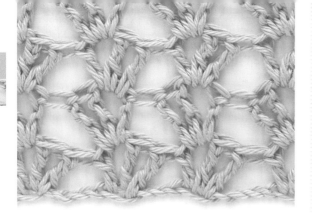

119 Offset Ladders

This is a pleasing stitch to crochet, with the offset stitches creating a very attractive fabric. It looks best in a smooth yarn, but you can experiment with different yarn fibers and weights to achieve different results. Use a smooth, medium-weight yarn to crochet a blanket or scarf, for example. The treble stitches naturally create a rounded effect because they are paired with a chain and the shorter double crochet.

Step 1

Step 2

Multiple 4 sts + 2, plus 1 for the foundation chain.

Step 1 (RS) [2tr, ch1, 1dc] in 4th ch from hk, *skip 3ch, [2tr, ch1, 1dc] in next ch; rep from * to last 3ch, skip 2ch, 1tr in last ch, turn.

Step 2 Ch3 (counts as 1dc), *[2tr, ch1, 1dc] in each ch1 sp across, 1tr in top of tch, turn.

Step 3 Repeat Step 2.

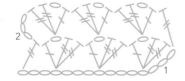

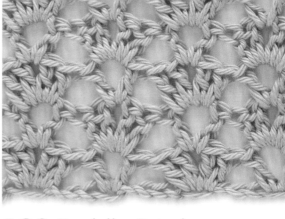

120 Paddle Stitch

This stitch is simple to memorize and works up quickly. After the initial row, you will always be crocheting into chain spaces, which creates a flowing and delicate fabric. Lace stitches are traditionally made in a lighter weight yarn, but you can use a range of yarn weights and fibers to achieve different effects. You could also try using a slightly larger hook than the one recommended for your yarn to create more drape and movement in the finished crochet.

Step 1

Step 2

Multiple 8 sts + 3, plus 3 for the foundation chain.

Step 1 (RS) [1dc, ch2, 1dc] in 7th ch from hk, *skip 3ch, [2dc, ch1, 2dc] in next ch, skip 3ch, [1dc, ch2, 1dc] in next ch; rep from * to last 7ch, skip 3ch, [2dc, ch1, 2dc] in next ch, skip 2ch, 1dc in last ch, turn.

Step 2 Ch3 (counts as 1dc), *[1dc, ch2, 1dc] in next ch1 sp, [2dc, ch1, 2dc] in next ch2 sp; rep from * to tch, 1dc in top of tch, turn.

Step 3 Repeat Step 2.

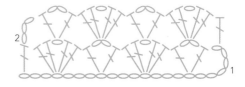

121 Sultan Stitch

This classic stitch makes a beautiful fabric that suits a variety of yarn weights and fibers. It is ideal for accessories and garments because it is firm enough to hold its shape. You could also use this stitch to make a scarf or wrap.

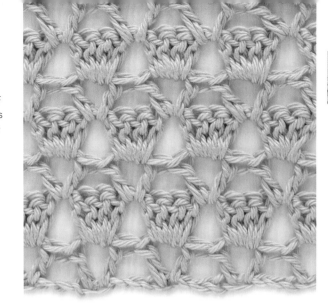

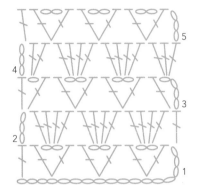

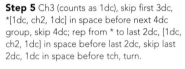

Step 2

Step 4

Step 5

Multiple 4 sts + 2, plus 3 for the foundation chain.

Step 1 (RS) [1dc, ch2, 1dc] in 6th ch from hk, *skip 3ch, [1dc, ch2, 1dc] in next ch; rep from * to last 3ch, skip 2ch, 1dc in last ch, turn.

Step 2 Ch3 (counts as 1dc), *4dc in each ch2 sp across, 1dc in top of tch, turn.

Step 3 Ch4 (counts as 1dc, ch1), 1dc in space between first 2dc, *skip 4dc, [1dc, ch2, 1dc] in space before next 4dc group; rep from * to last 4dc, skip 4dc, [1dc, ch1, 1dc] in space before tch, turn.

Step 4 Ch3 (counts as 1dc), 2dc in first ch1 sp, *4dc in next ch2 sp; rep from * to tch sp, 3dc in tch sp, turn.

Step 5 Ch3 (counts as 1dc), skip first 3dc, *[1dc, ch2, 1dc] in space before next 4dc group, skip 4dc; rep from * to last 2dc, [1dc, ch2, 1dc] in space before last 2dc, skip last 2dc, 1dc in space before tch, turn.

Step 6 Repeat Steps 2–5.

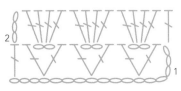

Steps 1–2

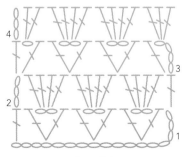

Steps 3–4

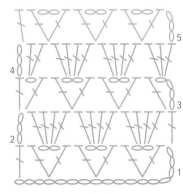

Step 5

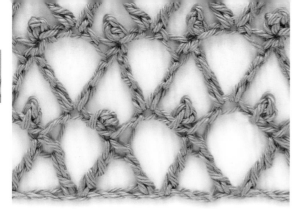

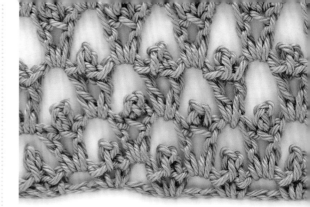

122 Picot Triangles

This pattern looks delicate, but the paired stitches make a strong fabric that holds its shape well. Use a smooth, lightweight yarn to show off the pattern. Be sure to work stitches into the chain and not the chain space on Step 2.

123 Little Arcs

This is an easy stitch to work and looks very effective for larger scale projects such as shawls and wraps. Picot stitches look best when you use a smooth yarn or crisp cotton and maintain a firm tension; the best way to achieve this is to use a hook that is one size smaller than recommended for the yarn. When you make the slip stitches, be sure to work through both loops of the chain to keep the picots looking neat.

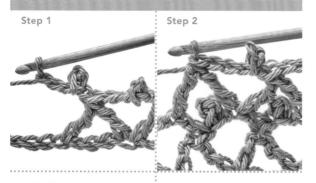

Step 1   **Step 2**

Multiple 4 sts + 1, plus 2 for the foundation chain.

Step 1 (RS) 1tr in 5th ch from hk, *ch3, tr2tog over same ch as previous tr and following 4th ch, Picot; rep from * across, working last leg of last tr2tog in last ch and finishing with a Picot, turn.

Step 2 Ch3, skipping all Picots, work 1tr in center ch of first ch3, *ch3, tr2tog over same ch as previous tr and center ch of next ch3, Picot; rep from * across, working last leg of last tr2tog in last tr and finishing with a Picot, turn.

Step 3 Repeat Step 2.

Special stitch *Picot: Ch3, 1sl st in first ch just made.*

Step 1   **Step 3**

Multiple 3 sts, plus 1 for the foundation chain.

Step 1 (RS) [1sc, ch3, 1sc] in 4th ch from hk, *ch2, skip 2ch, [1sc, ch3, 1sc] in next ch; rep from * to last 3ch, ch2, skip 2ch, 1sc in last ch, turn.

Step 2 Ch3 (counts as 1dc), *[Picot pair, ch2] in each ch2 sp across, 1dc in tch sp, turn.

Step 3 Ch3 (counts as 1dc), *[Picot pair, ch2] in each ch2 sp across, 1dc in top of tch, turn.

Step 4 Repeat Step 3.

Special stitch *Picot pair: [1dc, ch3, 1sl st in first ch just made, 1dc] in same ch sp.*

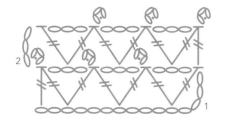

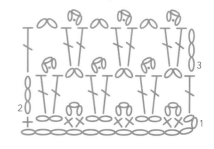

124 Offset Scallops

his is an example of a lace stitch with excellent strength and
rability. It would be ideal for accessories and wraps, where
e open structure allows plenty of drape and movement of
e fabric. It is best to use smooth yarns to show off the stitch
early, but you can achieve pleasing effects by experimenting
th different yarn types and hook sizes.

125 Garland Lace

This is an excellent stitch for many projects, including
accessories, bags, and homewares. A smooth cotton yarn
will really show off the shell pattern and little puff stitches.
The pattern creates an illusion of vertical columns, making
this a good choice for long, straight projects such as scarves
and wraps.

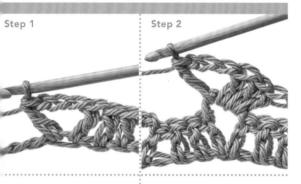

| Step 1 | Step 2 |

| Step 2 | Step 3 |

Multiple 4 sts, plus 2 for the
foundation chain.

Step 1 (RS) 1dc in 4th ch from
hk, 1dc in next ch, *[1dc, ch3,
1dc] in next ch, skip 1ch, 1dc
in each of next 2ch; rep from *
to last ch, 1dc in last ch, turn.

Step 2 Ch5 (counts as 1dc,
ch2), [3dc, ch3, 1dc] in each
ch3 sp across, 3dc in top of
tch, turn.

Step 3 Repeat Step 2.

Multiple 6 sts + 1, plus 1 for
the foundation chain.

Step 1 (RS) Fan in 5th ch from
hk, *skip 2ch, Puff in next ch,
skip 2ch, Fan in next ch; rep
from * to last 3ch, skip 2ch,
1hdc in last ch, turn.

Step 2 Ch2 (counts as 1hdc),
*[2sc, ch2, 2sc] in ch sp of next
Fan**, 1sc in next Puff; rep
from * across, ending last rep
at **, 1hdc in top of tch, turn.

Step 3 Ch2 (counts as 1hdc),
*Fan in next ch sp**, skip 2sc,
Puff in next sc; rep from *
across, ending last rep at **,
1hdc in top of tch, turn.

Step 4 Repeat Steps 2–3.

Special stitch Fan: [2hdc,
ch2, 2hdc] in same place.

Special stitch Puff: Hdc2tog
in same place.

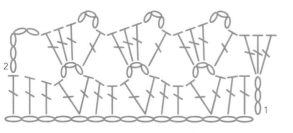

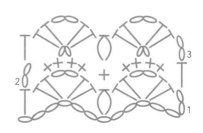

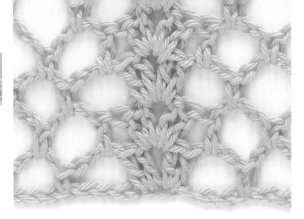

126 Climbing Vine

This stitch features columns of double crochet within a trellis of chain spaces to create a very attractive crochet pattern. You can use it for garments and accessories in a variety of yarn weights, but choose a smooth yarn to show off the lacy texture and block it well to reveal the lace.

127 Openwork Lace

This is a very useful stitch for projects where you will see both sides of the fabric, such as scarves and wraps. The repeating clusters create a lovely texture, and are combined with columns of chain spaces to produce a stable fabric that looks very attractive.

Step 2 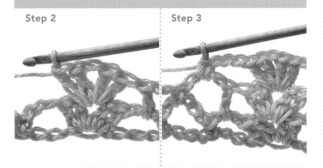 **Step 3**

Step 2  **Step 3**

Multiple 12 sts + 1, plus 3 for the foundation chain.

Step 1 (RS) 2dc in 4th ch from hk, *ch5, skip 3ch, 1sc in next ch, ch3, skip 3ch, 1sc in next ch, ch3, skip 3ch**, Fan in next ch; rep from * across, ending last rep at **, 3dc in last ch, turn.

Step 2 Ch3 (counts as 1dc), 2dc in first dc, *1dc in next ch3 sp, ch3, 1sc in next ch5 sp, ch3, 1dc in next ch3 sp**, Fan in ch1 sp of next Fan; rep from * across, ending last rep at **, 3dc in top of tch, turn.

Step 3 Ch3 (counts as 1dc), 2dc in first dc, *ch3, 1sc in next ch3 sp, ch5, 1sc in next ch3 sp, ch3 **, Fan in ch1 sp of next Fan; rep from * across, ending last rep at **, 3dc in top of tch, turn.

Step 4 Repeat Steps 2–3.

Special stitch Fan: [2dc, ch1, 2dc] in same place.

Multiple 6 sts + 1, plus 1 for the foundation chain.

Step 1 (RS) 1sc in 2nd ch from hk, *ch3, skip 1ch, CL in next ch, ch3, skip 3ch, 1sc in next ch; rep from * across, turn.

Step 2 Ch6 (counts as 1dc, ch3), *1sc in next CL, ch3, CL in next ch sp**, ch3; rep from * across, ending last rep at **, 1tr in last sc, turn.

Step 3 Ch1, 1sc in first tr, *ch3, CL in next ch sp, ch3, 1sc in next CL; rep from * across, working last sc in 3rd ch of tch, turn.

Step 4 Repeat Steps 2–3.

Special stitch CL (cluster): Dc3tog in same place.

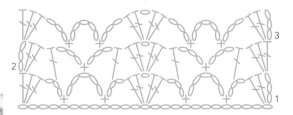

128 V-Stitch Shells

Suitable for many types of projects, this stitch has a very pleasing horizontal pattern. It would make an attractive shawl or wrap. You could also crochet this pattern in two or more colors, changing yarn after every repeat to make a colorful blanket.

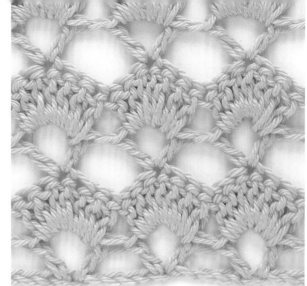

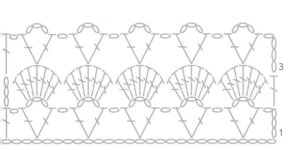

Step 1

Step 2

Step 3

Multiple 4 sts + 3.

Step 1 (RS) V-st in 8th ch from hk, *ch1, skip 4ch, V-st in next ch; rep from * to last 3ch, ch1, skip 2ch, 1dc in last ch, turn.

Step 2 Ch3 (counts as 1dc), *Shell in ch3 sp of next V-st; rep from * to tch, skip 1ch of tch, 1dc in next ch, turn.

Step 3 Ch4 (counts as 1dc, ch1), [V-st, ch1] in center dc of each Shell across, 1dc in top of tch, turn.

Step 4 Repeat Steps 2–3.

Special stitch V-st (V stitch): [1dc, ch3, 1dc] in same place.

Special stitch Shell: 7dc in same place.

Step 1

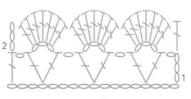

Step 2

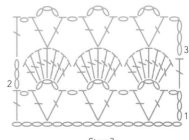

Step 3

129 Woven Lattice

Woven Lattice is a pretty crochet stitch made by combining double crochet and chains to create a woven effect. It is an ideal stitch for a novice crocheter looking for a challenge. This pattern makes a stable fabric that suits crisp cotton yarns. It is ideal for scarves and table runners.

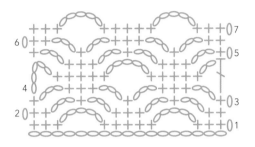

Step 3

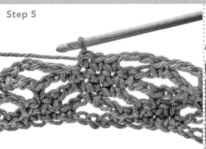

Step 5

Step 7

Multiple 8 sts + 1, plus 1 for the foundation chain.

Step 1 (RS) 1sc in 2nd ch from hk, 1sc in each of next 2ch, *ch5, skip 3ch**, 1sc in each of next 5ch; rep from * across, ending last rep at **, 1sc in each of last 3ch, turn.

Step 2 Ch1, 1sc in each of first 2sc, *ch3, skip 1sc, 1sc in next ch sp, ch3, skip 1sc**, 1sc in each of next 3sc; rep from * across, ending last rep at **, 1sc in each of last 2sc, turn.

Step 3 Ch1, 1sc in first sc, *ch3, skip 1sc, 1sc in next ch sp, 1sc in next sc, 1sc in next ch sp, ch3, skip 1sc, 1sc in next sc; rep from * across, turn.

Step 4 Ch5 (counts as 1dc, ch2), skip first sc, *1sc in next ch sp, 1sc in each of next 3sc, 1sc in next ch sp**, ch5, skip 1sc; rep from * across, ending last rep at **, ch2, 1dc in last sc, turn.

Step 5 Ch1, 1sc in first dc, *ch3, skip 1sc, 1sc in each of next 3sc, ch3, skip 1sc, 1sc in next ch5 sp; rep from * across, working last sc in tch sp, turn.

Step 6 Ch1, 1sc in first sc, *1sc in next ch sp, ch3, skip 1sc, 1sc in next sc, ch3, skip 1sc, 1sc in next ch sp, 1sc in next sc; rep from * across, turn.

Step 7 Ch1, 1sc in each of first 2sc, *1sc in next ch sp, ch5, skip 1sc, 1sc in next ch sp**, 1sc in each of next 3sc; rep from * across, ending last rep at **, 1sc in each of last 2sc, turn.

Step 8 Repeat Steps 2–7.

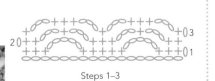

Steps 1–3

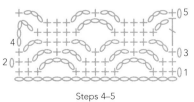

Steps 4–5

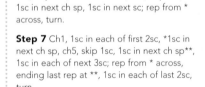

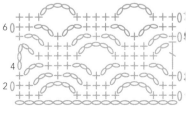

Steps 6–7

130 Victorian Lace Wave

he gentle wave pattern
eated by this stitch suits many
rns, but a smooth, crisp yarn
ll really show off the delicate
ce. You will need to block the
ochet to reveal the full effect
 the lace waves.

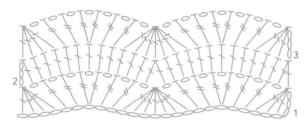

Step 1	Step 2	Step 3

Multiple 12 sts + 1, plus 2 for the foundation chain.

Step 1 (RS) Dc3tog over 4th, 5th, and 6th ch from hk, *ch1, [1tr in next ch, ch1] twice, [1tr, ch1, 1tr] in next ch, [ch1, 1tr in next ch] twice, ch1**, dc7tog over next 7ch; rep from * across, ending last rep at **, dc4tog over last 4ch, turn.

Step 2 Ch3 (counts as 1dc), 1dc in first ch sp, *[1dc in next tr, 1dc in next ch1 sp] 5 times, 1dc in next tr, dc2tog over next two ch sps (either side of dc7tog); rep from * across, working last dc2tog over last ch sp and dc3tog, turn.

Step 3 Ch3 (counts as 1dc), skip dc2tog, dc3tog over next 3dc, *ch1, [1tr in next dc, ch1] twice, [1tr, ch1, 1tr] in next dc, [ch1, 1tr in next dc] twice, ch1**, dc7tog over next 7 sts; rep from * across, ending last rep at **, dc4tog over last 4tr, turn.

Step 4 Repeat Steps 2–3.

Step 1

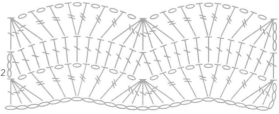

Steps 2–3

131 Trellis Garden

The pretty flowers that make up this pattern are created by a series of clusters framed by chain stitches. It is best to use a smooth, lightweight yarn and block the crochet firmly to reveal the pattern. The instructions for each step are quite long, but if you follow them carefully, you will be rewarded with a beautiful crochet fabric that suits many projects.

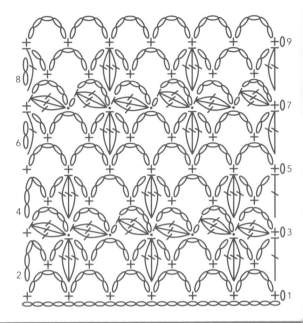

Step 2

Step 3

Step 4

Multiple 8 sts + 1, plus 1 for the foundation chain.

Step 1 (RS) 1sc in 2nd ch from hk, *ch5, skip 3ch, 1sc in next ch; rep from * across, turn.

Step 2 Ch5 (counts as 1dc, ch2), *1sc in next ch sp, ch2, CL in next sc, ch2, 1sc in next ch sp**; ch5; rep from * across, ending last rep at **, ch2, 1dc in last sc, turn.

Step 3 Ch1, [1sc, ch5, CL] in first dc, *[1sl st, ch5, CL] in next CL**, ch1, [1sl st, ch5, CL] in next ch sp; rep from * across, ending last rep at **, 1sc in tch sp, turn.

Step 4 Ch5 (counts as 1dc, ch2), *1sc in next ch5 sp, ch2, CL in next sl st, ch2, 1sc in next ch5 sp**; ch5; rep from * across, ending last rep at **, ch2, 1dc in last sc, turn.

Step 5 Ch1, 1sc in first dc, *ch5, 1sc in next CL, ch5, 1sc in next ch5 sp; rep from * across, working last sc in tch sp, turn.

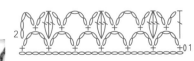

Steps 1–2

Step 3

Steps 4–5

Step 7

Step 8

Step 9

Step 6 Ch2, 1dc in first sc, *ch2, 1sc in next ch sp, ch5, 1sc in next ch sp, ch2**, CL in next sc; rep from * across, ending last rep at **, dc2tog in last sc, turn.

Step 7 Ch1, [1sc, ch5, CL] in first dc2tog, *ch1, [1sl st, ch5, CL] in next ch5 sp**, [1sl st, ch5, CL] in next CL; rep from * across, ending last rep at **, 1sc in last dc, turn.

Step 8 Ch2, 1dc in first sc, *ch2, 1sc in next ch5 sp, ch5, 1sc in next ch5 sp, ch2**, CL in next sl st; rep from * across, ending last rep at **, dc2tog in last sc, turn.

Step 9 Ch1, 1sc in first dc2tog, *ch5, 1sc in next ch5 sp, ch5, 1sc in next CL; rep from * across, working last sc in last dc, turn.

Step 10 Repeat Steps 2–9.

Special stitch CL (cluster): Dc3tog in same place.

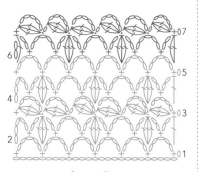

Steps 6–7

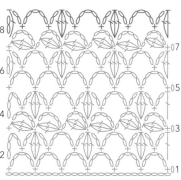

Step 8

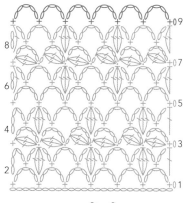

Step 9

132 Pineapple Stitch

There are many variations of this classic crochet stitch. It takes its name from the decreasing repeats of picots that look like pineapple fruits. You will need to block the crochet firmly to reveal the pattern's beauty. The columns of pineapples, separated by columns of fans, make this stitch ideal for long, straight projects such as table runners crocheted in crisp, cotton yarn using pale colors. You could also use this pattern for accessories.

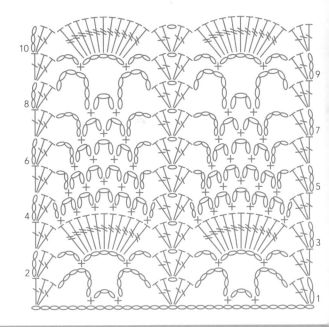

Step 1

Step 3

Step 4

Multiple 15 sts + 1, plus 2 for the foundation chain.

Step 1 (RS) 2dc in 3rd ch from hk, *ch7, skip 5ch, 1sc in next ch, ch3, skip 2ch, 1sc in next ch, ch7, skip 5ch**, Fan in next ch; rep from * across, ending last rep at **, 3dc in last ch, turn.

Step 2 Ch3 (counts as 1dc), 2dc in first dc, *ch3, 1sc in next ch7 sp, ch5, 1sc in next ch7 sp, ch3**, Fan in ch1 sp of next Fan; rep from * across, ending last rep at **, 3dc in top of tch, turn.

Step 3 Ch3 (counts as 1dc), 2dc in first dc, *Shell in next ch5 sp**, Fan in ch1 sp of next Fan; rep from * across, ending last rep at **, 3dc in top of tch, turn.

Step 4 Ch3 (counts as 1dc), 2dc in first dc, *ch2, 1sc in first tr of next Shell, [ch3, skip 1tr, 1sc in next tr] 5 times, ch2**, Fan in ch1 sp of next Fan; rep from * across, ending last rep at **, 3dc in top of tch, turn.

Step 5 Ch3 (counts as 1dc), 2dc in first dc, *ch3, skip ch2 sp, 1sc in next ch3 sp, [ch3, 1sc in next ch3 sp] 4 times, ch3, skip ch2 sp**, Fan in ch1 sp of next Fan; rep from * across, ending last rep at **, 3dc in top of tch, turn.

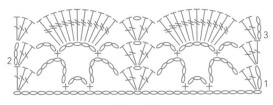

Steps 1–3

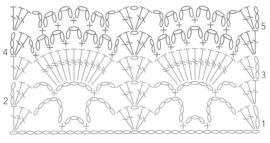

Steps 4–5

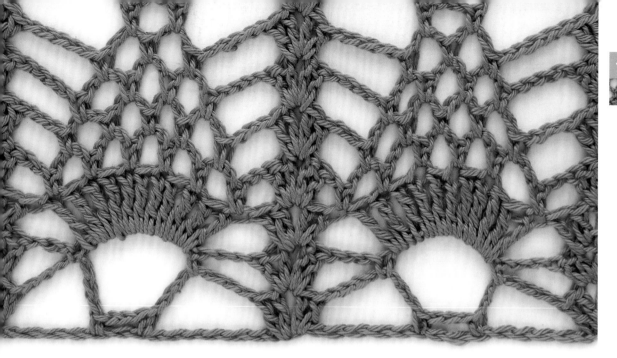

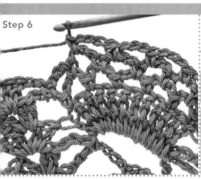

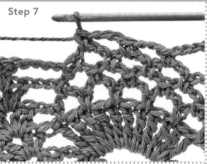

Step 6 Ch3 (counts as 1dc), 2dc in first dc, *ch4, skip next ch3 sp, 1sc in next ch3 sp, [ch3, 1sc in next ch3 sp] 3 times, ch4, skip next ch3 sp**, Fan in ch1 sp of next Fan; rep from * across, ending last rep at **, 3dc in top of tch, turn.

Step 7 Ch3 (counts as 1dc), 2dc in first dc, *ch5, skip ch4 sp, 1sc in next ch3 sp, [ch3, 1sc in next ch3 sp] twice, ch5, skip ch4 sp**, Fan in ch1 sp of next Fan; rep from * across, ending last rep at **, 3dc in top of tch, turn.

Step 8 Ch3 (counts as 1dc), 2dc in first dc, *ch7, skip ch5 sp, 1sc in next ch3 sp, ch3, 1sc in next ch3 sp, ch7, skip ch5 sp**, Fan in ch1 sp of next Fan; rep from * across, ending last rep at **, 3dc in top of tch, turn.

Step 9 Repeat Steps 2–8.

Special stitch Fan: [2dc, ch1, 2dc] in same place.

Special stitch Shell: 11tr in same place.

Steps 6–8

133 Wide Chevron

This is a very simple stitch that looks attractive in a single color. Chevron and wave patterns are made by balancing increases and decreases to give an undulating "wave" effect. Working into the front and back loops gives more texture to the fabric. This stitch has excellent drape and is ideal for accessories and blankets where you will see both sides of the fabric.

Step 1	Step 3

Multiple 14 sts +1, plus 3 for the foundation chain.

Step 1 (RS) 1dc in 4th ch from hk, *1dc in each of next 5ch, dc3tog over next 3ch, 1dc in each of next 5ch**, [1dc, ch1, 1dc] in next ch; rep from * across, ending last rep at **, 2dc in last ch, turn.

Step 2 Ch3 (counts as 1dc), 1FLdc in first dc, *1FLdc in each of next 5dc, FLdc3tog over next 3dc, 1FLdc in each

of next 5dc**, [1dc, ch1, 1dc] in ch sp; rep from * across, ending last rep at **, 2dc in top of tch, turn.

Step 3 Ch3 (counts as 1dc), 1BLdc in first dc, *1BLdc in each of next 5dc, BLdc3tog over next 3dc, 1BLdc in each of next 5dc**, [1dc, ch1, 1dc] in ch sp; rep from * across, ending last rep at **, 2dc in top of tch, turn.

Step 4 Repeat Steps 2–3.

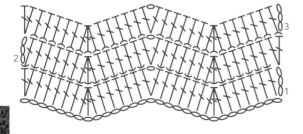

134 Ripple

This is another traditional stitch that can be worked in a single color. If you prefer to add stripes, you could use two colors and change color every two rows. You would not need to cut the yarn, so there would be few ends to weave in and the finished effect would be very attractive. After the initial row, this stitch is worked over a single-row repeat; decreases are made by skipping stitches to balance the increases.

Step 1	Step 2

Multiple 13 sts.

Step 1 (RS) 1dc in 4th ch from hk, 1dc in each of next 3ch, *3dc in next ch, 1dc in each of next 5ch, skip 2ch, 1dc in each of next 5ch; rep from * to last 6ch, 3dc in next ch, 1dc in each of last 5ch, turn.

Step 2 Skip first dc, 1sl st in next dc, ch3 (counts as 1dc), 1dc in each of next 4dc, *3dc in next dc, 1dc in each of next 5dc, skip 2dc, 1dc in each of next 5dc; rep from * to last 6dc, 3dc in next dc, 1dc in each of next 5dc, skip tch, turn.

Step 3 Repeat Step 2.

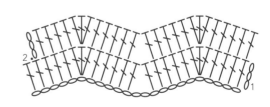

135 Traditional Chevron

This is one of the most useful chevron stitches because it allows you to make your own variations to create different effects and textures. By working in more than one color, you can create pretty stripes (see later stitches in this section for more colorful chevron stitches). You can also vary the placement of the hook, working into the front loops or back loops to create different textures. This stitch looks particularly effective made with variegated yarn. Use a slightly larger hook than recommended for the yarn to ensure that the work lies flat and does not pucker. In this example, you work into the back loops on alternate rows; this creates a subtle texture and gives the fabric excellent drape.

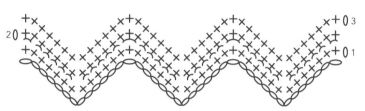

Step 1	Step 2	Step 3

Multiple 13 sts + 1, plus 1 for the foundation chain.

Step 1 (RS) 2sc in 2nd ch from hk, *1sc in each of next 5ch, skip 2ch, 1sc in each of next 5ch**, 3sc in next ch; rep from * across, ending last rep at **, 2sc in last ch, turn.

Step 2 Ch1, 2BLsc in first sc, *1BLsc in each of next 5sc, skip 2sc, 1BLsc in each of next 5sc**, 3BLsc in next sc; rep from * across, ending last rep at **, 2BLsc in last sc, turn.

Step 3 Ch1, 2sc in first sc, *1sc in each of next 5sc, skip 2sc, 1sc in each of next 5sc**, 3sc in next sc; rep from * across, ending last rep at **, 2sc in last sc, turn.

Step 4 Repeat Steps 2–3.

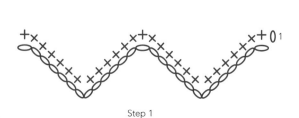

Step 1

Steps 2–3

136 Raised Chevron

This stitch is satisfying to crochet because it provides plenty of interest for crocheters at all skill levels. The single-row repeat is worked in two colors, with texture added by working into the back loop of each double crochet. Eyelets are formed by working chains instead of traditional increases. As you will be changing color every two rows, there is no need to cut the yarn. Change color on the last yarnover of the last stitch of the row.

137 Atlantic Wave

This classic chevron creates a colorful fabric ideal for blankets. You will be changing color at the end of every row, but as you are using three colors there will be no need to cut the yarn—after the initial three rows, the correct color will be waiting for you when you reach the end of each row. Change color on the last yarnover of the last stitch of the row to ensure smooth color transitions.

Step 1

Step 2

Step 1

Step 2

Multiple 10 sts + 2, plus 3 for the foundation chain.

Step 1 (WS) With yarn A, 1dc in 4th ch from hk, *1dc in each of next 4ch, skip 2ch, 1dc in each of next 4ch**, ch2; rep from * across, ending last rep at **, 2dc in last ch, turn.

Step 2 With yarn A, ch3 (counts as 1dc), 1BLdc in each of first 2dc, *1BLdc in each of next 3dc, skip 2dc, 1BLdc in each of next 3dc**, [1dc, ch2, 1dc] in ch sp; rep from * across, ending last rep at **, 1BLdc in next dc, 2BLdc in top of tch, change to yarn B, turn.

Step 3 Repeat Step 2, working two rows of each color in sequence.

Multiple 16 sts, plus 2 for the foundation chain.

Step 1 (RS) With yarn A, 1hdc in 3rd ch from hk, *1hdc in each of next 5ch, [hdc2tog over next 2ch] twice, 1hdc in each of next 5ch**, 2hdc in each of next 2ch; rep from * across, ending last rep at **, 2hdc in last ch, change to yarn B, turn.

Step 2 With yarn B, ch2 (counts as 1hdc), 1hdc in first hdc, *1hdc in each of next 5hdc, [hdc2tog over next 2 sts] twice, 1hdc in each of next 5hdc**, 2hdc in each of next 2hdc; rep from * across, ending last rep at **, 2hdc in top of tch, change to yarn C, turn.

Step 3 Repeat Step 2, working one row of each color in sequence.

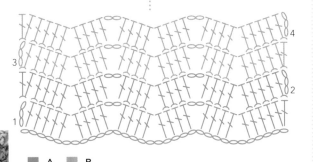

■ A   ■ B

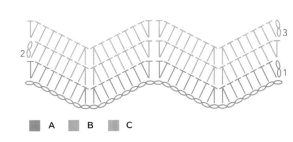

■ A   ■ B   ■ C

138 Ridged Chevron

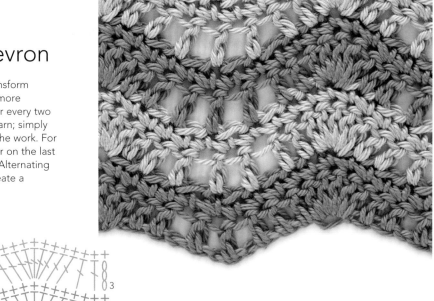

dding color to your projects can transform
simple stitch into something much more
pressive. You will be changing color every two
ws, so there is no need to cut the yarn; simply
rry the unused yarn up the side of the work. For
hooth color transitions, change color on the last
rnover of the last stitch of the row. Alternating
ws of single and double crochet create a
allow wave.

A
B

Step 1

Step 3

Step 5

Multiple 12 sts + 3, plus 2 for the
foundation chain.

Step 1 (RS) With yarn A, 1dc in 4th ch from
hk, *[skip 1ch, 1dc in next ch] twice, 1dc in
next ch, 5dc in next ch, 1dc in each of next
2ch, [skip 1ch, 1dc in next ch] twice; rep from
* to last ch, 1dc in last ch, turn.

Step 2 With yarn A, ch1, 1sc in each dc
across, 1sc in top of tch, change to yarn B,
turn.

Step 3 With yarn B, ch3 (counts as 1dc), skip
first sc, 1dc in next sc, *[skip 1sc, 1dc in next
sc] twice, 1dc in next sc, 5dc in next sc, 1dc in
each of next 2sc, [skip 1sc, 1dc in next sc]
twice; rep from * to last sc, 1dc in last sc,
turn.

Step 4 With yarn B, ch1, 1sc in each dc
across, 1sc in top of tch, change to yarn A,
turn.

Step 5 Repeat Steps 3–4, working two rows
of each color in sequence.

Steps 1–2

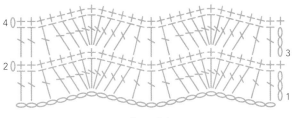

Steps 3–4

139 Wavy Chevron

This stitch is very relaxing to crochet. Once you have worked the first two rows, there is only a single-row repeat, which you will quickly learn. Change colors as often as you like to make bright, colorful blankets and accessories. Chevrons also create interesting effects when you use textured yarns such as bouclé or chainette.

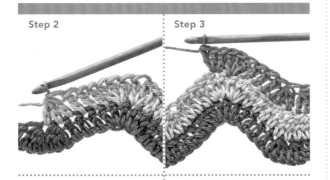

Step 2

Step 3

Multiple 14 sts, plus 3 for the foundation chain.

Step 1 (RS) With yarn A, 2dc in 4th ch from hk, *1dc in each of next 3ch, [dc3tog over next 3ch] twice, 1dc in each of next 3ch**, 3dc in each of next 2ch; rep from * across, ending last rep at **, 3dc in last ch, change to yarn B, turn.

Step 2 With yarn B, ch3 (counts as 1dc), 2dc in first dc, *1dc in each of next 3dc, [dc3tog over next 3dc] twice, 1dc in each of next 3dc**, 3dc in each of next 2dc; rep from * across, ending last rep at **, 3dc in top of tch, change to yarn C, turn.

Step 3 Repeat Step 2, working one row of each color in sequence.

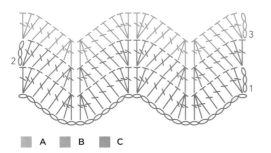

A   B   C

140 Deep Chevron

This is an attractive stitch that combines a simple pattern of single crochet worked into the back loops with skipped stitche to create a regular pattern of eyelets. It looks best in bright or strong colors, and would be a good choice for accessories suc as scarves and wraps.

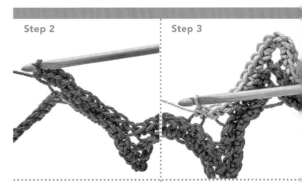

Step 2

Step 3

Multiple 19 sts + 1, plus 1 for the foundation chain.

Step 1 (RS) With yarn A, 3sc in 2nd ch from hk, *1sc in each of next 7ch, skip 4ch, 1sc in each of next 7ch**, 5sc in next ch; rep from * across, ending last rep at **, 3sc in last ch, turn.

Step 2 With yarn A, ch1, 3BLsc in first sc, *1BLsc in each of next 7sc, skip 4sc, 1BLsc in each of next 7sc**, 5BLsc in next sc; rep from * across, ending last rep at **, 3BLsc in last sc, change to yarn B, turn.

Step 3 Repeat Step 2, working two rows of each color in sequence.

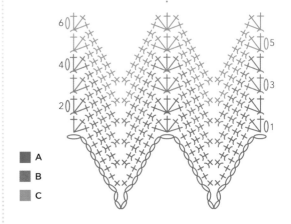

A
B
C

141 Textured Ripple

The textures in this stitch are created by working clusters on alternate rows. This creates gentle chevrons with lots of visual interest. You can use this stitch for many projects, including shawls and scarves. The textured stitches look their best when worked in a smooth yarn. If you wish, you could use more than one color for this stitch, changing color every two rows, or adding a splash of contrasting color at longer intervals on the textured rows (Step 3).

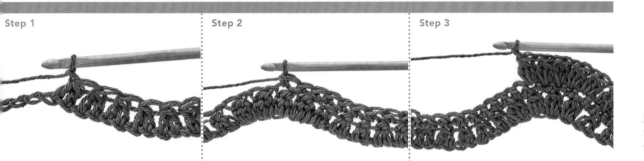

Step 1

Step 2

Step 3

Multiple 17 sts + 2, plus 2 for the foundation chain.

Step 1 (RS) Dc2tog over 4th and 5th ch from hk, *[dc2tog over next 2ch] twice, [ch1, CL in next ch] 5 times, ch1**, [dc2tog over next 2ch] 4 times; rep from * across, ending last rep at **, [dc2tog over next 2ch] 3 times, 1dc in last ch, turn.

Step 2 Ch1, 1sc in each st and ch sp across, 1sc in top of tch, turn.

Step 3 Ch3 (counts as 1dc), skip first sc, *[dc2tog over next 2sc] 3 times, [ch1, CL in next sc] 5 times, ch1, [dc2tog over next 2sc] 3 times; rep from * to last sc, 1dc in last sc, turn.

Step 4 Repeat Steps 2–3.

Special stitch *CL (cluster): Dc3tog in same place.*

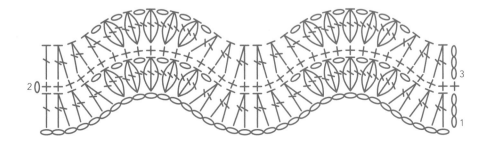

DIRECTORY OF STITCHES

142 Tweed Chevron

You need to work this stitch in multiple colors in order for the pattern to be shown off at its best. Making a large project such as a blanket in single crochet can be time-consuming, so try using a chunky yarn for a speedy make. As with all chevrons worked in single crochet, you will get better results if you use a slightly larger hook than the one recommended for the yarn.

A
B
C

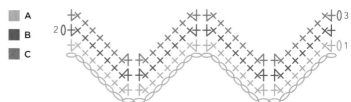

Step 1

Step 2

Step 3

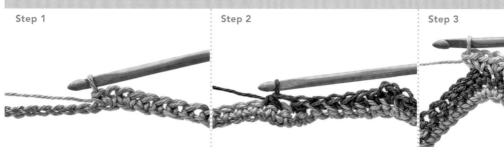

Multiple 16 sts, plus 1 for the foundation chain.

Step 1 (RS) With yarn A, 2sc in 2nd ch from hk, *1sc in each of next 5ch, [sc2tog over next 2ch] twice, 1sc in each of next 5ch**, [2sc in next ch] twice; rep from * across, ending last rep at **, 2sc in last ch, change to yarn B, turn.

Step 2 With yarn B, ch1, 2sc in first sc, *1sc in each of next 5sc, [sc2tog over next 2sc] twice, 1sc in each of next 5sc**, [2sc in next sc] twice; rep from * across, ending last rep at **, 2sc in last sc, change to yarn C, turn.

Step 3 Repeat Step 2, working one row of each color in sequence.

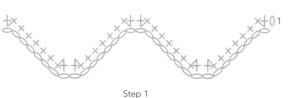

Step 1

Steps 2–3

143 Crossed Chevron

[Th]e use of crossed double crochet gives the fabric [an] unusual texture. You can use any number of [co]lors for this stitch. This example uses three [sh]ades of yarn and changes color every row, so you [ca]n simply carry the unused yarn up the side of the [wo]rk. Change color on the last yarnover of the last [sti]tch of the row for smooth color transitions.

WAVES AND CHEVRONS

Step 1   **Step 2**   **Step 3**

Multiple 21 sts + 1, plus 3 for the foundation chain.

Step 1 (RS) With yarn A, 1dc in 4th ch from hk, *[Crossed 2dc over next 2ch] 4 times, dc2tog over first and last of next 4ch (i.e. skipping 2ch), [Crossed 2dc over next 2ch] 4 times**, 3dc in next ch; rep from * across, ending last rep at **, 2dc in last ch, change to yarn B, turn.

Step 2 With yarn B, ch1, 2sc in first dc, *1sc in each of next 8dc, sc2tog over first and third of next 3 sts (i.e. skipping 1 st), 1sc in each of next 8dc**, 3sc in next dc; rep from * across, ending last rep at **, 2sc in top of tch, change to yarn C, turn.

Step 3 With yarn C, ch3 (counts as 1dc), 1dc in first dc, *[Crossed 2dc over next 2sc] 4 times, dc2tog over first and third of next 3 sts (i.e. skipping 1 st), [Crossed 2dc over next 2sc] 4 times**, 3dc in next sc; rep from * across, ending last rep at **, 2dc in last sc, change to yarn A, turn.

Step 4 Repeat Steps 2–3, working one row of each color in sequence.

Special stitch *Crossed 2dc: Skip 1 st, 1dc in next st, working in front of dc just made, 1dc in skipped st (work into foundation ch on row 1).*

A
B
C

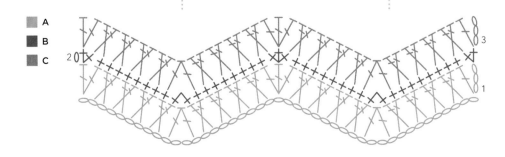

144 Eyelet Chevron

By adding chain spaces to chevron stitches, a lacy pattern of eyelets is formed. It looks particularly attractive in a single color, but you could also use a speckled or gradient yarn to make a stunning wrap or scarf.

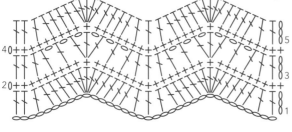

Step 2

Step 3

Step 5

Multiple 16 sts + 3, plus 2 for the foundation chain.

Step 1 (RS) 1dc in 4th ch from hk, *[skip 1ch, 1dc in next ch] twice, 1dc in each of next 3ch, 5dc in next ch, 1dc in each of next 4ch, [skip 1ch, 1dc in next ch] twice; rep from * to last ch, 1dc in last ch, turn.

Step 2 Ch1, 1sc in each dc across, 1sc in top of tch, turn.

Step 3 Ch3 (counts as 1dc), skip first sc, 1dc in next sc, *skip 1sc, 1dc in next sc, skip 1sc, [1dc in next sc, ch1, skip 1sc] twice, [1dc, ch1, 1dc, ch1, 1dc] in next sc, [ch1, skip 1sc, 1dc in next sc] twice, [skip 1sc, 1dc in next sc] twice; rep from * to last sc, 1dc in last sc, turn.

Step 4 Ch1, 1sc in each st and ch sp across, 1sc in top of tch, turn.

Step 5 Ch3 (counts as 1dc), skip first sc, 1dc in next sc, *[skip 1sc, 1dc in next sc] twice, 1dc in each of next 3sc, 5dc in next sc, 1dc in each of next 4sc, [skip 1sc, 1dc in next sc] twice; rep from * to last sc, 1dc in last sc, turn.

Step 6 Repeat Steps 2–5.

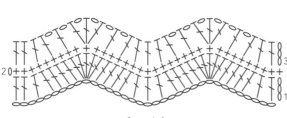

Steps 1–3

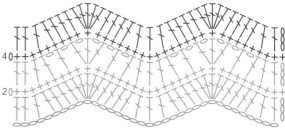

Steps 4–5

45 Simple Chevron

This is another example of a chevron stitch that uses eyelets to create visual interest. The stitch instructions look complicated, but the two-row repeat soon becomes familiar. It is a good idea to count your stitches after Step 2 to make sure you have not accidentally missed a chain space.

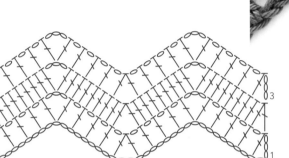

Step 1

Step 2

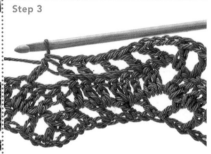

Step 3

Multiple 19 sts + 2, plus 2 for the foundation chain.

Step 1 (RS) 1dc in 5th ch from hk, *[ch1, skip 1ch, 1dc in next ch] 3 times, ch1, skip 1ch, [1dc, ch3, 1dc] in next ch, [ch1, skip 1ch, 1dc in next ch] 3 times, ch1, skip 1ch**, dc2tog over first and last of next 4ch (i.e. skipping 2ch); rep from * across, ending last rep at **, dc2tog over next and last ch (i.e. skipping 1ch), turn.

Step 2 Ch3 (counts as 1dc), skip first ch1 sp, 1dc in next dc, *[1dc in next ch1 sp, 1dc in next dc] 3 times, [2dc, ch3, 2dc] in ch3 sp, [1dc in next dc, 1dc in next ch1 sp] 3 times**, dc2tog over first and last of next 5 sts (i.e. skipping 1ch, dc2tog, 1ch); rep from * across, ending last rep at **, dc2tog over next dc and top of tch (i.e. skipping 1ch, 1dc), turn.

Step 3 Ch3 (counts as 1dc), skip first 2 sts, 1dc in next dc, *[ch1, skip 1dc, 1dc in next dc] 3 times, ch1, [1dc, ch3, 1dc] in ch3 sp, ch1, [1dc in next dc, ch1, skip 1dc] 3 times**, dc2tog over first and last of next 5 sts (i.e. skipping 1dc, dc2tog, 1dc); rep from * across, ending last rep at **, dc2tog over next dc and top of tch (i.e. skipping 2dc), turn.

Step 4 Repeat Steps 2–3.

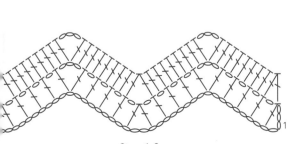

Steps 1–2

Step 3

146 Textured Wave

Wave stitches are made by combining different-height stitches across the row. The results are very effective and can be used for many projects, including blankets and accessories. This stitch has a loose, open texture that looks best in a smooth yarn.

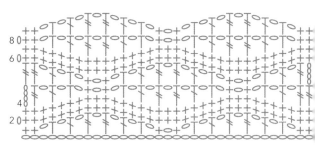

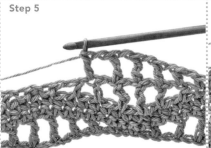

Step 2

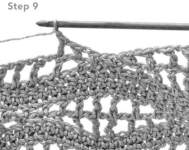

Step 5

Step 9

Multiple 16 sts + 1, plus 1 for the foundation chain.

Step 1 (RS) 1sc in 2nd ch from hk, *1sc in next ch, ch1, skip 1ch, 1hdc in next ch, ch1, skip 1ch, 1dc in next ch, [ch1, skip 1ch, 1tr in next ch] twice, ch1, skip 1ch, 1dc in next ch, ch1, skip 1ch, 1hdc in next ch, ch1, skip 1ch, 1sc in next ch**, ch1, skip 1ch; rep from * across, ending last rep at **, 1sc in last ch, turn.

Step 2 Ch1, 1sc in each st and ch sp across, turn.

Step 3 Ch1, 1sc in each sc across, turn.

Step 4 Ch4 (counts as 1tr), skip first sc, *1tr in next sc, ch1, skip 1sc, 1dc in next sc, ch1, skip 1sc, 1hdc in next sc, [ch1, skip 1sc, 1sc in next sc] twice, ch1, skip 1sc, 1hdc in next sc, ch1, skip 1sc, 1dc in next sc, ch1, skip 1sc, 1tr in next sc**, ch1, skip 1sc; rep from * across, ending last rep at **, 1tr in last sc, turn.

Step 5 Ch4 (counts as 1tr), skip first tr, *1tr in next tr, ch1, 1dc in next dc, ch1, 1hdc in next hdc, [ch1, 1sc in next sc] twice, ch1, 1hdc in next hdc, ch1, 1dc in next dc, ch1, 1tr in next tr**, ch1; rep from * across, ending last rep at **, 1tr in top of tch, turn.

Steps 6–7 Work as Steps 2–3.

Step 8 Ch1, 1sc in each of first 2sc, *ch1, skip 1sc, 1hdc in next sc, ch1, skip 1sc, 1dc in next sc, [ch1, skip 1sc, 1tr in next sc] twice, ch1, skip 1sc, 1dc in next sc, ch1, skip 1sc, 1hdc in next sc, ch1, skip 1sc, 1sc in next sc**, ch1, skip 1sc, 1sc in next sc; rep from * across, ending last rep at **, 1sc in last sc, turn.

Step 9 Ch1, 1sc in each of first 2sc, *ch1, 1hdc in next hdc, ch1, 1dc in next dc, [ch1, 1tr in next tr] twice, ch1, 1dc in next dc, ch1, 1hdc in next hdc, ch1, 1sc in next sc**, ch1, 1sc in next sc; rep from * across, ending last rep at **, 1sc in last sc, turn.

Step 10 Repeat Steps 2–9.

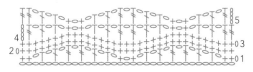

Steps 1–5

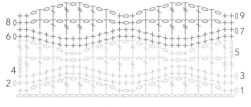

Steps 6–9

47 Three-Color Textured Wave

This elegant stitch looks effective in a single color or in multiple colors. Working into the back loops creates ridges and also ensures that the fabric drapes well. You can use this stitch for homewares and accessories. Change color on the last yarnover of the last stitch of the row to ensure smooth color transitions. There is no need to cut the yarn; simply carry the unused yarn up the side of the work.

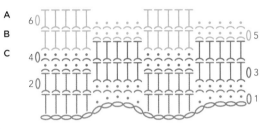

Step 2

Step 4

Step 6

Multiple 10 sts, plus 1 for the foundation chain.

Step 1 (RS) With yarn A, 1sl st in 2nd ch from hk, 1sl st in each of next 4ch, *1hdc in each of next 5ch, 1sl st in each of next 5ch; rep from * to last 5ch, 1hdc in each of last 5ch, turn.

Step 2 With yarn A, ch1, *1BLhdc in each of next 5 sts, 1BLsl st in each of next 5 sts; rep from * across, change to yarn B, turn.

Step 3 With yarn B, ch1, *1BLhdc in each of next 5 sts, 1BLsl st in each of next 5 sts; rep from * across, turn.

Step 4 With yarn B, ch1, *1BLsl st in each of next 5 sts, 1BLhdc in each of next 5 sts; rep from * across, change to yarn C, turn.

Step 5 With yarn C, ch1, *1BLsl st in each of next 5 sts, 1BLhdc in each of next 5 sts; rep from * across, turn.

Step 6 With yarn C, ch1, *1BLhdc in each of next 5 sts, 1BLsl st in each of next 5 sts; rep from * across, change to yarn A, turn.

Step 7 Repeat Steps 3–6, working two rows of each color in sequence.

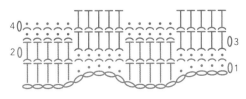

Steps 1–4

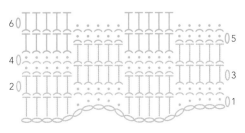

Steps 5–6

148 Offset Diamonds

This attractive stitch can be used for many projects and is suitable for novice crocheters. The simple repeat creates a pattern of offset diamond shapes that can most clearly be seen when using a smooth yarn.

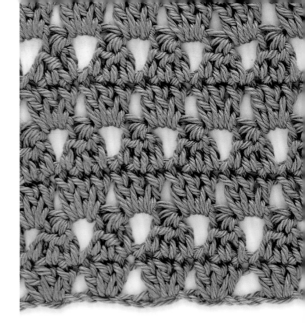

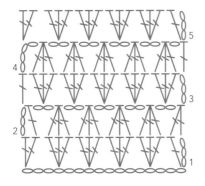

Step 2

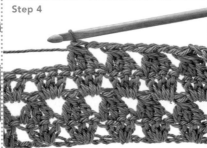

Step 4

Step 5

Multiple 3 sts + 1, plus 3 for the foundation chain.

Step 1 (RS) 1dc in 4th ch from hk, skip 2ch, *3dc in next ch, skip 2ch; rep from * to last ch, 2dc in last ch, turn.

Step 2 Ch3 (counts as 1dc), skip first dc, 1dc in next dc, ch2, *dc3tog over next 3dc, ch2; rep from * to last dc, dc2tog over last dc and top of tch, turn.

Step 3 Ch3 (counts as 1dc), 3dc in each ch2 sp across, 1dc in top of tch, turn.

Step 4 Ch4 (counts as 1dc, ch1), skip first dc, dc3tog over next 3dc, *ch2, dc3tog over next 3dc; rep from * to tch, ch1, 1dc in top of tch, turn.

Step 5 Ch3 (counts as 1dc), 1dc in first dc, skip ch1 sp, 3dc in each ch2 sp across, 2dc in 3rd ch of tch, turn.

Step 6 Repeat Steps 2–5.

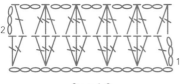

Steps 1–2

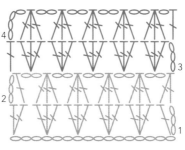

Steps 3–4

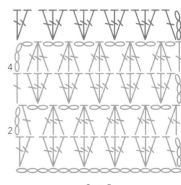

Step 5

149 Picot Texture Stitch

s is a lightweight pattern that is suitable for garments and cessories. The fabric drapes well and holds its shape. The ain spaces are anchored by single crochet stitches on the owing row, which means the fabric does not distort.

150 Waffle Rib

This stitch has a lovely texture that suits garments and homewares such as blankets. The fabric is quite dense, which means that it can be very warm to wear. Try using a lighter weight yarn for accessories such as scarves and cowls.

Step 1

Step 2

Step 1

Step 2

Multiple 3 sts + 2, plus 1 for he foundation chain.

Step 1 (RS) Picot over 2nd and 3rd ch from hk, *skip 1ch, Picot over next 2ch; rep from * across, turn.

Step 2 Ch1, Picot in each ch sp across, turn.

Step 3 Repeat Step 2.

Special stitch *Picot: In Step 1, work 1sc in next ch, ch3, 1sc in following ch. In Step 2, work [1sc, ch3, 1sc] in same ch sp.*

Multiple An odd number of sts, plus 1 for the foundation chain.

Step 1 (RS) 1hdc in 3rd ch from hk and in each ch across, turn.

Step 2 Ch2 (counts as 1hdc), skip first hdc, *1BLhdc in next hdc, 1FLhdc in next hdc; rep from * to last hdc, 1BLhdc in last hdc, 1hdc in top of tch, turn.

Step 3 Repeat Step 2.

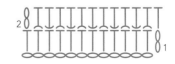

151 Textured Nub Stitch

This is an easy way to add an accent color or texture to your crochet. The contrast color (yarn B) is not joined in the traditional way. Instead, on each nub stitch row, hold the yarn tail at the back of the work and weave it in over the first two stitches of the row to secure it in place. Cut the contrast yarn at the end of the row and weave in the yarn tails at the beginning of the next row to secure them.

152 Braided Crochet

This stitch works very well in two or more colors, because the contrast will show off the slanting stitches to their best. Change color after every two rows. There is no need to cut the yarn; simply carry the unused yarn up the side of the work. This stit looks stunning as a scarf or for largescale projects.

Step 1

Step 3

Step 2

Step 3

Multiple 3 sts + 2, plus 1 for the foundation chain.

Step 1 (RS) With yarn A, 1sc in 2nd ch from hk, 1sc in next ch, *Nub st in next ch, 1sc in each of next 2ch; rep from * across, cut yarn B, turn.

Step 2 Ch1, 1sc in each sc across, turn.

Step 3 Ch1, 1sc in each of first 2sc, *Nub st in next sc, 1sc in each of next 2sc; rep from * across, cut yarn B, turn.

Step 4 Repeat Steps 2–3.

Special stitch *Nub st: After completing the previous sc with yarn A, bring yarn B forward under the working yarn, complete 1sc with yarn A, then take yarn B to back under the working yarn.*

Multiple Any number of sts.

Step 1 (RS) With yarn A, 1Bdc in 4th ch from hk and in each ch across, turn.

Step 2 With yarn A, ch3 (counts as 1Bdc), skip first Bdc, 1Bdc in each Bdc across, 1Bdc in top of tch, change to yarn B, turn.

Step 3 Repeat Step 2, working two rows of each color in sequence.

Special stitch *Bdc (braided double crochet): Yo, insert hk in next st, yo and pull through st and first loop on hk, ch1, yo and pull through both loops on hk.*

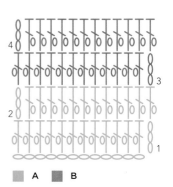

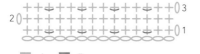

■ A ■ B

■ A ■ B

153 Alternating Stitch

ombining different-height stitches is an easy and popular
y to create texture in crochet projects. This stitch creates a
ntle wave that can be used for many different projects, such
accessories or a textured bag. The pattern can be seen most
early when worked in a smooth yarn, and looks effective in
unky or heavier weight yarns using a large hook.

154 Textured Lace

Lace stitches do not have to be complicated; this easy pattern
has a lovely texture and plenty of drape. You can use it for a
variety of projects, either on its own or combined with panels
of single or double crochet for shawls and wraps.

Step 2	Step 3

Step 2	Step 3

Multiple 10 sts + 5, plus 1 for
the foundation chain.

Step 1 (RS) 1sc in 2nd ch from
hk, 1sc in each of next 4ch,
*1dc in each of next 5ch, 1sc
in each of next 5ch; rep from *
across, turn.

Step 2 Ch3 (counts as 1dc),
skip first sc, 1dc in each of
next 4sc, *1sc in each of next
5dc, 1dc in each of next 5sc;
rep from * across, turn.

Step 3 Ch1, 1sc in each of
first 5dc, *1dc in each of next
5sc, 1sc in each of next 5dc;
rep from * across, working last
sc in top of tch, turn.

Step 4 Repeat Steps 2–3.

Multiple 6 sts + 1, plus 2 for
the foundation chain.

Step 1 (RS) 1dc in 4th ch from
hk and in each ch across, turn.

Step 2 Ch8 (counts as 1dc,
ch5), skip first 6dc, 1dc in next
dc, *ch5, skip 5dc, 1dc in next
dc; rep from * across, working
last dc in top of tch, turn.

Step 3 Ch6 (counts as 1dc,
ch3), skip first dc, *1sc in next
ch sp, ch3, 1dc in next dc, ch3;
rep from * to tch sp, 1sc in tch
sp, ch3, 1dc in 3rd ch of tch,
turn.

Step 4 Ch8 (counts as 1dc,
ch5), skip first dc, *1dc in next
dc, ch5; rep from * to tch, 1dc
in 3rd ch of tch, turn.

Step 5 Repeat Steps 3–4.

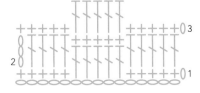

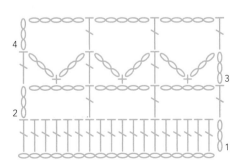

155 Corner to Corner

This stitch is sometimes known as Diagonal Box Stitch. Worked from corner to corner, you start with one box and increase on each row until the work is the desired size, then you decrease on each row to form a square. It has become universally known as "corner to corner" crochet. It is very satisfying to see your work grow and there are lots of opportunities to add color by working in alternating colors or using variegated yarn. This has become a popular stitch for crocheting blankets.

Step 2

Step 3

Step 5

Multiple Start with 6ch.

Step 1 (RS) 1dc in 4th ch from hk and in each of next 2ch, turn (1 box made).

Step 2 Ch6, 1dc in 4th ch from hk and in each of next 2ch, 1sl st in ch3 sp of previous box, ch3, 3dc in same ch3 sp, turn (2 boxes made).

Step 3 Ch6, 1dc in 4th ch from hk and in each of next 2ch, 1sl st in ch3 sp of last box made on previous row, *ch3, 3dc in same ch3 sp**, 1sl st in ch3 sp of next box on previous row; rep from * across, ending last rep at ** (1 box increased).

Step 4 Repeat Step 3 until work is desired size, then continue with Step 5.

Step 5 Ch1, 1sl st in each of 3dc and in ch3 sp of last box made on previous row, *ch3, 3dc in same ch3 sp, 1sl st in ch3 sp of next box on previous row; rep from * across (1 box decreased).

Step 6 Repeat Step 5 until work is square.

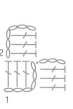

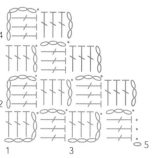

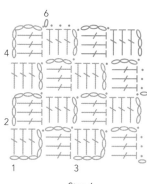

Steps 1–2

Steps 3–4

Step 5

Step 6

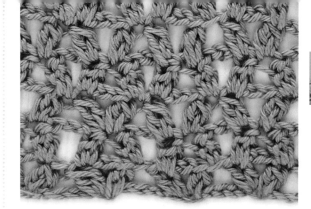

156 Butterfly Stitch

e unusual construction of this stitch creates a highly textured
ric with plenty of visual interest. The multiple rows of chains
e gathered together with a slip stitch that is worked under
e chains. You can use a variety of yarn weights and textures
create interesting effects.

157 Parterre Stitch

Inspired by the symmetrical patterns of formal parterre
gardens, this pattern has a subtle texture that needs a smooth
yarn to show it off properly. The regular repeat makes this a
good choice for garments and accessories. Combining chains
and puff stitches creates a fabric with plenty of drape and
visual interest.

Step 2

Step 4

Step 1

Step 3

Multiple 12 sts + 3, plus 1 for
the foundation chain.

Step 1 (RS) 1sc in 2nd ch from
hk, 1sc in each of next 3ch,
*ch7, skip 7ch**, 1sc in each of
next 5ch; rep from * across,
ending last rep at **, 1sc in
each of last 4ch, turn.

Step 2 Ch1, 1sc in each of
first 4sc, *ch7, skip 7ch**, 1sc
in each of next 5sc; rep from *
across, ending last rep at **,
1sc in each of last 4sc, turn.

Step 3 Work as Step 2.

Step 4 Ch1, 1sc in each of
first 4sc, *ch3, 1sl st in ch7 sp
three rows below, ch3**, 1sc in
each of next 5sc; rep from *
across, ending last rep at **,
1sc in each of last 4sc, turn.

Step 5 Ch1, 1sc in each of
first 4sc, *ch7, skip [3ch, 1sl st,
3ch]**, 1sc in each of next 5sc;
rep from * across, ending last
rep at **, 1sc in each of last
4sc, turn.

Step 6 Repeat Steps 2–5.

Multiple 5 sts + 2, plus 2 for
the foundation chain.

Step 1 (RS) [CL, ch3, CL]
in 6th ch from hk, *skip 4ch,
[CL, ch3, CL] in next ch; rep
from * to last 3ch, skip 2ch,
1dc in last ch, turn.

Step 2 Ch5 (counts as 1dc,
ch2), *CL in each of next
2CL**, ch3; rep from * across,
ending last rep at **, ch2,
1dc in top of tch, turn.

Step 3 Ch3 (counts as 1dc),
*CL in next CL, ch3, CL in next
CL**; rep from * across,
ending last rep at **, 1dc in
3rd ch of tch, turn.

Step 4 Repeat Steps 2–3.

Special stitch CL (cluster):
Dc2tog in same place.

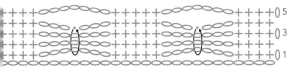

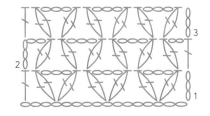

158 Marguerite Stitch

This pretty crochet stitch is traditionally used for garments and accessories, but also works well for smaller homewares such as dishcloths. Use a smooth, medium-weight yarn to display the texture most clearly. It may also help to use a slightly larger hook than usual and pull up the stitches to the full height of the previous stitch so that your work does not pucker.

159 Blanket Stitch

The crossed stitches that make up this pattern create a subtle texture and a dense, warm fabric that is ideal for cozy accessories and blankets. Choose smooth yarns and single colors to show the pattern at its best.

Step 2	Step 4

Step 2	Step 4

Multiple An odd number of sts, plus 1 for the foundation chain.

Step 1 (RS) 1sc in 2nd ch from hk and in each ch across, turn.

Step 2 Ch3, hdc5tog over [2nd and 3rd ch from hk and first 3sc], *ch1, CL; rep from * across, turn.

Step 3 Ch1, *1sc in next CL**, 1sc in next ch1 sp; rep from * across, ending last rep at **, 1sc in tch sp, 1sc in 2nd ch of tch, turn.

Step 4 Repeat Steps 2–3.

Special stitch CL (cluster): Hdc5tog over [top of hdc5tog just made, post of last hdc of hdc5tog just made, last sc just worked into, and each of next 2sc].

Multiple 8 sts + 1, plus 1 for the foundation chain.

Step 1 (WS) 1sc in 2nd ch from hk and in each ch across, turn.

Step 2 Ch3 (counts as 1dc), skip first sc, *C3B over next 3sc, 1dc in next sc, C3F over next 3sc, 1dc in next sc; rep from * across, turn.

Step 3 Ch1, 1sc in each st across, 1sc in top of tch, turn.

Step 4 Repeat Steps 2–3.

Special stitch C3B (cross 3 back): Skip 2sc, 1tr in next sc, working behind tr just made, 1dc in each of skipped 2sc.

Special stitch C3F (cross 3 front): Skip 1sc, 1dc in each of next 2sc, working in front of 2dc just made, 1tr in skipped sc.

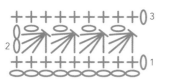

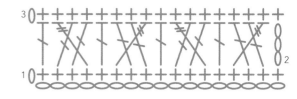

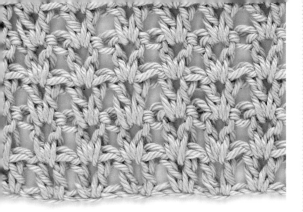

160 V-Stitch

e single-row repeat of this stitch makes it easy to memorize d suitable for all skill levels. You will be working into the ace between double crochets made on the previous row, not to the double crochet itself, which gives the fabric plenty of ape. It would be the ideal choice for masculine accessories ch as scarves or for blankets. This stitch also works well in xtured yarns such as angora and mohair.

161 Offset V-Stitch

This pattern is similar to V-Stitch, but the rows of double crochet are alternated with rows of single crochet, which gives the fabric more stability. You can use two or more colors to make a striped fabric, changing color after every two rows (at the end of Step 3). This would make a pretty blanket or it could be used for garments.

Step 1	Step 2

Step 2	Step 4

Multiple 2 sts, plus 2 for the foundation chain.

Step 1 (RS) 2dc in 4th ch from hk, skip 1ch, *2dc in next ch (2dc group made), skip 1ch; rep from * to last ch, 1dc in last ch, turn.

Step 2 Ch3 (counts as 1dc), skip first dc, 2dc in space between sts in center of each 2dc group across, 1dc in top of tch, turn.

Step 3 Repeat Step 2.

Multiple An odd number of sts, plus 1 for the foundation chain.

Step 1 (RS) 1sc in 2nd ch from hk and in each ch across, turn.

Step 2 Ch3 (counts as 1dc), 1dc in first sc, skip 1sc, *2dc in next sc, skip 1sc; rep from * to last sc, 1dc in last sc, turn.

Step 3 Ch1, 1sc in each dc across, 1sc in top of tch, turn.

Step 4 Repeat Steps 2–3.

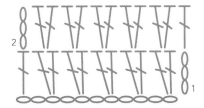

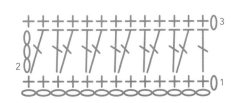

162 Raised Columns

This stitch has a pleasing pattern of vertical columns, which makes it ideal for long projects such as scarves and blankets that will show them off. You can also use it for summer tops and lightweight garments.

163 Baby Blanket

As the name suggests, this is a popular choice for baby blankets. It can also be used for shawls and accessories. The regular pattern is pleasing to the eye, easy to memorize, and works up quickly. It is an excellent choice for the novice crocheter looking for a challenge.

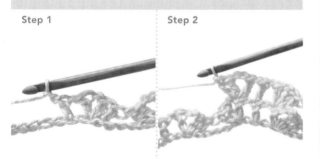

Step 1

Step 2

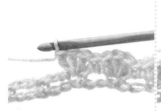

Step 2

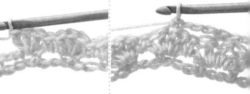

Step 3

Multiple 10 sts + 7, plus 5 for the foundation chain.

Step 1 (RS) 2dc in 6th ch from hk, *skip 5ch, [2dc, ch2, 1dc] in next ch**, ch1, skip 1ch, 1dc in next ch, ch1, skip 1ch, [1dc, ch2, 2dc] in next ch; rep from * across, ending last repeat at **, turn.

Step 2 Ch5 (counts as 1dc, ch2), 2dc in first dc, skip first two ch2 sps, *[2dc, ch2, 1dc] in next dc, ch1, 1dc in next dc, ch1, [1dc, ch2, 2dc] in next dc**, skip next two ch2 sps; rep from * across, ending last rep at **, [2dc, ch2, 1dc] in 3rd ch of tch, turn.

Step 3 Repeat Step 2.

Multiple 4 sts + 1, plus 1 for the foundation chain.

Step 1 (RS) 1sc in 2nd ch from hk, *ch3, skip 2ch, 1sc in next ch; rep from * across, turn.

Step 2 Ch3 (counts as 1dc), 1dc in first sc, *1sc in next ch sp**, Shell in next sc; rep from * across, ending last rep at **, 2dc in last sc, turn.

Step 3 Ch1, 1sc in first dc, ch3, *1sc in center dc of next Shell, ch3; rep from * to tch, 1sc in top of tch, turn.

Step 4 Repeat Steps 2–3.

Special stitch Shell: 3dc in same place.

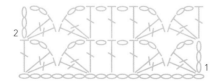

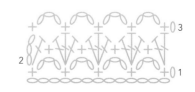

164 Pebbles

e clusters in this pattern create a highly textured fabric of
-over bobbles that can be used to make striking accessories.
e clusters are worked on wrong-side rows, so be sure to
sh them through to the right side of the fabric when you
mplete your project.

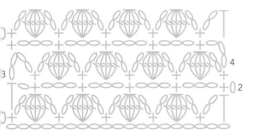

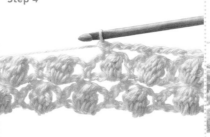
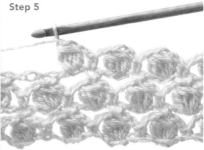

Multiple 4 sts + 3, plus 1 for the foundation
chain.

Step 1 (WS) 1sc in 2nd ch from hk, *ch2, skip
1ch, CL in next ch, ch2, skip 1ch, 1sc in next
ch; rep from * to last 2ch, ch2, skip 1ch, 1hdc
in last ch, turn.

Step 2 Ch1, 1sc in first hdc, *ch3, 1sc in next
CL; rep from * to last sc, ch1, 1hdc in last sc,
turn.

Step 3 Ch4 (counts as 1hdc, ch2), 1sc in first
sc, *ch2, skip 1ch, CL in next ch, ch2, 1sc in
next sc; rep from * across, turn.

Step 4 Ch3 (counts as 1hdc, ch1), *1sc in
next CL, ch3; rep from * to tch sp, ch3, 1sc in
tch sp, turn.

Step 5 Ch1, 1sc in first sc, *ch2, skip 1ch,
CL in next ch, ch2, 1sc in next sc; rep from *
to tch, ch2, 1hdc in 2nd ch of tch, turn.

Step 6 Repeat Steps 2–5.

Special stitch CL (cluster): Dc5tog in
same place.

Steps 1–2

Steps 3–4

Step 5

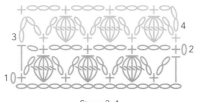
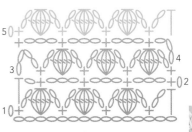

165 Tunisian Simple Stitch

This stitch is the basis for all Tunisian crochet patterns. You do not need a special hook to practice on a small number of stitches, but you will need a long, straight shaft. You can purchase special Tunisian hooks with extra-long shafts with a stop on the end so you don't lose your stitches. As a general rule, use a hook two sizes larger than usually recommended for the yarn because Tunisian crochet makes a very dense fabric. Each row of the chart represents a forward pass worked from right to left to create multiple loops on the hook, followed by a return pass worked from left to right to work the loops off the hook. The work is not turned. Unless the pattern indicates otherwise, the loop remaining on the hook after the return pass counts as the first stitch of the next forward pass. With all Tunisian stitches, the chain multiple and the stitch multiple are the same because the loop on the hook counts as a stitch.

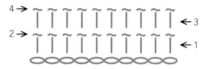

Step 1

Step 2

Step 4 (row 5)

Multiple Any number of sts.

Step 1 (RS) 1Tss in 2nd ch from hk and in each ch across, do not turn.

Step 2 (return pass) Yo and pull through 1 loop on hk, *yo and pull through 2 loops on hk; rep from * until 1 loop remains on hk, do not turn.

Step 3 Skip first st (loop on hk counts as 1Tss), 1Tss in each st across, do not turn.

Step 4 Repeat Steps 2–3, ending with a Step 2.

Special stitch Tss (Tunisian simple stitch): Insert hk from right to left under front vertical bar of st (or into ch when working Step 1), yo and pull a loop through.

Steps 1–2

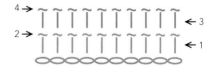

Steps 3–4

166 Tunisian Knit Stitch

is stitch closely resembles knitted stockinette stitch and
akes a sturdy, dense fabric. You can use it for garments and
ccessories. Tunisian stitches look best in smooth yarns; use a
ger hook than recommended and experiment with different
eights of yarn to see which you prefer. If you are following a
itten pattern, you will be given details of hook size and
uge recommended for the project.

167 Tunisian Purl Stitch

This stitch looks similar to purl stitch in knitting and creates
a fabric that is very dense and full of texture; the slightly blurry
appearance is an optical illusion. It works well for accessories
and homewares such as pillows because the fabric is quite
hard-wearing. The yarn is moved to the front of the fabric
before making the purl stitch, which might feel awkward for
the first few stitches, but your hands will quickly adjust as you
become familiar with the stitch.

Step 2	Step 3	Step 1	Step 3

Multiple Any number of sts.

Step 1 (RS) 1Tss in 2nd ch
from hk and in each ch across,
do not turn.

Step 2 (return pass) Yo and
pull through 1 loop on hk,
*yo and pull through 2 loops
on hk; rep from * until 1 loop
remains on hk, do not turn.

Step 3 Skip first st (loop on
hk counts as 1Tss), 1Tks in
each st across, do not turn.

Step 4 Repeat Steps 2–3,
ending with a Step 2.

Special stitch Tss (Tunisian
simple stitch): Insert hk in ch,
yo and pull a loop through.

Special stitch Tks (Tunisian
knit stitch): Insert hk from front
to back through center of st
between the vertical bars,
yo and pull a loop through.

Multiple Any number of sts.

Step 1 (RS) 1Tss in 2nd ch
from hk and in each ch across,
do not turn.

Step 2 (return pass) Yo and
pull through 1 loop on hk,
*yo and pull through 2 loops
on hk; rep from * until 1 loop
remains on hk, do not turn.

Step 3 Skip first st (loop on
hk counts as 1Tss), 1Tps in
each st across, do not turn.

Step 4 Repeat Steps 2–3,
ending with a Step 2.

Special stitch Tss (Tunisian
simple stitch): Insert hk in ch,
yo and pull a loop through.

Special stitch Tps (Tunisian
purl stitch): Bring yarn to front
of work, insert hk from right to
left under front vertical bar of
st, take yarn to back, yo and
pull a loop through.

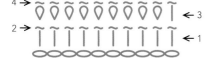

168 Tunisian Rib Stitch

This pattern alternates Tunisian knit stitch and purl stitch to create a fabric that looks like knitted ribbing. It is best to familiarize yourself with the basic Tunisian stitches before attempting this pattern. Once you are comfortable working Tunisian rib, you can experiment with different combinations—for example, one knit followed by one purl, or three knit followed by three purl. Although you are using the most basic stitches, the resulting fabric is very attractive.

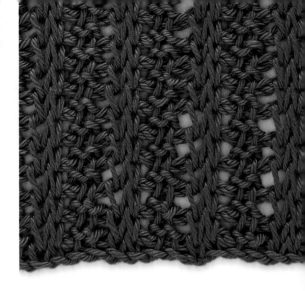

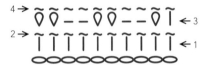

Step 1	Step 3	Step 3 (cont.)

Multiple 4 sts + 2.

Step 1 (RS) 1Tss in 2nd ch from hk and in each ch across, do not turn.

Step 2 (return pass) Yo and pull through 1 loop on hk, *yo and pull through 2 loops on hk; rep from * until 1 loop remains on hk, do not turn.

Step 3 Skip first st (loop on hk counts as 1Tss), 1Tks in next st, *1Tps in each of next 2 sts, 1Tks in each of next 2 sts; rep from * across, do not turn.

Step 4 Repeat Steps 2–3, ending with a Step 2.

Special stitch Tss (Tunisian simple stitch): Insert hk in ch, yo and pull a loop through.

Special stitch Tks (Tunisian knit stitch): Insert hk from front to back through center of st between the vertical bars, yo and pull a loop through.

Special stitch Tps (Tunisian purl stitch): Bring yarn to front of work, insert hk from right to left under front vertical bar of st, take yarn to back, yo and pull a loop through.

Steps 1–2

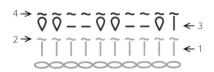

Steps 3–4

69 Tunisian Openwork

[Thi]s is a lovely, lacy stitch that makes attractive accessories [suc]h as shawls and wraps. You will be working two stitches [tog]ether, which takes a little bit of practice. Once you have [ma]stered this technique, however, the two-row repeat quickly [be]comes easier and the resulting fabric is worth the effort. Like [all] Tunisian stitches, you will need to use a hook at least two [siz]es larger than recommended for the yarn so that the lace [fab]ric has plenty of drape. The slightly blurry appearance [is a]n optical illusion.

Step 2	Step 3	Step 3 (cont.)

Multiple An even number of sts.

Step 1 (RS) 1Tss in 2nd ch from hk and in [e]ach ch across, do not turn.

Step 2 (return pass) Yo and pull through [1] loop on hk, *yo and pull through 2 loops [o]n hk; rep from * until 1 loop remains on hk, [do] not turn.

Step 3 Skip first st (loop on hk counts as 1Tss), *Tss2tog over next 2 sts, 1Tbs in space before next st; rep from * to last st, 1Tss in last st, do not turn.

Step 4 Repeat Steps 2–3, ending with a Step 2.

Special stitch Tss (Tunisian simple stitch): Insert hk from right to left under front vertical bar of st (or into ch when working Step 1), yo and pull a loop through.

Special stitch Tss2tog (Tunisian simple stitch 2 together): Insert hk from right to left under front vertical bar of each of next 2 sts, yo and pull a loop through.

Special stitch Tbs (Tunisian between stitch): Insert hk from front to back between indicated sts, yo and pull a loop through.

Steps 1–2

Steps 3–4

170 Tunisian Honeycomb

Honeycomb has a lovely texture that suits many kinds of projects, especially homewares. It is made using Tunisian simple stitch and purl stitch, so it is best to familiarize yourself with these basic stitches before attempting this pattern. Use smooth yarns in natural fibers to show off the texture, and use a larger hook than recommended for the yarn because the fabric is quite dense. The number of chains you make will be the same as the number of stitches made on the first row, so there is no need to add turning chains.

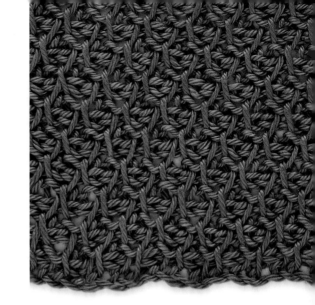

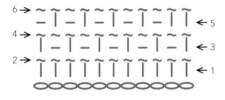

Step 1

Step 3

Step 5

Multiple An odd number of sts.

Step 1 (RS) 1Tss in 2nd ch from hk and in each ch across, do not turn.

Step 2 (return pass) Yo and pull through 1 loop on hk, *yo and pull through 2 loops on hk; rep from * until 1 loop remains on hk, do not turn.

Step 3 Skip first st (loop on hk counts as 1Tss), *1Tps in next st, 1Tss in next st; rep from * across, do not turn.

Step 4 Work as Step 2.

Step 5 Skip first st (loop on hk counts as 1Tss), *1Tss in next st, 1Tps in next st; rep from * across, do not turn.

Step 6 Repeat Steps 2–5, ending with a Step 2.

Special stitch Tss *(Tunisian simple stitch): Insert hk from right to left under front vertical bar of st (or into ch when working Step 1), yo and pull a loop through.*

Special stitch Tps *(Tunisian purl stitch): Bring yarn to front of work, insert hk from right to left under front vertical bar of st, take yarn to back, yo and pull a loop through.*

Steps 1–2

Steps 3–4

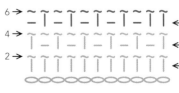

Steps 5–6

71 Tunisian Lace 1

s easy variation on Tunisian simple stitch is ideal for
cessories and blankets. It has a loose, open structure that
ds its shape. To give the fabric a neat edge, you can work
nal row of single crochet, inserting the hook into each
tical bar and then completing the stitch as for a standard
gle crochet.

172 Tunisian Lace 2

This lace stitch has a lovely open texture that is made using
Tunisian double crochet. The longer stitches help to give the
fabric excellent drape, while the crossed stitches provide extra
stability so it holds its shape. To give the fabric a firm edge,
you can use a smaller hook for the last row.

Step 2	Step 3

Step 3	Step 5

Multiple Any number of sts.

Step 1 (RS) 1Tss in 2nd ch
rom hk and in each ch across,
do not turn.

Step 2 (return pass) Yo and
pull through 1 loop on hk, *yo
and pull through 2 loops on
hk; rep from * until 1 loop
emains on hk, do not turn.

Step 3 Skip first st (loop on
hk counts as 1Tss), ch1, *1Tss
in next st, ch1; rep from *
across, do not turn.

Step 4 Repeat Steps 2–3,
ending with a Step 2.

Special stitch *Tss (Tunisian
simple stitch): Insert hk from
right to left under front vertical
bar of st (or into ch when
working Step 1), yo and pull
a loop through.*

Multiple An odd number
of sts.

Steps 1–2 Work as for
Tunisian Lace 1.

Step 3 Skip first st (loop on
hk counts as 1Tss), ch1, *skip
1 st, 1Tdc in next st, 1Tdc in
skipped st; rep from * to last
2 sts, 1Tdc in next st, 1Tss in
last st, ch1, do not turn.

Step 4 Work as Step 2.

Step 5 Skip first st (loop on
hk counts as 1Tss), ch1, 1Tdc
in next st, *skip 1 st, 1Tdc in

next st, 1Tdc in skipped st; rep
from * to last st, 1Tss in last st,
ch1, do not turn.

Step 6 Repeat Steps 2–5,
ending with a Step 2.

Special stitch *Tss: As for
Tunisian Lace 1.*

Special stitch *Tdc (Tunisian
double crochet): Yo, insert
hk from right to left under
front vertical bar of next st,
yo and pull a loop through,
yo and pull through 2 loops
on hk.*

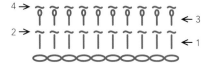

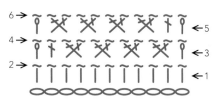

DIRECTORY OF STITCHES

173 Tunisian Mesh

This stitch creates a firm mesh fabric that has plenty of drape, perfect for making shawls and wraps. The pattern also includes a variation on the standard return pass. To make a firm edge, work a final row of single crochet, inserting the hook through each vertical bar and chain space along the row.

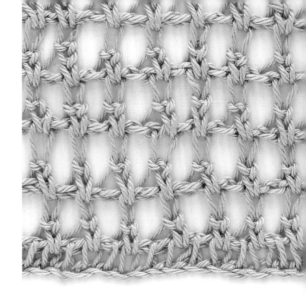

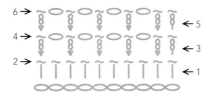

Step 2

Step 4

Step 5

Multiple An even number of sts.

Step 1 (RS) 1Tss in 2nd ch from hk and in each ch across, do not turn.

Step 2 (return pass) Yo and pull through 1 loop on hk, *yo and pull through 2 loops on hk; rep from * until 1 loop remains on hk, do not turn.

Step 3 Skip first st (loop on hk counts as 1Tss), ch2, *1Tks in next st, ch2, skip 1 st; rep from * to last st, 1Tks in last st, ch2, do not turn.

Step 4 (return pass) Yo and pull through 1 loop on hk, *ch1, yo and pull through 2 loops on hk; rep from * to last 2 loops on hk, yo and pull through last 2 loops (1 loop remains on hk).

Step 5 Skip first st (loop on hk counts as 1Tss), ch2, *1Tks in next st, ch2, skip ch sp (made on return pass); rep from * to last st, 1Tks in last st, ch2, do not turn.

Step 6 Repeat Steps 4–5, ending with a Step 4.

Special stitch Tss (Tunisian simple stitch): Insert hk in ch, yo and pull a loop through.

Special stitch Tks (Tunisian knit stitch): Insert hk from front to back through center of st between the vertical bars, yo and pull a loop through.

Steps 1–2

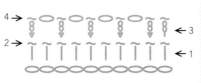

Steps 3–4

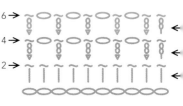

Steps 5–6

74 Tunisian Chevron

This is a very simple variation of traditional crochet chevron stitches that uses Tunisian simple stitch combined with yarnovers and a simple decrease to create the familiar chevron pattern. The swatch shown here is made in just one color, but you can use as many colors as you like, changing yarn after a return pass. This is also an excellent stitch for variegated or self-striping yarns. On each return pass, the yarnover is treated as a stitch; on the next forward pass they can look slanted, but just work them as a normal stitch.

Step 1	Step 3	Step 4 (row 5)

Multiple 14 sts + 1.

Step 1 (RS) 1Tss in 2nd ch from hk and in each ch across, do not turn.

Step 2 (return pass) Yo and pull through 1 loop on hk, *yo and pull through 2 loops on hk; rep from * until 1 loop remains on hk, do not turn.

Step 3 Skip first st (loop on hk counts as 1Tss), *yo, 1Tss in each of next 5 sts, Tss3tog over next 3 sts, 1Tss in each of next 5 sts; rep from * to last st, yo, 1Tss in last st, do not turn.

Step 4 Repeat Steps 2–3, ending with a Step 2.

Special stitch Tss (Tunisian simple stitch): Insert hk from right to left under front vertical bar of st (or into ch when working Step 1), yo and pull a loop through.

Special stitch Tss3tog (Tunisian simple stitch 3 together): Insert hk from right to left under front vertical bar of each of next 3 sts, yo and pull a loop through.

Steps 1–2

Steps 3–4

175 Block Stitch Stripes

Combining simple texture and colorwork, this pattern can be used for a variety of projects. It looks best in a smooth, medium-weight yarn. After Step 3, you will be changing color every two rows. There is no need to cut the yarn; simply carry the unused yarn up the side of the work. Change color on the last yarnover of the last stitch of the row for smooth color transitions.

■ A
■ B

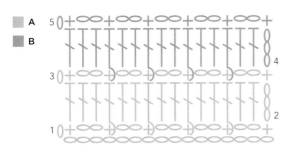

Step 2

Step 4

Step 6

Multiple 3 sts + 1, plus 1 for the foundation chain.

Step 1 (WS) With yarn A, 1sc in 2nd ch from hk, *ch2, skip 2ch, 1sc in next ch; rep from * across, turn.

Step 2 With yarn A, ch3 (counts as 1dc), skip first sc, *2dc in next ch sp, 1FPdc around next sc; rep from * to last ch sp, 2dc in last ch sp, 1dc in last sc, turn.

Step 3 With yarn A, ch1, 1sc in first dc, *ch2, skip 2dc, 1sc in next dc; rep from * across, working last sc in top of tch, change to yarn B, turn.

Step 4 With yarn B, ch3 (counts as 1dc), skip first sc, *2dc in next ch sp, 1FPdc around next sc; rep from * to last ch sp, 2dc in last ch sp, 1dc in last sc, turn.

Step 5 With yarn B, ch1, 1sc in first dc, *ch2, skip 2dc, 1sc in next dc; rep from * across, working last sc in top of tch, change to yarn A, turn.

Step 6 Repeat Steps 4–5, working two rows of each color in sequence.

Special stitch FPdc (front post dc): Inserting hk from front, work dc around post of indicated st.

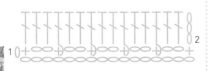

Steps 1–2

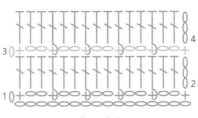

Steps 3–4

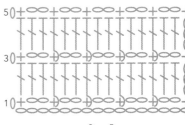

Step 5

76 Three-Color Checks

imple way to add color to your crochet, the check effect is
ieved by working over the chains and into the row below
m. It is a lovely stitch to use for accessories and homewares
h as pillows. There is no need to cut the yarn when
anging color; after the first three rows, the correct color in
sequence will be waiting for you at the end of each row.

177 Vertical Stripes

Vertical stripes can be tricky in crochet, because they often
involve working with more than one color across the row. This
variation of Three-Color Checks is an effective way to achieve a
striped fabric that can be tackled even by the novice. You will
only be working with one color on each row. Change color on
the last yarnover of the last stitch of the row, and cut the old
yarn. Weave in the yarn ends as you work each row.

Step 2

Step 3

Step 2

Step 3

Multiple 6 sts + 3, plus 2 for
he foundation chain.

Step 1 (RS) With yarn A, 1dc
n 4th ch from hk, 1dc in next
h, *ch3, skip 3ch, 1dc in each
f next 3ch; rep from * across,
change to yarn B, turn.

Step 2 With yarn B, *ch3, skip
3dc, 1Spike dc in each of next
3 sts two rows below; rep from
* to last 2dc, ch2, skip last 2dc,
sl st in top of tch, change to
arn C, turn.

Step 3 With yarn C, ch3
(counts as 1dc), skip sl st,
1Spike dc in each of next 2dc
two rows below, *ch3, skip
3dc, 1Spike dc in each of next
3dc two rows below; rep from
* across, change to yarn A,
turn.

Step 4 Repeat Steps 2–3,
working one row of each color
in sequence.

Special stitch Spike dc:
Work dc in specified st
two rows below (work into
foundation ch on row 1).

Multiple 6 sts + 3, plus 2 for
the foundation chain.

Step 1 (RS) With yarn A, 1dc
in 4th ch from hk, 1dc in next
ch, *ch3, skip 3ch, 1dc in each
of next 3ch; rep from * across,
change to yarn B, turn.

Step 2 With yarn B, *ch3, skip
3dc, 1Spike dc in each of next
3 sts two rows below; rep from
* to last 2dc, ch2, skip last 2dc,
1sl st in top of tch, change to
yarn A, turn.

Step 3 With yarn A, ch3
(counts as 1dc), skip sl st,
1Spike dc in each of next 2dc
two rows below, *ch3, skip
3dc, 1Spike dc in each of next
3dc two rows below; rep from
* across, change to yarn B,
turn.

Step 4 Repeat Steps 2–3,
working one row of each color
in sequence.

Special stitch Spike dc:
Work dc in specified st
two rows below (work into
foundation ch on row 1).

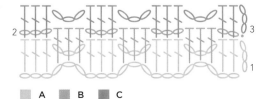

A   B   C

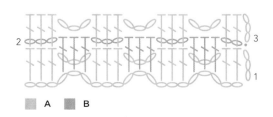

A   B

178 Three-Color Shells

This shell stitch is an easy way to play with color. Whether you choose neutrals or brights, or three tones of the same color, this simple pattern will appeal to crocheters of all skill levels. You will be changing color at the end of every row, so simply carry the unused yarn up the side of the work. If you prefer to cut the yarn, weave in the ends as you go, because they will be less daunting than if left until the project is completed.

179 Jacquard Stripes

Tapestry crochet patterns are generally worked in single crochet and the technique creates a sturdy, hard-wearing fabric. You will be working with two colors of yarn on every ro change color on the last yarnover of the last stitch in the old color and carry the unused yarn across the back of the work until needed again. Carry the unused yarn to the end of the row and up the side of the work so that the fabric is the same thickness throughout.

Step 2	Step 3

Step 1	Step 2

Multiple 6 sts + 1, plus 1 for the foundation chain.

Step 1 (RS) With yarn A, 1sc in 2nd ch from hk, *skip 2ch, Shell in next ch, skip 2ch, 1sc in next ch; rep from * across, change to yarn B, turn.

Step 2 With yarn B, ch3 (counts as 1dc), 2dc in first sc, *1sc in center dc of next Shell**, Shell in next sc; rep from * across, ending last rep at **, 3dc in last sc, change to yarn C, turn.

Step 3 With yarn C, ch1, 1sc in first dc, *Shell in next sc, 1sc in center dc of next Shell; rep from * across, working last sc in top of tch, change to yarn A, turn.

Step 4 Repeat Steps 2–3, working one row of each color in sequence.

Special stitch Shell: 5dc in same place.

Multiple 8 sts + 4, plus 1 for the foundation chain.

Step 1 (RS) With yarn A, 1sc in 2nd ch from hk and in each ch across, turn.

Step 2 With yarn A, ch1, 1sc in each of first 4sc, *change to yarn B, 1sc in each of next 4sc, change to yarn A, 1sc in each of next 4sc; rep from * across, turn.

Step 3 Repeat Step 2, changing color as indicated on the chart.

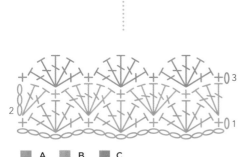

A   B   C

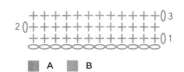

A   B

80 V-Stitch Stripes

Combining single and double crochet creates a light fabric that can be used for garments. Using two or more colors gives the crochet the appearance of tweed. Experiment with different color combinations, changing colors every two rows. This example uses two colors, so there is no need to cut the yarn when changing color; simply carry the unused yarn up the side of the work. Change color on the last yarnover of the last stitch of the row to ensure smooth color transitions.

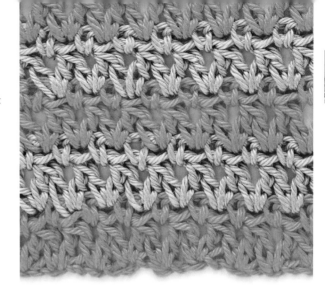

■ A
■ B

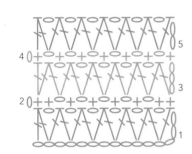

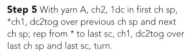

Step 1

Step 3

Step 5

Multiple An odd number of sts, plus 2 for the foundation chain.

Step 1 (RS) With yarn A, 1dc in 4th ch from hk, *ch1, dc2tog working first leg of st in same ch as previous dc, then skip 1ch and work 2nd leg of st in next ch; rep from * to last ch, ch1, dc2tog over last 2ch, turn.

Step 2 With yarn A, ch1, 1sc in first dc2tog, *1sc in next ch sp, ch1; rep from * to last ch sp, 1sc in last ch sp, 1sc in top of tch, change to yarn B, turn.

Step 3 With yarn B, ch3 (counts as 1dc), dc2tog over first sc and ch sp, *ch1, dc2tog over previous ch sp and next ch sp; rep from * to last 2sc, ch1, dc2tog over last ch sp and last sc, 1dc in last sc, turn.

Step 4 With yarn B, ch1, 1sc in first dc, *ch1, 1sc in next ch sp; rep from * to tch, ch1, 1sc in top of tch, change to yarn A, turn.

Step 5 With yarn A, ch2, 1dc in first ch sp, *ch1, dc2tog over previous ch sp and next ch sp; rep from * to last sc, ch1, dc2tog over last ch sp and last sc, turn.

Step 6 Repeat Steps 2–5, working two rows of each color in sequence.

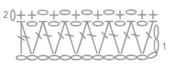

Steps 1–2

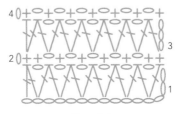

Steps 3–4

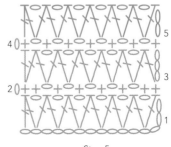

Step 5

181 Interlocking V-Stitch

You can create a very attractive woven effect by working over skipped stitches on previous rows. This pattern makes a thick, dense fabric that is ideal for cozy accessories and textured homewares. You will be changing color every two rows, so there is no need to cut the yarn; simply carry the unused yarn up the side of the work. Change color on the last yarnover of the last stitch of the row to ensure smooth color transitions.

A
B

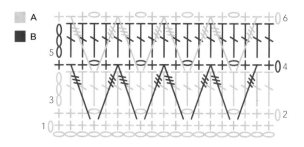

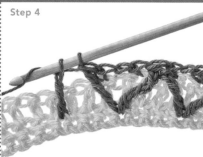

Step 3

Step 4

Step 6

Multiple 4 sts + 3, plus 1 for the foundation chain.

Step 1 (WS) With yarn A, 1sc in 2nd ch from hk and in each ch across, turn.

Step 2 With yarn A, ch1, 1sc in each of first 3sc, *ch1, skip 1sc, 1sc in each of next 3sc; rep from * across, turn.

Step 3 With yarn A, ch3 (counts as 1dc), skip first sc, 1dc in each st and ch sp across, change to yarn B, turn.

Step 4 With yarn B, ch1, 1sc in first dc, 1Spike dtr in first skipped st three rows below, 1sc in next dc, *ch1, skip 1dc, 1sc in next dc, Spike dtr2tog in same skipped st and next skipped st three rows below, 1sc in next dc; rep from * to last 3dc, ch1, skip 1dc, 1sc in next dc, 1Spike dtr in last skipped st three rows below (same place as previous Spike dtr2tog ended), 1sc in top of tch, turn.

Step 5 With yarn B, ch3 (counts as 1dc), skip first sc, 1dc in each st and ch sp across, change to yarn A, turn.

Step 6 With yarn A, work as Step 4.

Step 7 Repeat Steps 3–6, working two rows of each color in sequence.

Special stitch Spike dtr or dtr2tog: *Work dtr or dtr2tog in specified sts three rows below.*

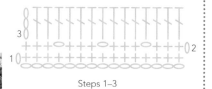

Steps 1–3

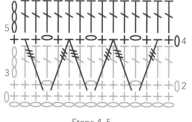

Steps 4–5

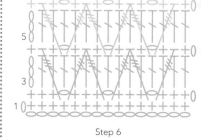

Step 6

182 Granny Stripes

is stitch is simple and versatile. You can use a single color to
eate fabric with a soft texture, but for maximum impact and
ual interest use a combination of three or more colors. Like
e traditional granny square motif, this stitch is an ideal way to
e up leftover yarn from your stash to create brightly colored
ankets and accessories.

183 Two-Color Granny Stripes

Working in stripes is a simple way to add color and visual
interest to your crochet. This stitch is simple to work and,
because you will be working two rows in each color, there is no
need to cut the yarn. Simply carry the unused yarn up the side
of the work. Change color on the last yarnover of the last stitch
of the row for smooth color transitions.

Step 2	Step 4

Step 3	Step 5

 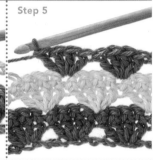

Multiple 4 sts + 3, plus 1 for
the foundation chain.

Step 1 (RS) With yarn A, 2dc
in 4th ch from hk, *ch1, skip
3ch, 3dc in next ch; rep from *
across, change to yarn B, turn.

Step 2 With yarn B, ch4
(counts as 1dc, ch1), *3dc in
next ch sp, ch1; rep from * to
tch, 1dc in top of tch, change
to yarn C, turn.

Step 3 With yarn C, ch3
(counts as 1dc), 2dc in first ch
sp, *ch1, 3dc in next ch sp; rep
from * across, working last 3dc
in tch sp, change to yarn A,
turn.

Step 4 Repeat Steps 2–3,
working one row of each color
in sequence.

Multiple 4 sts, plus 1 for the
foundation chain.

Step 1 (RS) With yarn A, 4dc
in 5th ch from hk, *skip 3ch,
4dc in next ch; rep from * to
last 4ch, skip 3ch, 3dc in last
ch, turn.

Step 2 With yarn A, ch1, 1sc
in each dc across, 1sc in top of
tch, change to yarn B, turn.

Step 3 With yarn B, ch3
(counts as 1dc), skip first sc,
2dc in next sc, *skip 3sc, 4dc
in next sc; rep from * to last
2sc, skip 1sc, 1dc in last sc,
turn.

Step 4 With yarn B, ch1, 1sc
in each dc across, 1sc in top of
tch, change to yarn A, turn.

Step 5 With yarn A, ch3
(counts as 1dc), skip first 3sc,
*4dc in next sc, skip 3sc; rep
from * to last sc, 3dc in last sc,
turn.

Step 6 Repeat Steps 2–5,
working two rows of each
color in sequence.

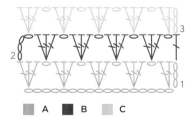

■ A   ■ B   ▨ C

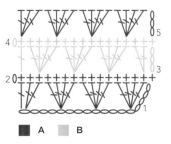

■ A   ▨ B

184 Diamond Stripes

This stitch creates defined stripes that work well for large projects such as blankets. You will be changing color every two rows, but you can simply carry the unused yarn up the side of the work. If you prefer to cut the yarn, weave in the ends as you work, especially for larger projects.

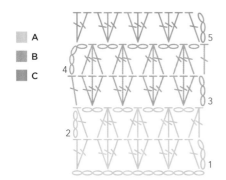

- A
- B
- C

Step 2

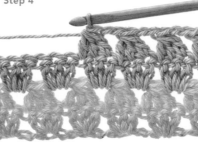

Step 4

Step 5

Multiple 3 sts + 1, plus 3 for the foundation chain.

Step 1 (RS) With yarn A, 1dc in 4th ch from hk, *skip 2ch, 3dc in next ch; rep from * to last 3ch, skip 2ch, 2dc in last ch, turn.

Step 2 With yarn A, ch3 (counts as 1dc), skip first dc, 1dc in next dc, *ch2, dc3tog over next 3dc; rep from * to last dc, ch2, dc2tog over last dc and top of tch, change to yarn B, turn.

Step 3 With yarn B, ch3 (counts as 1dc), 3dc in each ch sp across, 1dc in top of tch, turn.

Step 4 With yarn B, ch4 (counts as 1dc, ch1), skip first dc, *dc3tog over next 3dc**, ch2; rep from * across, ending last rep at **, ch1, 1dc in top of tch, change to yarn C, turn.

Step 5 With yarn C, ch3 (counts as 1dc), 1dc in first dc, skip ch1 sp, 3dc in each ch2 sp across, 2dc in 3rd ch of tch, turn.

Step 6 Repeat Steps 2–5, working two rows of each color in sequence.

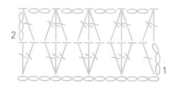

Steps 1–2

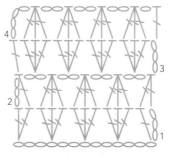

Steps 3–4

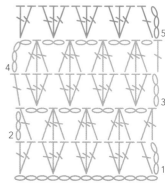

Step 5

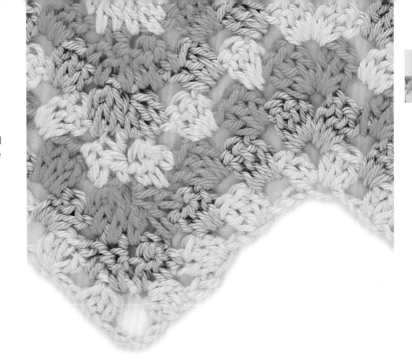

.85 Granny Ric Rac

s attractive chevron stitch pays homage to
e traditional granny square. You can use as
ny colors as you like. Three colors are used
this example, which means there is no need
cut the yarn when changing color. After the
t three rows, the correct yarn in the color
quence will be waiting for you as you finish
ch row.

Step 1

Step 2

Step 3

Multiple 26 sts + 1, plus 4 for the
foundation chain.

Step 1 (RS) With yarn A, 3dc in 5th ch from
hk, *[ch1, skip 2ch, 3dc in next ch] twice, ch1,
skip 2ch, dc3tog over next 3ch, skip 3ch,
dc3tog over next 3ch, [ch1, skip 2ch, 3dc in
next ch] twice, ch1, skip 2ch**, [3dc, ch2, 3dc]
in next ch; rep from * across, ending last rep
at **, [3dc, ch1, 1dc] in last ch, change to
yarn B, turn.

Step 2 With yarn B, ch4 (counts as 1dc, ch1),
3dc in first ch1 sp, *[ch1, 3dc in next ch1 sp]
twice, ch1, skip 2dc, dc3tog over next [dc,
ch1 sp, dc3tog], dc3tog over next [dc3tog,
ch1 sp, dc], [ch1, 3dc in next ch1 sp] twice,
ch1**, [3dc, ch2, 3dc] in ch2 sp; rep from *
across, ending last rep at **, 3dc in tch sp,
ch1, 1dc in 3rd ch of tch, change to yarn C,
turn.

Step 3 Repeat Step 2, working one row of
each color in sequence.

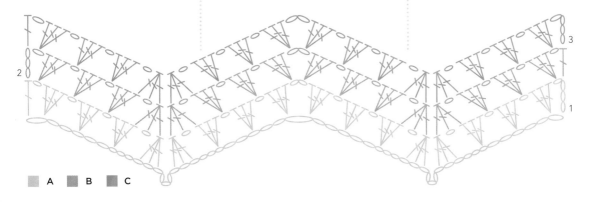

■ A ■ B ■ C

186 Three-Color Heart Braid

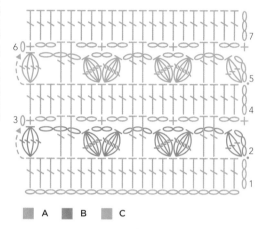

■ A ■ B ■ C

This pattern uses clusters to make pairs of bobbles that give the crochet fabric the appearance of little hearts; it is a very simple stitch to make. You must work the cluster rows in a contrasting color to see the full effect. Pay special attention to the instructions as you do not turn your work at the end of every row.

Step 2

Step 3

Step 5

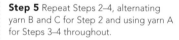

Multiple 7 sts + 1, plus 2 for the foundation chain.

Step 1 (RS) With yarn A, 1dc in 4th ch from hk and in each ch across, slip working loop from hk and secure with a stitch marker, do not turn.

Step 2 With RS facing, join yarn B with sl st to top of tch of previous row, ch3, 3dc CL in same place as join, ch3, skip 6dc, *[5dc CL, ch2, 5dc CL] in next dc, ch3, skip 6dc; rep from * to last dc, 4dc CL in last dc, fasten off yarn, remove stitch marker from yarn A and place yarn A loop back onto hk, turn.

Step 3 With yarn A, ch1, 1sc in first CL, ch2, *1Spike dc in each of 3rd and 4th dc of skipped 6dc two rows below, ch2**, 1sc in ch2 sp between next 2CL, ch2; rep from * across, ending last rep at **, 1sc in top of tch, turn.

Step 4 With yarn A, ch3 (counts as 1dc), skip first sc, 1dc in each ch and st across, slip working loop from hk and secure with a stitch marker, do not turn.

Step 5 Repeat Steps 2–4, alternating yarn B and C for Step 2 and using yarn A for Steps 3–4 throughout.

Special stitch 3dc, 4dc, or 5dc CL (cluster): Dc3tog, dc4tog, or dc5tog in same place.

Special stitch Spike dc: Work dc in specified st two rows below.

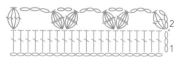

Steps 1–2

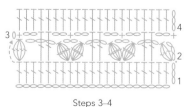

Steps 3–4

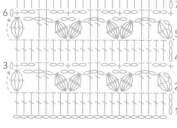

Step 5

187 Flower Garden

is is another example of a stitch that combines textured
tches and different colors to good effect. The stitches look
e rows of flowers. You can carry yarn A up the side of the
ork, but you will need to cut yarns B and C each time you
ange color. It is best to weave in the ends as you go,
cause this will be less daunting than leaving them all
til your project is finished.

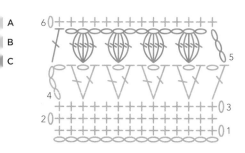

Multiple 3 sts + 2, plus 1 for the foundation
chain.

Step 1 (RS) With yarn A, 1sc in 2nd ch from
hk and in each ch across, turn.

Step 2 With yarn A, ch1, 1sc in each sc
across, turn.

Step 3 With yarn A, 1sc in each sc across,
change to yarn B, turn.

Step 4 With yarn B, ch4 (counts as 1dc, ch1),
*skip 2sc, V-st in next sc; rep from * to last
2sc, ch1, skip 1sc, 1dc in last sc, change to
yarn C, turn.

Step 5 With yarn C, ch4 (counts as 1dc, ch1),
*PC in ch1 sp of next V-st**, ch2; rep from *
across, ending last rep at **, ch1, 1dc in
3rd ch of tch, change to yarn A, turn.

Step 6 With yarn A, ch1, 1sc in first dc, 1sc in
next ch, *1sc in next PC**, 1sc in each of next
2ch; rep from * across, ending last rep at **,
1sc in each of top 2ch of tch, turn.

Step 7 Repeat Steps 3–6, maintaining color
sequence as set.

Special stitch *V-st (V-stitch):* [1dc, ch1, 1dc]
in same place.

Special stitch *PC (popcorn):* 5dc in same
place, withdraw hk from loop, insert hk in top
of first of these 5dc, catch empty loop and
pull it through dc.

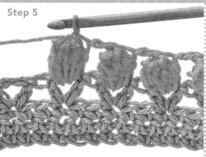

Step 4 | Step 5 | Step 6

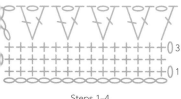

Steps 1–4

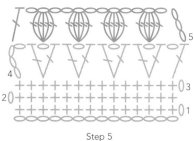

Step 5

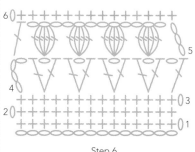

Step 6

188 Striped Fans

Crocheting with multiple colors of yarn can be very rewarding. This stitch uses three colors to create the appearance of columns of tiny hearts. It is a good choice for blankets, because the open-weave texture and the mesh pattern give the fabric plenty of drape. You do not need to cut the yarn when changing color. Carry the unused yarn up the side of the work and, after the first three rows, the correct color in the sequence will be waiting for you at the end of each row.

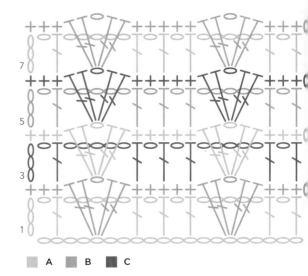

A   B   C

Step 1

Step 2

Step 3

Multiple 10 sts + 1, plus 3 for the foundation chain.

Step 1 (WS) With yarn A, 1dc in 6th ch from hk, *ch5, skip 5ch, 1dc in next ch, ch1, skip 1ch, 1dc in next ch**, ch1, skip 1ch, 1dc in next ch; rep from * across, ending last rep at **, change to yarn B, turn.

Step 2 With yarn B, ch1, 1sc in first dc, *1sc in next ch1 sp, 1sc in next dc, Fan in center ch of skipped 5 foundation ch two rows below, 1sc in next dc**, 1sc in next ch1 sp, 1sc in next dc; rep from * across, ending last rep at **, 1sc in tch sp, 1sc in 4th ch of tch, change to yarn C, turn.

Step 3 With yarn C, ch4 (counts as 1dc, ch1), skip first 2sc, 1dc in next sc, *ch5, skip Fan, [1dc in next sc, ch1, skip 1sc] twice, 1dc in next sc; rep from * to last Fan, ch5, skip last Fan, 1dc in next sc, ch1, skip 1sc, 1dc in last sc, change to yarn A, turn.

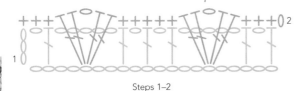

Steps 1–2

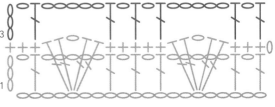

Step 3

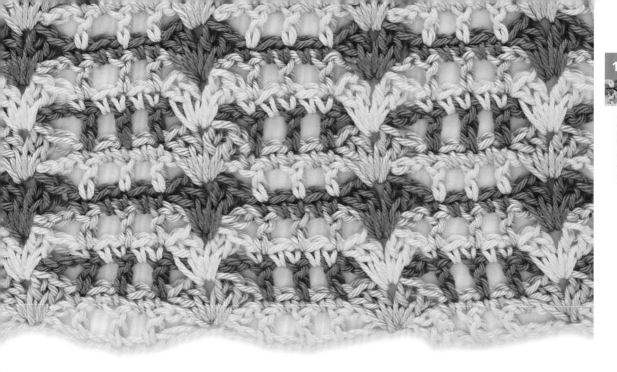

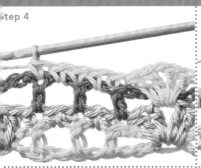

Step 4

Step 5 (row 5)

Step 5 (row 6)

Step 4 With yarn A, ch1, 1sc in first dc, *1sc in next ch1 sp, 1sc in next dc, Fan in center ch1 sp of skipped Fan two rows below, 1sc in next dc**, 1sc in next ch1 sp, 1sc in next dc; rep from * across, ending last rep at **, 1sc in ch sp, 1sc in 3rd ch of tch, change to yarn B, turn.

Step 5 Repeat Steps 3–4, working one row of each color in sequence.

Special stitch *Fan: [2dc, ch1, 2dc] in specified ch or ch sp two rows below.*

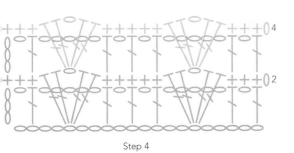

Step 4

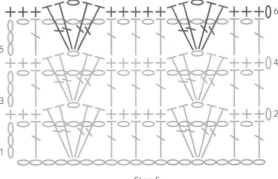

Step 5

189 Catherine Wheel

This striking stitch looks best in a smooth, medium-weight yarn. The pattern does require some concentration at first, but the finished effect is very rewarding. You will not need to cut the yarn each time you change color; simply carry the unused yarn up the side of the work.

A ■ B

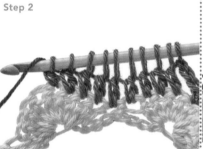

Step 1

Step 2

Step 3

Multiple 8 sts + 1, plus 1 for the foundation chain.

Step 1 (WS) With yarn A, 1sc in 2nd ch from hk, *skip 3ch, 9dc in next ch, skip 3ch, 1sc in next ch; rep from * across, change to yarn B, turn.

Step 2 With yarn B, ch3 (counts as 1dc), skip first sc, dc4tog over next 4dc, *ch3, 1sc in next dc, ch3**, dc9tog over next [4dc, 1sc, 4dc]; rep from * across, ending last rep at **, dc5tog over last 4dc and 1sc, turn.

Step 3 With yarn B, ch3 (counts as 1dc), 4dc in first dc5tog, *1sc in next sc**, 9dc in next dc9tog; rep from * across, ending last rep at **, 5dc in last dc4tog, change to yarn A, turn.

Steps 1–2

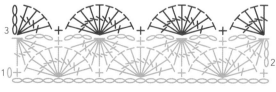

Step 3

Step 4 With yarn A, ch1, 1sc in first dc, *ch3, dc9tog over next [4dc, 1sc, 4dc], ch3, 1sc in next dc; rep from * across, working last sc in top of tch, turn.

Step 5 With yarn A, ch1, 1sc in first sc, *9dc in next dc9tog, 1sc in next sc; rep from * across, change to yarn B, turn.

Step 6 Repeat Steps 2–5, working two rows of each color in sequence.

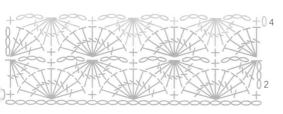

Step 4

Steps 5–6

190 Shell Edging

This pretty shell edging looks attractive on many projects. It is a useful stitch for edging household items such as pillowcases and blankets. If you wish to add the edging to an existing project, start at Step 2.

191 Picot Edging

This is a lovely stitch to use as the edging on any project. Use the same yarn, or a contrasting color to add visual intere If you wish to add the edging to an existing project, start at Step 2.

Step 3

Step 3 (cont.)

Step 3

Step 3 (cont.)

Multiple 4 sts + 1, plus 1 for the foundation chain.

Step 1 (RS) 1sc in 2nd ch from hk and in each ch across, turn.

Step 2 Ch1, 1sc in each sc across, turn.

Step 3 Ch1, 1sc in first sc, *skip 1sc, Shell in next sc, skip 1sc, 1sc in next sc; rep from * across.

Special stitch Shell: 5dc in same place.

Multiple 2 sts + 1, plus 1 for the foundation chain.

Step 1 (RS) 1sc in 2nd ch from hk and in each ch across, turn.

Step 2 Ch1, 1sc in each sc across, turn.

Step 3 Ch1, 1sc in first sc, *Picot, skip 1sc, 1sc in next sc rep from * across.

Special stitch Picot: Ch3, 1sl st in 3rd ch from hk.

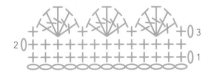
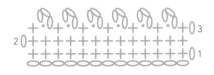

92 Crown Picot Edging

s is a very simple edging that is usually worked into the final
v of the fabric. You can also use it to edge blankets and
rments. If you wish to add the edging to an existing project,
rt at Step 2.

193 Lace Edging

This deep edging adds a feminine touch to homewares
and accessories. To add the edging to an existing project,
begin with a row of double crochet and then start the pattern
at Step 2.

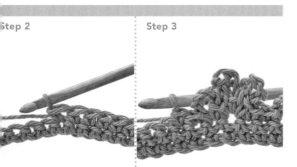

Step 2

Step 3

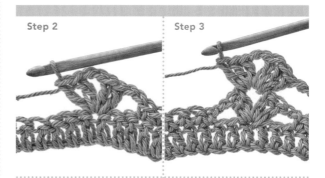

Step 2

Step 3

Multiple 5 sts, plus 1 for the
oundation chain.

Step 1 (RS) 1sc in 2nd ch from
k and in each ch across, turn.

Step 2 Ch1, 1sc in each sc
across, turn.

Step 3 Ch1, 1sc in first sc,
*Picot Crown over next 3sc**,
1sc in each of next 2sc; rep
from * across, ending last rep
at **, 1sc in last sc.

Special stitch Picot Crown:
[1sc, ch5, 1sl st] in next sc,
[1sc, ch7, 1sl st] in next sc,
[1sc, ch5, 1sl st] in next sc.

Multiple 10 sts + 1, plus 2 for
the foundation chain.

Step 1 (RS) 1dc in 4th ch from
hk and in each ch across, turn.

Step 2 Ch1, 1sc in each of
first 3dc, *ch2, skip 2dc, Small
Fan in next dc, ch2, skip 2dc**,
1sc in each of next 5dc; rep
from * across, ending last rep
at **, 1sc in each of last 2sc,
1sc in top of tch, turn.

Step 3 Ch1, 1sc in each of
first 2sc, *ch3, Large Fan in
center ch sp of next Small Fan,
ch3, skip 1sc**, 1sc in each of
next 3sc; rep from * across,
ending last rep at **, 1sc in
each of last 2sc.

Special stitch Small Fan:
[2dc, ch2, 2dc] in same place.

Special stitch Large Fan:
[3dc, ch2, 3dc] in same place.

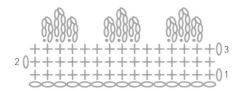

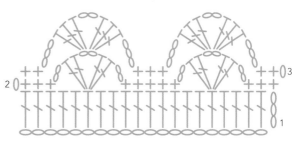

194 Chain Edging

This edging looks most attractive in two colors. It is a good choice for projects made with more than one color, because the edging will reflect the colorwork in the crochet.

195 Ruffle Fringe

This is a good choice for edging accessories such as scarves. is made lengthwise, so you can easily adjust the length to sui the project. When finished, sew the edging to your project o join it using a single crochet seam.

Step 2	Step 3

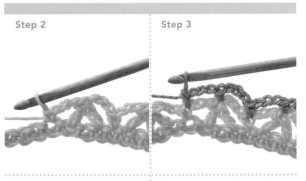

Step 5	Step 6 (row 9)

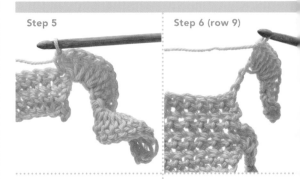

Multiple 4 sts + 1, plus 1 for the foundation chain.

Step 1 (WS) With yarn A, 1sc in 2nd ch from hk and in each ch across, turn.

Step 2 With yarn A, ch1, 1sc in first sc, *ch3, dc2tog over first and last of next 3sc, ch3, 1sc in next sc; rep from * across, do not turn.

Fasten off yarn A.

Step 3 Join yarn B with sl st to first sc of previous row, ch1, 1sc in same place as join, *ch3, 1sc in next dc2tog, ch3, 1sc in next sc; rep from * across.

Fasten off yarn B.

Multiple Start with 6ch.

Step 1 (RS) 1sc in 2nd ch from hk and in each ch across, turn.

Step 2 Ch1, 1sc in each sc across, turn.

Step 3 Work as Step 2.

Step 4 Work as Step 2.

Step 5 Ch12, 3dc in 4th ch from hk and in each ch across, 1sc in each of next 5sc, turn.

Step 6 Repeat Steps 2–5 for desired length.

A   B

96 Picot Sprigs

s is a very attractive trim that is suitable for edging
ments and accessories. It works best in smooth yarns and
p cottons, which help the delicate stitches hold their shape.
ce made, you can stitch it to necklines or hemlines or use
o edge homewares.

197 Simple Ruffle

Simple and practical, this edging can be used for a variety of
projects. If you are adding it to an existing project, begin with a
row of half double crochet and then start the pattern at Step 2.

Step 1	Step 2

Multiple 7 sts, plus 1 for the
foundation chain.

tep 1 (RS) 1sc in 2nd ch from
k and in each of next 5ch,
Arch over previous 6sc**,
sc in each of next 7ch; rep
rom * across, ending last rep
t **, 1sc in last ch, turn.

Step 2 Ch4 (counts as 1tr),
*[(1dc, Picot) 4 times, 1dc] in
ch sp at center of next Arch,
1tr in single unworked sc after
Arch; rep from * across,
working last tr in tch.

Special stitch *Arch: Turn,
ch7, skip 5sc, 1sc in next sc,
turn, [6sc, ch5, 6sc] in ch7 sp.*

Special stitch *Picot: Ch3,
1sl st in 3rd ch from hk.*

Step 3	Step 5

Multiple 2 sts + 1, plus 1 for
the foundation chain.

Step 1 (RS) 1hdc in 3rd ch
from hk and in each ch across,
turn.

Step 2 Ch3 (counts as 1dc),
skip first hdc, 1dc in each hdc
across, 1dc in top of tch, turn.

Step 3 Ch2 (counts as 1hdc),
skip first dc, 1hdc in each dc
across, 1hdc in top of tch,
turn.

Step 4 Ch1, 1sc in each hdc
across, 1sc in top of tch, turn.

Step 5 Ch3 (counts as 1dc),
1dc in first sc, *3dc in next sc,
2dc in next sc; rep from *
across, turn.

Step 6 Ch1, 1sc in each dc
across, 1dc in top of tch.

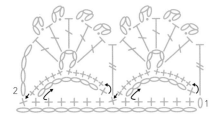

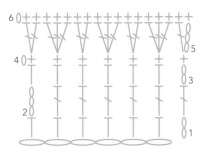

198 Bobble Sprig

LEFT: This pretty edging can be used for shawls and accessories. It looks quite complicated, but follow the instructions step by step and you will see how the spr develop. You can work the edging onto a existing project, or sew it onto your croch once it is completed.

199 Chain Fringe

RIGHT: This fun edging is great for scarve and accessories. If you wish to add this to an existing project, begin with a row of ha double crochet and then start the pattern at Step 2.

Step 1	Step 2	Step 3

Multiple 11 sts + 1, plus 2 for the foundation chain.

Step 1 (RS) 1dc in 4th ch from hk and in each ch across, turn.

Step 2 Ch1, 1sc in first dc, *ch6, Picot, ch6, skip 10dc, 1sc in next dc; rep from * across, working last sc in top of tch, turn.

Step 3 Ch7 (counts as 1dtr, ch2), *CL group in ch3 sp of next Picot, ch2, 1dtr in next sc**, ch2; rep from * across, ending last rep at ** and working last dtr in last sc.

Special stitch Picot: Ch3, 1sl st in 3rd ch from hk.

Special stitch CL (cluster) group: [(Dc3tog, ch5) twice, dc3tog] in same place.

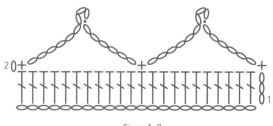

Steps 1–2

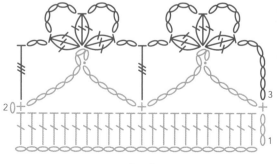

Step 3

200 Pompom Edging

This is a fun edging for almost any kind of crochet project. The clusters are slip stitched together to make each pompom. The technique can feel a little awkward at first, so it is best to practice before attempting this on your project. Use a smooth yarn because this will make it easier to work the clusters.

Step 2

Step 4

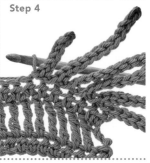

Step 3

Step 3 (cont.)

Multiple 3 sts, plus 1 for the foundation chain.

Step 1 (RS) 1hdc in 3rd ch from hk and in each ch across, turn.

Step 2 Ch4 (counts as 1tr), skip first hdc, 1tr in each hdc across, 1tr in top of tch, turn.

Step 3 Ch2 (counts as 1hdc), skip first tr, 1hdc in each tr across, 1hdc in top of tch, turn.

Step 4 *Ch16, 1sl st in 2nd ch from hk and in each of next 14ch, 1sl st in next hdc (work into first hdc of row for first fringe), ch12, 1sl st in 2nd ch from hk and in each of next 10ch, 1sl st in next hdc, ch8,

1sl st in 2nd ch from hk and in each of next 6ch, 1sl st in next hdc; rep from * across, working last sl st in top of tch.

Multiple 6 sts + 5, plus 1 for the foundation chain.

Step 1 (RS) 1sc in 2nd ch from hk and in each ch across, turn.

Step 2 Ch1, 1sc in each sc across, turn.

Step 3 Ch1, 1sc in first sc, *ch5, Pompom, ch5, skip 3sc**, 1sc in each of next 3sc; rep from * across, ending last rep at **, 1sc in last sc.

Special stitch *Pompom:* [Ch4, dc3tog in 4th ch from hk] twice, 1sl st in same ch as first dc3tog.

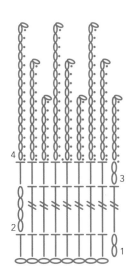

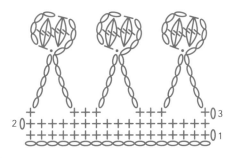

2 Crochet skills

From learning about hook sizes to taking care of finished pieces, this chapter will walk you through the essentials of crocheting. Basic stitches and useful techniques are covered with step-by-step instructions and illustrated with clear line drawings, so you can develop your skills and become a confident crocheter.

Materials

Yarn

Yarn is the generic term used to describe the material you crochet with. It can be a synthetic fiber such as acrylic, a natural fiber such as wool, or a blend of different fibers. It is easy to be overwhelmed by the variety of yarns available, and knowing how to choose the right yarn for your project is a skill you will learn with experience. The ideal yarn for a beginner is a smooth (rather than textured) yarn in a single color.

Smooth yarn

Smooth, firm yarns are suitable for crochet. These are sold in various weights, from fingering (the finest) through sport, double knitting, and worsted weight, to bulky and jumbo weights (see table opposite). They may be cotton, wool, or synthetic.

Fine crochet cotton

Yarns sold specifically for crochet are fine, smooth cottons, usually described by a number ranging from 5 (the coarsest) to 60 (very fine yarn used for traditional crochet). These cotton yarns are often described as "mercerized," which means they have been treated with an alkali to improve their strength and luster. They are ideal for showing off intricate patterns and textures.

Special yarn

Special yarns such as silk, glossy viscose, and metallic Lurex are equally suitable for crochet. Avoid any that are loosely spun; they may easily catch on the hook. Fine, natural-linen yarns are also suitable for crochet, and give a crisp finish to the work.

TIPS

- Yarn supplied in hanks must be wound into a ball before you begin to crochet.
- When choosing an unfamiliar yarn, it is a good idea to buy just one ball and experiment with it before purchasing all the yarn for a large project.

Pearl-cotton yarn

Pearl-cotton yarns are sold for use in crochet, knitting, and embroidery, and give a softer and less tightly twisted finish than traditional crochet yarns. They are manufactured in a range of thicknesses.

Novelty yarn

Novelty yarns are fun to try, adding another dimension to your work. Beware of any yarn that is very heavily textured, because the patterns made by many stitches will be lost if the yarn is too complex, plus it may be difficult to see the stitch structure when inserting the hook.

Unusual materials

You can crochet with any fine, flexible, continuous material—try string (natural or synthetic), raffia, or leather thonging. Many novelty threads such as metallic tapes are sold as embroidery materials.

Yarn Weights

Yarn is generally categorized by the thickness of each strand, known as its weight. This table shows the most common weight categories, with the usual gauge range and hook sizes for each category.

Category	Names	Gauge range to 4in (10cm)	Hook size range
0 LACE	fingering, 2ply, 10-count crochet thread	32–42 single crochet stitches	steel 6–8 (1.6–1.4mm); regular hook B (2.25mm)
1 SUPER FINE	sock, fingering, baby	21–32 single crochet stitches	B–E (2.25–3.5mm)
2 FINE	sport, baby, 4ply	16–20 single crochet stitches	E–7 (3.5–4.5mm)
3 LIGHT	DK, light worsted	12–17 single crochet stitches	7–I (4.5–5.5mm)
4 MEDIUM	worsted, afghan, aran	11–14 single crochet stitches	I–K (5.5–6.5mm)
5 BULKY	chunky, bulky, craft, rug	8–11 single crochet stitches	K–M (6.5–9mm)
6 SUPER BULKY	super bulky, roving	7–9 single crochet stitches	M–Q (9–15mm)
7 JUMBO	jumbo, roving	6 or fewer single crochet stitches	Q (15mm) and larger

Embellishments

Buttons, beads, and ribbon can add a professional finish to otherwise simple crochet items. Novelty buttons for baby clothes, pretty ribbon trims on housewares, and beads or sequins added to a simple crochet scarf will all add a personal touch. Beads and sequins for crochet should have holes large enough to thread easily onto the yarn.

Equipment

Hooks

Crochet hooks may be made from aluminum, steel, wood, bamboo, or plastic. They are available in a variety of sizes to suit different types of yarn and gauge requirements. Sizes range from 0.6mm (the smallest) up to 15mm or more, and the hooks are normally between 5in (13cm) and 8in (20cm) long. The shaft behind the hook may be cylindrical, or with a flattened area to help you hold it at the correct angle. Try out the different options to decide which suits you best.

Tunisian crochet requires a special Tunisian hook. There are two common types. The first is like a standard hook, but with a much longer shaft and a fixed stopper at the end to prevent stitches from sliding off. The second type has a flexible cord (with stopper) attached to a standard hook.

Hook sizes

The internationally used metric system of sizing known as the International Standard Range (ISR) gives the diameter of the hook shaft in millimeters. Before metric sizing, crochet hooks were sized in two ranges: steel hooks (small sizes for fine work) and aluminum or plastic hooks (larger sizes, sometimes called wool hooks). US sizes were used in America, and imperial sizes were used in the UK and Canada, and it is useful to understand these—you may have old hooks in your collection, or wish to follow an old crochet pattern.

You can see from the table at right how hooks labeled under different systems may be confused. Always measure your own gauge.

International standard range (ISR)	Imperial steel hooks	Imperial aluminum or plastic hooks	US steel hooks	US aluminum or plastic hooks
0.6mm	6		14	
0.75mm	5		13	
1mm	4		12	
	3½		11	
1.25mm	3		10	
			9	
1.5mm	2½		8	
			7	
1.75mm	2		6	
	1½		5	
2mm	1	14	4	
			3	
2.25mm	1/0 or 0	13	2	B
2.5mm	2/0 or 00	12	1	C
3mm	3/0 or 000	11	0	D
		10		
3.5mm		9	00	E
				F
4mm		8		
				G
4.5mm		7		
5mm		6		H
5.5mm		5		I
6mm		4		J
6.5mm		3		K
7mm		2		L
8mm		1		M
9mm		0		N
10mm				O
12mm				P
15mm				Q

Approximate Equivalent Hook Sizes
For guidance only; sizes given do not necessarily correspond exactly.

Standard crochet hooks

These come in many different materials and sizes. Some have a flat thumb rest or comfort grip.

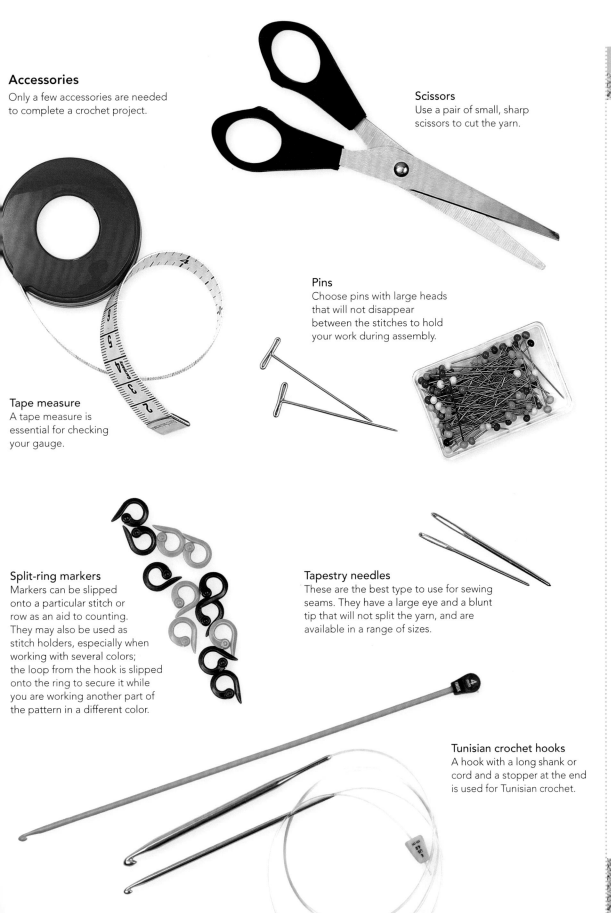

Accessories
Only a few accessories are needed to complete a crochet project.

Scissors
Use a pair of small, sharp scissors to cut the yarn.

Tape measure
A tape measure is essential for checking your gauge.

Pins
Choose pins with large heads that will not disappear between the stitches to hold your work during assembly.

Split-ring markers
Markers can be slipped onto a particular stitch or row as an aid to counting. They may also be used as stitch holders, especially when working with several colors; the loop from the hook is slipped onto the ring to secure it while you are working another part of the pattern in a different color.

Tapestry needles
These are the best type to use for sewing seams. They have a large eye and a blunt tip that will not split the yarn, and are available in a range of sizes.

Tunisian crochet hooks
A hook with a long shank or cord and a stopper at the end is used for Tunisian crochet.

Basic Techniques

Holding the hook

The hook is held in the right hand (if you are right-handed). There is no right or wrong way to hold a hook but most people find it most comfortable to hold the hook either like a pencil (A), with the tips of your right thumb and index finger centered over the flat section of the hook, or by grasping the flat section of the hook between your right thumb and index finger, as if you were holding a knife (B). The hook should face downward.

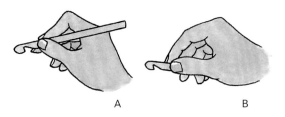

A   B

Making a slip knot

Almost every piece of crochet begins with a slip knot.

Step 1
Leaving a tail of about 6in (15cm), loop the yarn in the direction shown, insert the hook through the loop to catch the yarn leading to the ball (not the short tail), and pull it through to make a loop.

Step 2
Pull gently on both yarn ends to tighten the knot against the hook.

Holding the yarn

The left hand (if you are right-handed) controls the supply of yarn. It is important to maintain an even tension on the yarn. One method is to wind the yarn around the fingers, as shown below.

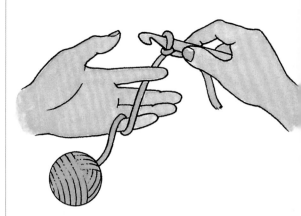

To form a stitch, use the first finger to bring the yarn into position so it may be caught by the hook and pulled through to make a new loop. Note the direction of the yarn over the tip of the hook.

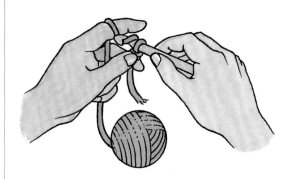

TIP

If you are left-handed, hold the hook in your left hand and the yarn in your right and look at the reflection of these illustrations in a mirror.

Foundation chains and multiples

The foundation chain is the crochet equivalent of casting on in knitting. It is the foundation from which your crochet fabric grows. It is important to make sure that you have made the required number of chain stitches for the pattern you are going to work (instructions for forming chain stitches can be found on page 176). This number will be given as a multiple of a certain number before the instructions for each stitch: for example, "Multiple 3 sts + 2" means any number that divides by 3, with 2 more added, such as 9 + 2 (a total of 11) or 33 + 2 (a total of 35). Extra stitches are sometimes required for the foundation chain: for example, "Multiple 3 sts + 2, plus 2 for the foundation chain" means begin with a number of foundation chain stitches that divides by 3, add 2, and then add 2 more, such as 33 + 2 + 2 (a total chain of 37).

The front of the foundation chain looks like a series of "V"s or little hearts, while the back of the chain forms a distinctive bump of yarn behind each "V." Count each V-shaped loop on the front of the chain as one chain stitch, but do not count the slip knot or the loop that is on the hook. You can also turn the chain over and count the stitches on the back if you find that easier.

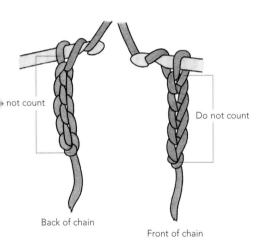

not count

Do not count

Back of chain

Front of chain

Turning Chains

single crochet	1 chain
extended single crochet	2 chains
half double crochet	2 chains
double crochet	3 chains
treble crochet	4 chains
double treble crochet	5 chains

Note: These are the usual numbers of turning chains used for the basic stitches. Sometimes two chains are needed for single crochet, and the requirements of more complicated stitch patterns may vary.

Working in rows

The basic stitches described on the following pages may be repeated in rows to make simple textured fabrics. When you work the first row onto the foundation chain, you begin the first stitch in the second, third, fourth, or fifth chain from the hook and so on, depending on the height of the stitch you are making. Every following row begins with a similar number of chains, called the turning chain(s)—referred to as the "tch" in the directory. The turning chains may count as the first stitch of the first row; the patterns in the directory tell you if this is the case. The example below shows rows of double crochet stitches, with three turning chains that count as the first stitch of each row. More complicated stitch patterns usually follow the same principle.

Turning the work

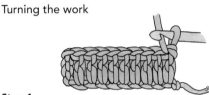

Step 1
When the first row is complete, unless otherwise instructed in the steps, turn the work. You can turn it either clockwise or counterclockwise, but a neater edge will result if you are consistent.

At the beginning of the next row, work a number of turning chains to correspond with the stitch in use, as described in the chart below left. These chains will stand for the first stitch of the new row and are counted as one stitch.

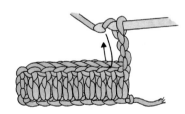

Step 2
Work the appropriate number of chains (three are shown here). Skip the last stitch of the previous row and work into the next stitch. The hook is normally inserted under the top two threads of each stitch, as shown. (When the hook is to be inserted elsewhere, pattern instructions will indicate this.)

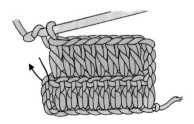

Step 3
At the end of the row, work the last stitch into the top of the chains at the beginning of the previous row. Then repeat Steps 1–3.

Joining yarn and changing colors

When working in one color, try to join in a new ball of yarn at the end of the row rather than in the middle to make the join less noticeable. You can do this by making an incomplete stitch and then using the new yarn to work the final yarnover of the stitch. Alternatively, join the new yarn at the beginning of the row you are about to work using the slip-stitch method.

Many of the stitches detailed in this book look particularly striking when worked in more than one color. When you are working a piece of crochet in more than one color, join the new color of yarn wherever the pattern or chart indicates by leaving the last stitch in the old color incomplete and using the new color to work the final yarnover of the stitch.

Carrying yarn up side of work

When working stripe patterns, you can often carry the color or colors not in use up the side of the work instead of breaking off each color of yarn when you change to another one. As well as being faster, this means that you will have fewer yarn ends to weave in. You can use this technique when working a stripe pattern in which each color (no matter how many colors) is used to work an even number of rows, or when using an odd number of colors and each color is used to work an odd number of rows. The example below is worked in single crochet using two colors and an even number of rows per stripe.

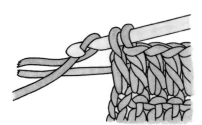

Joining a new yarn on final yarnover of stitch

To change color at the end of a row, work as far as the last stitch of the row in the old color. To change color mid-row, work as far as the last stitch before you need to start the new color. Using the old color, work this last stitch as normal but stop before the final "yo, pull through." To make the color change, wrap the new color over the hook and pull it through the loops on the hook to complete the stitch. Continue working the pattern using the new color.

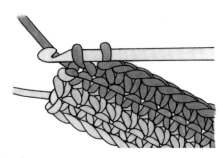

Step 1
Work the foundation chain and the first two rows using the first color (yarn A—gray). Join in the second color (yarn B—blue) without breaking off yarn A. Work the last stitch of the row up to the final "yo, pull through."

Joining a new yarn using slip stitch

At the beginning of the row, make a slip knot in the new yarn and place it on the hook. Insert the hook into the first stitch on the row and make a slip stitch with the new yarn through both slip stitch and slip knot. Continue along the row using the new yarn.

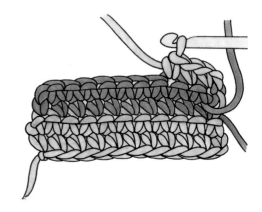

Step 2
Drop yarn B and pick up yarn A at the side of the work. Complete the final yarnover of the stitch with yarn A, then turn and work the next two rows using yarn A.

Fastening off and weaving in ends

It is very easy to fasten off yarn when you have finished a piece of crochet, but do not cut the yarn too close to the work because you need enough yarn to weave in the end. It is important to weave in yarn ends securely so they do not unravel. Do this as neatly as possible so that the woven yarn does not show through on the front of the work.

Fastening off

To fasten off the yarn securely, work one chain, then cut the yarn at least 4in (10cm) away from the work and pull the tail through the loop on the hook, tightening it gently.

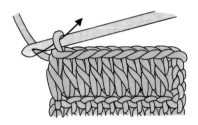

Weaving in yarn ends

To weave in a yarn end along the top or lower edge of a piece of crochet, start by threading the end into a tapestry needle. Take the needle through several stitches on the wrong side of the crochet, working stitch by stitch. Trim the remaining yarn.

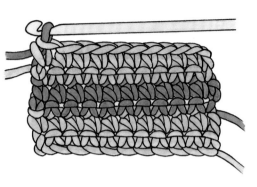

Step 3
At the end of the second row in yarn A, drop yarn A and complete the final yarnover of the last stitch with yarn B. Continue working with yarn B for two rows, then repeat the two-row stripes, alternating the yarn colors as required.

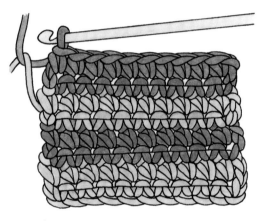

Step 4
When working a stripe wider than two rows, continue to carry the color not in use up the side of the work as before, but twist the yarns together every two rows to avoid making big loops at the edge.

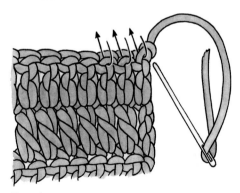

Top edge

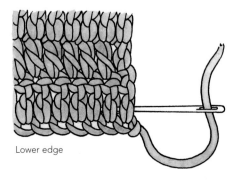

Lower edge

TIP

Try to avoid running out of yarn in the middle of a row. When you think you have enough yarn left for two rows, tie a loose overhand knot at the center of the remaining yarn. Work one row. If you need to undo the knot, there is not enough yarn left for another complete row. Fasten off the old ball at the side edge and use a new ball for the next row.

Seams

Crochet pieces may be seamed either by sewing them with a tapestry needle or by crocheting them together with a hook. In either case, use the same yarn as used for the main pieces, if possible. If this is too bulky, choose a matching, finer yarn, preferably with the same fiber content to avoid problems when the article is washed.

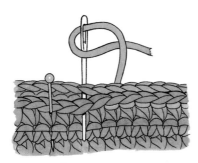

Backstitch seam

This is a firm seam that resists stretching, and is used for hard-wearing garments and projects such as bags, and for areas where firmness is an advantage, such as the shoulder seams of a garment. Hold the pieces with right sides together (pin them if necessary), matching the stitches or row ends, and use a tapestry needle and matching yarn to work the backstitches.

Woven seam

This seam is flexible and flat, making it suitable for fine work and for baby clothes. Lay the pieces with edges touching, wrong sides up, and use a tapestry needle and matching yarn to weave around the centers of the edge stitches. Do not pull the stitches too tightly—the seam should stretch as much as the work itself. When joining row ends, work in a similar way.

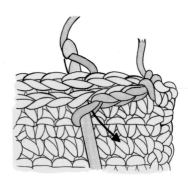

Slip stitch seam

This seam may be worked with right sides together, so that the seam is inside, or with wrong sides together, so that the seam shows as a ridge on the right side of the work. Insert the hook through the corresponding stitches of each edge and work one slip stitch through each pair of stitches along the seam. Fasten off securely.

You can insert the hook under two threads of each stitch, as shown here; or, for a less bulky seam, insert the hook under the back loop of the nearer edge and the front loop of the further edge. When working this seam along side edges, match the row ends carefully. Make a suitable number of slip stitches to the side edge of each row so that the seam is not too tight—for example, two or three slip stitches along the side edge of each row of doubles.

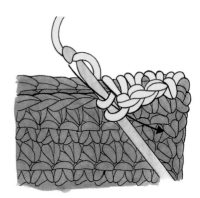

Single crochet seam

Again, this seam may be worked with wrong or right sides together, so that it appears on the inside or outside of the project. Work as for the slip stitch seam (see above), but in single crochet stitches.

Measuring gauge

Most crochet patterns recommend a "gauge." This is the number of stitches (or pattern repeats) and rows to a given measurement (usually 4in or 10cm). For your work to be the correct size, you must match this gauge as closely as possible. To work out a design of your own, you need to measure your gauge to calculate the stitches and rows required.

The hook size recommended by any pattern or ball band is only a suggestion. Gauge depends not only on the hook and yarn but also on personal technique.

If you have too many stitches (or pattern repeats) or rows to 4in (10cm), your work is too tight; repeat the process described at right with another sample made with a larger hook. If you have too few stitches (or pattern repeats) or rows, your work is too loose; try a smaller hook. It is usually more important to match the number of stitches exactly, rather than the number of rows.

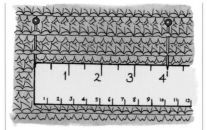

Step 1
Work a piece of crochet about 6in (15cm) square, using the hook, yarn, and stitch pattern required. Press if this is recommended on the ball band. Lay the sample flat and place two pins 4in (10cm) apart along the same row, near the center. Count the stitches (or pattern repeats) between them.

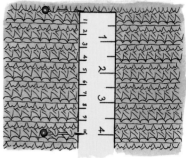

Step 2
Place two pins 4in (10cm) apart on a vertical pattern line near the center, and count the number of rows between them.

Crochet aftercare

It is a good idea to keep a ball band from each project you complete as a reference for washing instructions. Crochet items are best washed gently by hand and dried flat, to keep their shape. Crochet garments should not be hung on coat hangers, but folded and stored flat, away from dust, damp, heat, and sunlight. Clean tissue paper is better than a plastic bag.

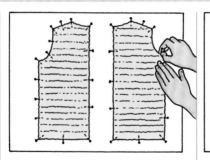

Step 1
Lay each piece right side down on a well-padded surface. With all the rows straight, pin the pieces in place, inserting pins evenly all around at right angles to the edges. If necessary, ease the piece gently to size, checking the measurements. (Matching pieces, such as the two garment fronts shown here, may be pinned out side by side.)

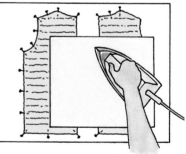

Step 2
Check the ball band for pressing instructions. For natural fibers, such as wool or cotton, a clean damp cloth and a warm iron are usually suitable. Lift and replace the iron lightly; do not rub. Allow to cool and dry completely before removing the pins. After assembly, press the seams gently.

TIP

Some yarns (such as some synthetics) should not be pressed. Pin out the work as above, mist with water, and allow to dry.

Blocking
Crochet often needs to be blocked (see steps above) before assembly, to "set" the stitches and give a professional finish.

Basic Stitches

Chain stitch

Most pieces of crochet begin with a foundation chain of a certain number of chain stitches, and this information will be provided before the step instructions for each stitch. Chains worked at the beginning of a row, or as part of a stitch pattern, are worked in the same way.

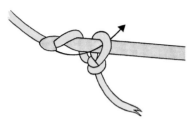

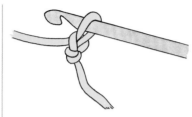

Step 1
Begin with a slip knot on the hook. Wrap the yarn over the hook in the direction shown (or catch it with the hook).

Step 2
Pull a new loop through the loop on the hook. One chain made.

Step 3
Repeat Steps 1–2 as required, moving your left hand every few stitches to hold the chain just below the hook. Tighten the slip knot by pulling on the short yarn tail.

Slip stitch

Step 1
Begin with a length of chains. Insert the hook in the second chain from the hook, wrap the yarn over the hook, and pull a new loop through both the work and the loop on the hook. One slip stitch made.

Step 2
Repeat Step 1 in each chain to the end to complete one row of slip stitches.

Single crochet

Step 1
Begin with a length of chains. Insert the hook in the second chain from the hook, wrap the yarn over the hook, and pull the new loop through the chain only.

Step 2
Wrap the yarn over the hook and pull a loop through both loops on the hook.

Step 3
One loop remains on the hook. One single crochet stitch made. Repeat Steps 1–2 in each chain to the end to complete one row of single crochet stitches.

Extended single crochet

Extended stitches are taller, slightly elongated, and looser versions of the standard crochet stitches. This example shows extended single crochet, but the same technique can be used with all the basic stitches. They are all made by working an extra yarnover, as described in Step 2.

TIPS

- Making the correct number of foundation chains is crucial when working a pattern. Count the chains as you make them and count them again before continuing. Do not count the slip knot as a chain. See page 171 for more on foundation chains.
- When working into a foundation chain, you can insert the hook under either one or two threads of each chain, but be consistent. For a firm edge, insert under two threads; for a looser edge, insert under one thread.

Step 1
Begin with a length of chains. Work the first stage of the stitch in the usual way. For single crochet, insert the hook in the third chain from the hook, wrap the yarn over the hook, and pull the new loop through the chain.

Step 2
Wrap the yarn over the hook and pull it through the first loop only. This is the extra yarnover that creates the extended stitch and leaves you with the same number of loops on the hook.

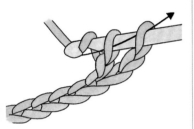

Step 3
Complete the stitch in the usual way. For single crochet, wrap the yarn over the hook again and pull it through both loops on the hook.

Step 4
One loop remains on the hook. One extended single crochet stitch made. Repeat Steps 1–3 in each chain to the end to complete one row of extended single crochet stitches.

Half double crochet

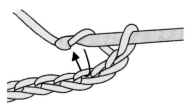

Step 1
Begin with a length of chains. Wrap the yarn over the hook and insert the hook in the third chain from the hook.

Step 2
Pull a loop through this chain. You now have three loops on the hook. Wrap the yarn over the hook again. Pull through all three loops on the hook.

Step 3
One loop remains on the hook. One half double crochet stitch made. Repeat Steps 1–3 in each chain to the end to complete one row of half double crochet stitches.

Double crochet

Step 1
Begin with a length of chains. Wrap the yarn over the hook and insert the hook in the fourth chain from the hook.

Step 2
Pull a loop through this chain to make three loops on the hook. Wrap the yarn over the hook again. Pull a new loop through the first two loops on the hook. Two loops remain on the hook. Wrap the yarn over the hook again. Pull a new loop through both loops on the hook.

Step 3
One loop remains on the hook. One double crochet stitch made. Repeat Steps 1–2 in each chain to the end to complete one row of double crochet stitches.

Treble crochet

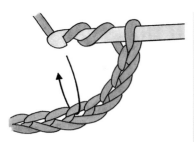
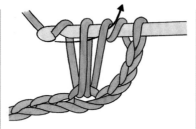
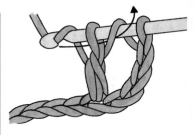

Step 1
Begin with a length of chains. Wrap the yarn twice over the hook and insert the hook in the fifth chain from the hook.

Step 2
Pull a loop through this chain. You now have four loops on the hook. Wrap the yarn over again and pull through the first two loops.

Step 3
Three loops remain on the hook. Wrap the yarn over the hook and pull through the first two loops.

Step 4
Two loops remain on the hook. Wrap the yarn over again and pull through the two remaining loops.

Step 5
One treble crochet stitch made. Repeat Steps 1–4 in each chain to the end to complete one row of treble crochet stitches.

Double treble crochet

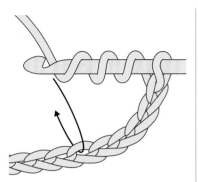

Step 1
Begin with a length of chains. Wrap the yarn three times over the hook and insert the hook in the sixth chain from the hook.

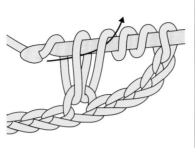

Step 2
Pull a loop through this chain. You now have five loops on the hook. Wrap the yarn over the hook again and pull through the first two loops on the hook.

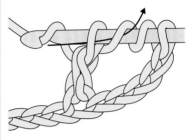

Step 3
Four loops remain on the hook. Wrap the yarn over the hook and pull through the first two loops.

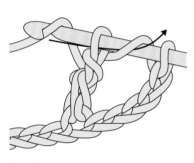

Step 4
Three loops remain on the hook. Wrap the yarn over again and pull through the first two loops.

Step 5
Two loops remain on the hook. Wrap the yarn over again and pull through the remaining loops. One double treble stitch made. Repeat Steps 1–4 in each chain to the end to complete one row of double treble stitches.

TIPS

- For any stitch, the yarn is always wrapped over the hook in the direction shown, unless specific instructions direct otherwise.
- Make triple trebles, quadruple trebles, quintuple trebles, and so on in a similar way. Wrap the yarn three (or four or five) times over the hook, insert the hook, pull a loop through, then *wrap the yarn over the hook, pull a loop through the first two loops, and repeat from * until one loop remains.

A seemingly infinite number of stitch patterns can be created by combining just two or three different-height stitches.

Stitch Variations

Basic stitches may be varied in many ways to achieve different effects. For example, by working several stitches in the same place, by inserting the hook in a different place, by working several stitches together, or by working in the reverse direction you can alter the appearance of basic stitches and create really dazzling crochet designs.

Working into one loop

If the hook is inserted under just one loop at the top of a stitch, the empty loop creates a ridge on either the front or the back of the fabric. Throughout this book, "front loop" means the loop nearest to you, at the top of the stitch, and "back loop" means the farther loop, whether you are working a right-side or a wrong-side row.

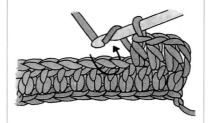

Front loop only
If the hook is inserted under the front loop only, the empty back loop will show as a ridge on the other side of the work.

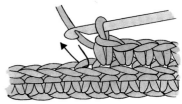

Back loop only
If the hook is inserted under the back loop only, the empty front loop creates a ridge on the side of the work facing you.

Working into the middle bar

This technique is much the same as working into the front or back loop only. Working into the horizontal middle bar at the back of each stitch raises the front and back loops to add some textural interest.

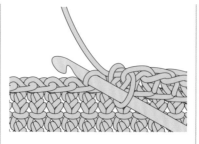

Step 1
To insert the hook into the middle bar, fold the top of the stitches forward and insert the hook from top to bottom under the horizontal middle bar, or "bump," at the back of the stitch.

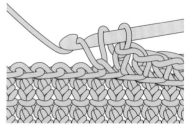

Step 2
Work the stitch as normal.

Working into spaces

Some patterns require the hook to be inserted into spaces rather than directly into stitches. These may be spaces formed by a loop of chains or spaces between stitches.

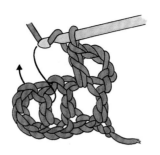

Working into a chain space
The hook is inserted into the space below one or more chains. Here, a double crochet stitch is being worked into the space below a single chain.

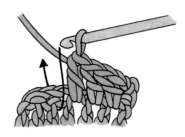

Working into the space between stitches
Here, the hook is inserted between the stitches of the previous row, instead of into the top of a stitch.

Working into a different row

Many pattern variations can be made by inserting the hook one or more rows below the previous row. The insertion may be directly below the next stitch, or one or more stitches to the right or left.

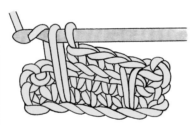

Spike stitch
Insert the hook as directed, wrap the yarn over the hook, and pull the loop through the work, lengthening the loop to the height of the working row. Complete the stitch as instructed.

Working several stitches in the same place

This technique is used to increase the total number of stitches when shaping a garment or other item. Increases may be worked at the edges of flat pieces, or at any point along a row. The technique is also used to create decorative effects such as shells.

Fans and shells
Two, three, or more stitches may be worked into the same place to make a group of stitches in the form of a shell or fan shape. The total number of stitches is increased, so when working a stitch pattern, other stitches are worked together or skipped to compensate. Here, five double crochet stitches are shown worked into the same foundation chain, making a shell.

Working several stitches together

Two or more stitches may be joined together at the top to decrease the total number of stitches when shaping the work, using the same method as for clusters (see right).

Joining groups of stitches together makes several decorative stitch formations: clusters, puffs, bobbles, and popcorns. These add beautiful features to crochet stitch patterns and feature repeatedly in the directory.

Cluster

The term "cluster" may be used for groups of stitches joined closely together at the top (shown below), or joined together at both top and bottom (see examples at right). This can be denoted in the pattern using the abbreviation "tog" along with the type and number of stitches—for example, a cluster made from four double crochet stitches worked together would be "dc4tog."

Step 1
Work each of the stitches to be joined up to the last "yo, pull through" that will complete it. One loop from each stitch to be joined should remain on the hook, plus the loop from the previous stitch. Wrap the yarn over the hook once again.

Step 2
Pull a loop through all the loops on the hook. One loop now remains on the hook. Three double crochet stitches are shown worked together here, but any number of any type of stitch may be worked together in a similar way.

Bobble

A bobble is a type of cluster formed by several double crochet stitches (or longer stitches) joined at both top and bottom. It is often surrounded by shorter stitches to put the bobble into high relief. Bobbles are usually worked on wrong-side rows. A three double crochet bobble (dc3tog) is demonstrated here.

Step 1
*Wrap the yarn over the hook, insert the hook where required, pull a loop through, wrap the yarn over the hook, pull through the first two loops; repeat from * two (or more) times in the same place. Wrap the yarn over the hook and pull through all loops.

Step 2
Sometimes a single chain is worked to complete the bobble, depending on the stitch pattern.

Puff stitch

A puff is normally a group of three or more half double crochet stitches joined at both top and bottom. A three half double crochet puff (hdc3tog) is demonstrated here.

Popcorn

A popcorn is formed when several complete double crochet stitches (or longer stitches) are worked in the same place, and the top of the first stitch is joined to the last to make a "cup" shape. A four double crochet popcorn is shown here.

Step 1
*Wrap the yarn over the hook, insert the hook where required, pull a loop through; repeat from * two (or more) times in the same place. You now have seven loops (or more) on the hook. Wrap the yarn over the hook again and pull through all the loops on the hook.

Step 1
Work four doubles (or the number required) in the same place.

Step 3
Pull this loop through to close the top of the popcorn.

Step 2
Often, one chain is worked in order to close the puff.

Step 2
Slip the last loop off the hook. Reinsert the hook in the top of the first double of the group and catch the empty loop. (On a wrong-side row, reinsert the hook from the back, to push the popcorn to the right side of the work.)

Raised stitches

These are created by inserting the hook around the post, or stem, of the stitch below, from the front or the back. The two examples here show raised doubles, but shorter or longer stitches may be worked in a similar way.

Front post double crochet

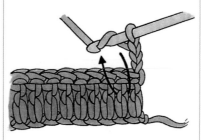

Step 1
Wrap the yarn over the hook, insert the hook from the front to the back to the right of the next stitch, and bring it out to the left of the same stitch. The hook is now around the post of the stitch.

Step 2
Complete the double in the usual way. A ridge forms on the other side of the work.

Back post double crochet

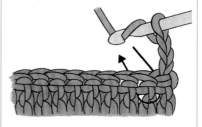

Step 1
Wrap the yarn over the hook, insert the hook from the back to the front to the right of the next stitch, and through to the back again to the left of the same stitch.

Step 2
Complete the double in the usual way. A ridge forms on the side of the work facing you.

Picots

A picot is formed by three or more chains closed into a ring with a slip stitch or a single crochet stitch.

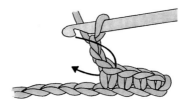

Step 1
Work three chains (or the number required). Insert the hook as instructed. The arrow shows how to insert the hook down through the top of the previous single crochet stitch.

Step 2
Wrap the yarn over the hook and pull through all the loops to close the picot with a slip stitch.

Tunisian stitches

Tunisian crochet is worked in rows, but without turning the work. On the "forward" pass, worked from right to left, all the loops that are made are kept on the hook. On the "return" pass, worked from left to right, the loops are worked off the hook in turn, leaving a single loop on the hook at the end of the pass. A Tunisian crochet hook is required for work of any width, but you can try out a few stitches with an ordinary straight-shafted hook.

Most Tunisian work begins with a foundation chain of the required length, followed by two "base rows" comprising a forward pass and then a return pass. The base rows are equivalent to Tunisian simple stitch and are charted with the same symbols.

Tunisian base rows

Step 1
Start by making a forward pass. Insert the hook in the second chain from the hook, wrap the yarn over the hook, and pull the loop through.

Step 2
Repeat this process in each chain to the end. Do not turn.

Step 3
Now work the return pass. Make one chain. *Wrap the yarn over the hook and pull it through the first two loops on the hook. Repeat from * to end.

Step 4
One loop now remains on the hook. As a rule, this loops stands for the first stitch of the next row, so the next row begins by inserting the hook in the second stitch.

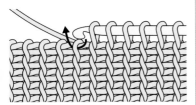

Tunisian simple stitch
To work the forward pass, insert the hook under the single vertical bar of the stitch below, from right to left, then wrap the yarn over the hook and pull through, keeping the loop on the hook. Repeat as required to the end of the forward pass. Work the return pass as for the base row (see Steps 3–4 above).

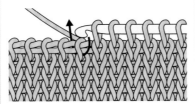

Tunisian knit stitch
To work the forward pass, insert the hook through the center of the stitch below, from front to back, then wrap the yarn over the hook and pull through, keeping the loop on the hook. Repeat as required to the end of the forward pass. Work the return pass as for the base row (see Steps 3–4 above).

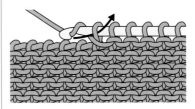

Tunisian purl stitch
To work the forward pass, bring the yarn to the front of the work and insert the hook under the single vertical bar of the stitch below, from right to left. Then take the yarn to the back of the work, wrap it over the hook, and pull through, keeping the loop on the hook. Repeat as required to the end of the forward pass. Work the return pass as for the base row (see Steps 3–4 above).

Symbols and Abbreviations

These are the abbreviations and symbols used in this book. There is no worldwide standard, so, in other publications, you may find different abbreviations and symbols. Always read the list provided with the pattern you are using before starting a project.

Abbreviations

Below is an alphabetical list of abbreviations used in the written patterns in this book.

Abbreviation	Meaning
Bdc	braided double crochet
BL	back loop
BP	back post
ch	chain
CL	cluster
dc	double crochet
dec	decrease
dtr	double treble crochet
exsc	extended single crochet
FL	front loop
FP	front post
hdc	half double crochet
hk	hook
PC	popcorn
rep	repeat
RS	right side
sc	single crochet
sl st	slip stitch
sp(s)	space(s)
Ssc	shallow single crochet
st(s)	stitch(es)
Tbs	Tunisian between stitch
tch	turning chain
Tdc	Tunisian double crochet
Tks	Tunisian knit stitch
tog	together
Tps	Tunisian purl stitch
tr	treble crochet
trtr	triple treble crochet
Tss	Tunisian simple stitch
WS	wrong side
yo	yarn over

Basic Stitches

See pages 176–179 for instructions on how to work the basic stitches. Note that American crochet terms are used throughout this book (see page 188).

Stitch	Abbreviation	Symbol
chain	ch	⌒
slip stitch	sl st	•
single crochet	sc	+ †
extended single crochet	exsc	⸶
half double crochet	hdc	⊤
double crochet	dc	⨏
treble crochet	tr	⨎
double treble crochet	dtr	⨎
triple treble crochet	trtr	⨎

Special Stitches and Variations

Many stitch patterns use special stitch constructions and, where these occur in this book, the abbreviation is indicated in the Special Stitch instructions at the end of the pattern. Always refer to Special Stitch instructions where they occur. Any published pattern should include a list of all the abbreviations and symbols used, which may differ from those below.

Description	Abbreviation	Symbol	Description	Abbreviation	Symbol
stitch worked in front loop only	e.g. FLhdc		increase (such as to make a shell)	e.g. 5dc in same place	
stitch worked in back loop only	e.g. BLhdc		decrease	e.g. dc5tog	
stitch worked in middle bar	e.g. hdc in middle bar		spike stitch	e.g. Spike sc	
stitch worked around front post	e.g. FPdc		spike cluster	Spike CL	
stitch worked around back post	e.g. BPdc		wrapped cluster	wrapped CL	
shallow single crochet	Ssc		cluster	e.g. CL made of dc3tog	
nub stitch	nub st		puff stitch	e.g. Puff made of hdc4tog	
braided double crochet	bdc		popcorn	PC made of 5dc	
V-stitch	e.g. V-st made of [1dc, ch1, 1dc]		picot	–	
crossed stitches	e.g. Crossed 2dc		direction of working	–	

Tunisian Stitches

The following symbols are used for the Tunisian patterns on pages 136–143. The curved line that indicates the return pass makes it easy to distinguish a Tunisian chart. In some publications, the symbol for each Tunisian stitch is enclosed inside a rectangular box.

Description	Abbreviation	Symbol	Description	Abbreviation	Symbol
forward pass	–	←	chain 1 after a Tunisian stitch	e.g. 1Tss, ch1	
return pass	–	→	chain 2 after a Tunisian stitch	e.g. 1Tks, ch2	
Tunisian simple stitch	Tss		Tunisian double crochet	Tdc	
Tunisian decrease	e.g. Tss2tog or Tss3tog		crossed Tunisian stitches	e.g. Crossed 2Tdc	
Tunisian knit stitch	Tks		Tunisian between stitch	Tbs	
Tunisian purl stitch	Tps		yarn over	yo	

American/English Terminology

Some English terms differ from the American system, as shown below. Patterns you may encounter that are published using English terminology can be very confusing unless you understand the difference.

American stitch name	American abbreviation	English stitch name	English abbreviation
single crochet	sc	double crochet	dc
extended single crochet	exsc	extended double crochet	exdc
half double crochet	hdc	half treble crochet	htr
double crochet	dc	treble crochet	tr
treble crochet	tr	double treble crochet	dtr
double treble crochet	dtr	triple treble crochet	trtr
triple treble crochet	trtr	quadruple treble crochet	quadtr

Arrangement of Symbols

It is helpful to understand the different arrangements of symbols on crochet charts, but note that the chart represents how a stitch pattern is constructed and may not bear much resemblance to the appearance of the finished stitch. Always read the written instructions together with the chart.

Description	Examples	Explanation
symbols joined at top		A group of symbols may be joined at the top, indicating that these stitches should be worked together as a cluster, as page 182.
symbols joined at base		Symbols joined at the base should all be worked into the same place below, as page 181.
symbols joined at top and base		Sometimes a group of stitches is joined at both top and bottom, making a bobble, puff, or popcorn, as pages 182–183.
symbols on a curve or angle		Sometimes symbols are drawn along a curve or at an angle, depending on the construction of the stitch pattern.
distorted symbols		Some symbols may be lengthened, curved, or spiked to indicate where the hook is inserted below, as for spike stitches, page 181.

Index

Credits

All photographs and illustrations are the copyright of Quarto Publishing plc. While every effort has been made to credit contributors, Quarto would like to apologize should there have been any omissions or errors—and would be pleased to make the appropriate correction for future editions of the book.

We would like to thank Yarn and Colors for generously supplying all of the yarns used to make the swatches in this book. The yarns are from the "Must-Have" range: sport-weight 100% mercerized cotton. The colors used are: 009 Limestone, 010 Vanilla, 014 Sunflower, 020 Orange, 023 Brick, 026 Satay, 045 Blossom, 048 Antique Pink, 056 Lavender, 062 Larimar, 066 Blue Lake, 067 Pacific Blue, 068 Sapphire, 075 Green Ice, 077 Green Beryl, 083 Peridot, 084 Pistachio, 089 Gold, and 095 Silver.

YARN AND COLORS.

www.yarnandcolors.com

Author's acknowledgments

Every book is a team effort, so first of all to everyone at Quarto who has helped my life run smoothly over the past year: thank you! A special mention to Michelle Pickering; your meticulous eye for detail has made a beautiful book and I am so grateful to you for your persistence and encouragement when I doubted myself!

The ladies at Frodsham Knit and Natter, and my crochet pupils, have been a personal cheerleading team—always interested in the latest book news, testing ideas, and offering suggestions.

Thank you to my non-crafting friends and family, who always have time for coffee when I need a break and never complain when day trips involve a detour to visit a yarn shop. Thank you Colin and Nicola, for being the best husband and daughter I could wish for and always being proud of my designs and my job.

Finally, a special thank you to all the crochet designers, bloggers, and podcasters who give so much of their time to encourage a new generation of crocheters to discover this wonderful craft.